Tony Eccles

Under New Management

The story of Britain's largest worker cooperative –
its successes and failures

Pan Original
Pan Books London and Sydney

First published 1981 by Pan Books Ltd,
Cavaye Place, London SW10 9PG
© Tony Eccles 1981
ISBN 0 330 26285 8
Printed and bound in Great Britain by
Cox and Wyman Ltd, Reading

*To my mother, Louise,
whose kindness and integrity have
made her many life-long friends*

Under New Management

Tony Eccles is Professor of Business Administration at London Business School. He comes from the shop-floor on Merseyside. Originally an engineering fitter, he won a scholarship from night school to Liverpool University where he obtained a first-class degree in mechanical engineering. Following a spell as a ship's engineer, he became a management trainee at Unilever, with whom he spent ten years in production management posts. He joined the faculty of Manchester Business School in 1968 and later became a Senior Lecturer in Business Environment, as well as undertaking consultancy projects – mainly on employee relations, and presenting a number of television programmes for both the BBC and independent television. Since 1977 he has directed London Business School's Centre for Management Development and also advises organizations as diverse as the Cooperative Development Agency and GEC. In October 1974 he was Labour Parliamentary candidate for Runcorn.

Contents

Introduction

This is the story of Britain's largest worker cooperative – KME; its birth, life, success and ultimate failure. It was a strange phenomenon; a product of its time. You wouldn't expect a major challenge to traditional ways of organizing capital and labour to emerge from a bleak trading estate outside Liverpool, and it seems hard now to remember the fluxing days in 1974 when the Heath Government departed and Tony Benn was actually Secretary of State for Industry.

It is a chastening story about the performance of politicians, the ideologies and behaviour of civil servants, the constraints on shop stewards, the abilities of workers, the aims of trade unions, and the roles of managers – all of them caught up in a strange and compelling saga which assumed an importance out of all proportion to its economic influence, bound up in struggles over the Labour Government's industrial strategy, over issues of worker participation (remember the Bullock Report?) and whether workers ought even to try to manage their own affairs.

The book is not a heroic tale of working-class politicization of the style beloved by radicals who inflate every worker initiative into the birth of the revolution. It incorporates a sobering strand of caution about the prospects for developing socialism in British workplaces. Yet, nor is it a salutary reminder that the iron rule of free market capitalism will always triumph. It is not a story of the constitutional complications between ministers and civil servants – well not much anyway. It is a book about some ordinary – and a few extraordinary – people acting as they thought best in a difficult situation; forced into behaviour which surprised even themselves.

The story of KME is a piece of contemporary social

history; of wider interest in the context of industrial Britain in the 1980s. Writing it posed a dilemma. Academics frequently feel the need to pepper their works with vast arrays of reference to the works of others, thus setting the scene for rigorous analysis of concepts, hypotheses and issues. This is occasionally done to lend weight to some pretty meagre data. KME's history produces the near opposite problem, for the story is so rich in fact and incident that it is difficult to find space for analysis without making the book hopelessly overlong. Even now it is only half its original draft length. Hence, surveys of the wider worker-control movement and of the participation literature are not included and nor is an elaborate discussion of hypotheses and theories. These are being written elsewhere.*

Consequently, the book's principal aim is to be useful to shop stewards and managers, wherever they are, as they grapple with the problem of developing more effective ways of working in the last fraction of the twentieth century, for I believe that we will continue to suffer if we do not find a more sophisticated accommodation between the interests of capital and the interests of labour.

Worker cooperatives may provide such a bridge. Despite Britain's pioneering role in the cooperative movement, only the consumer retailing cooperatives have remained of any note. The nineteenth-century worker cooperatives have all but faded from view. The formation rate of worker cooperatives has been low and more energy has gone into founding consumer cooperatives and other cooperative organizations such as banks, building societies and insurance companies. Their motives are divergent, for there is a world of difference between consumer cooperatives, where consumers bond together to secure their supplies, and worker cooperatives where workers are trying to secure their livelihoods.

* See 'Control in the democratized enterprise' in *The Control of Work*, eds. Purcell and Smith (Macmillan, 1979).

The result is that, outside a few surviving cooperatives from the nineteenth century, the sector has primarily comprised the endowed cooperatives, such as Scott Bader and the John Lewis Partnership, where the controlling shareholder has handed over ownership in some form to the employees. There are also worker cooperatives in the timber industry in the USA, a major centre of cooperative activity in the Basque region of Spain round Mondragon, some worker cooperatives in France and Italy and, of course, the extensive network of state-encouraged worker cooperatives in Yugoslavia. Over three hundred million people are in cooperatives of some kind. Apart from a number of tiny British ventures, until Tony Benn began to back worker cooperatives, that part of the cooperative movement was stagnant in Britain.

The picture in 1981 is different, for cooperatives like KME have been path-breakers. The idea of worker co-operatives is now viewed more sympathetically, indeed to the point where some see it as the only road ahead for matching the aspirations of workers to the needs of society for efficiently produced goods and services. Whatever route is chosen for improving relationships and performance at work, worker cooperatives display all the dilemmas of power, accountability, democracy, leadership, efficiency, legitimacy and goals – often in a stark form – which we need to face in some measure, no matter what kind of organization is under debate.

I became involved in KME almost by accident. Living in Liverpool and working at Manchester Business School, I had been engaged in research on Liverpool docks in the late 1960s, where I had first learned of the difficulties of doing action research in contentious situations – particularly where the various parties develop an interest in your not writing up the events and where they fear that your real purpose is to test their feet for clay in public.

I had first met one of the pair who were to become key leaders at KME at a public meeting arranged by a mutual friend at a school in Kirkby, outside Liverpool. Jack

Spriggs and I were speaking about the ill-fated 1971 Industrial Relations Act – which both of us criticized as largely unworkable. We had not met again.

Late in 1974 I was undertaking a consultancy project at Kraft Foods in Kirkby. As the assignment ended, I was leaving the Kraft factory one evening in December when a steward, Ray Spriggs, said that his brother Jack was returning from a London meeting with Tony Benn and would I like to meet Jack and his partner Dick Jenkins for a drink.

Jack and Dick told me that they wanted me to analyse some papers concerning the plans to turn a nearby factory into a worker cooperative. At that stage I knew nothing about the proposed Government-funded worker cooperative, though my worker participation research made me basically in favour of workers being given more control and more responsibility for their work lives.

I read Jack and Dick's papers over Christmas 1974 and became quietly enraged. Not so much because KME's eight hundred workers were up the creek with an inadequate paddle, but because of the derogatory style of the Government's analysis of their business.

Jack Spriggs and Dick Jenkins received my report on 5 January 1975 and I began to explore their future plans, little realizing that I would spend a lot of time over the next five years doing my best to help the cooperative to succeed. Apart from Labour politicians Tony Benn, Eric Heffer and local MP Robert Kilroy-Silk, they seemed to have no friends and certainly none with business experience. I began to advise the two leaders and also took them to Manchester Business School to obtain help from executives in other companies. Initially it was another form of unpaid consultancy. Only later did I conceive the idea of writing up the story, not wanting another project to slip through my fingers as the docks work had done.

My research and management advice had to be done on their terms because of their suspicion of outsiders of all political persuasions, and so the methodology emerged as my being a participant observer at meetings within the cooperative and in negotiations with Government. As in most novel, fast-moving situations, the cascading events are not designed to fit into a researcher's framework and the only way to work is to grab the thing by the tail and hang on as best you can.

The observations were virtually all recorded as notes taken in meetings, including meetings with Government ministers. Not only did this enable people to relax, feeling that they could always claim that I had mis-recorded words, but I am sure that I could never have taken a tape-recorder into meetings with officials and ministers. Indeed, if I had applied to them to carry out the work as research, it would have been refused. As it was, they couldn't have excluded me as a part of KME's delegation ('Are you, Minister, refusing to meet the chosen representatives of the workforce?') and they couldn't easily prevent me from taking notes – particularly since the civil servants were recording the meetings too. This intermittently caused concern amongst Government lawyers, but no attempt was ever made to exclude me from the KME delegations. It's a useful research rule: attach yourself to a project in a way which makes you an integral element of the system.

I have all but written myself out of the story, partly to avoid intruding on the events and partly to avoid self-justification. Occasionally an unidentified comment can be traced back to me or I surface in the course of conversation. Sometimes I am identified because the interjection could otherwise be puzzlingly attributed to someone else of quite different views, or else it would appear that one of the principal actors was talking to himself.

Thanks are due to the forbearance of all the people mentioned in the book, who, knowing that I was writing it, were all prepared to talk to me, both at the time and in the writing of the story. My particular thanks are due to the people of KME led by Jack Spriggs and Dick Jenkins.

I would like to thank Raymond Ashton, Mike Bett, Giles Gordon, Jack Robertson, Rosemary Smith, Stephen Wellings and Mimi Wheldon for making valuable comments on the draft of the book; they enabled me to refine it substantially.

There are many academic and journalistic sources which lie behind my interpretations and which remain anonymous to avoid turning the story into an academic tract, but I would like to mention the valuable help which came from Paul Chaplin, Tom Clarke, Roger Cowe, Mike Jalland and Harvie Ramsay.

Thanks are also due to the Foundation for Management Education, which gave me a grant to cover my travel costs from Scotland during 1976; and to Mike Unger and the *Liverpool Daily Post* for access to their library.

Many thanks also to Isabel Carrick, Katherine Boutineau, Brenda Collins, Sue Harris, Janice Martin, Nicola Parker and Gail Newmark for typing up the endless drafts and edits.

Finally, I would like to express my gratitude to my wife Jackie, whose forbearance and support were major factors in my investing the enormous amount of time which went into the research and the writing of this book.

The people and organizations involved

The factory, and its owners

1960–1968	Fisher & Ludlow (subsidiary of British Motor Corporation Ltd)
1968–1971	Fisher Bendix (subsidiary of Parkinson Cowan Ltd)
1971–1972	Fisher Bendix (subsidiary of Thorn Electrical Industries Ltd)
1972–1974	Clohurst Ltd, later IPD (Industrial) Ltd (subsidiaries of International Property Development Ltd)

July 1974– January 1975	In receivership
January 1975 onwards	KME (Kirkby Manufacturing and Engineering Co. Ltd) – a State-funded workers' cooperative

KME

Jack Spriggs	convenor of shop stewards for Amalgamated Union of Engineering Workers (AUEW) and also worker director of KME Ltd
Dick Jenkins	convenor of shop stewards for Transport & General Workers' Union (TGWU) and also worker director of KME Ltd
Bob Lewis	ex-production director of IPD (I); later general manager of KME Ltd
John Bandell	ex-office manager of IPD (I); later financial controller of KME Ltd

Labour politicians

Rt Hon. Harold Wilson	MP for Huyton (including Kirkby until February 1974) and Prime Minister February 1974 to March 1976
Rt Hon. Tony Benn	Secretary of State for Industry, February 1974 to June 1975
Eric Heffer	Minister of State, Industry Department, February 1974 to April 1975
Rt Hon. Eric Varley	Secretary of State for Industry, June 1975 to May 1979
Rt Hon. Alan Williams	Minister of State, Industry Department, March 1976 to May 1979

Bob Cryer	Under-Secretary of State for Industry, April 1976 to November 1978
Robert Kilroy-Silk	MP for Ormskirk (including Kirkby) from February 1974

Civil servants & officials

Sir Antony Part	Permanent Secretary, Industry Department, until retiring in June 1976. Later director of Metal Box Ltd
Sir Peter Carey	Secretary (Industry) and then Permanent Secretary, Industry Department from June 1976
John Lippitt	Under-Secretary, Regional Industrial Finance Division. Later Deputy Secretary, Industry Department and, since March 1980, group export director, GEC Ltd
Ken Binning	Under-Secretary, Regional Industrial Finance Division, Industry Department
Brian Hilton	Assistant Secretary, Regional Industrial Finance Division, Industry Department
John Andrewes	Deputy Director, Industrial Development Unit, Industry Department

Other individuals & institutions

Jack Marsden	Senior Consultant, P. A. Management Consultants
Derek Hartland	Consultant, P. A. Management Consultants
Professor Douglas Hague	Manchester Business School

Paul Chaplin   Manchester Business School

Roger Cowe   Manchester Business School

Arthur Ward   Regional Industrial Director (North-West) Department of Industry. Later Regional Director, National Enterprise Board

Lord Oram   Chairman, Cooperative Development Agency

Harold King   Chairman and Managing Director, International Property Development Co. Ltd

Roger Cork   Cork, Gully, chartered accountants

Peter Lowell   Independent consultant

Robert Maxwell   Chairman, Pergamon Press

Cyril Duckworth   Managing Director, Worcester Engineering Co. Ltd

Industrial Development Advisory Board (Department of Industry)
National Westminster Bank
Inbucon, management consultants
Hill Foster Ltd
Stelrad (subsidiary of Metal Box Co. Ltd)

1. How it all began: 1960–71

- **The first takeover**
- **Thorn makes a bid**
- **The atmosphere sours**
- **Nine weeks' stoppage**

The story of the KME Cooperative really began in 1849 when Mr Fisher started making kettle spouts for travelling tinkers in a little shop up an entry in Birmingham's Sherlock Street.

The business flourished and Fisher was joined by Ludlow. By 1884 they were making kettle lids and necks as well and the South African war saw them turning out thousands of mess tins and camp kettles. In the 1914–18 war the firm worked day and night to supply gun parts, field kitchens, exhaust manifolds, ammunition cases and yet more mess tins and kettles. During the 1920s it extended its operations into making car body parts and shortly after the Second World War occupied a large site near Birmingham. Fisher & Ludlow joined the British Motor Corporation (BMC) and by 1959 it employed 13,000 people turning out 6,000 car bodies per week and 6,500 washing machines, dryers, refrigerators and sink units.

The fortunes of the motor and domestic appliance industries looked bright. Britain seemed to be back on its feet. The year 1959 had seen a beautiful summer. Harold Macmillan had just won the 'You've never had it so good' general election, and it was entirely in keeping that BMC should announce a £49 million expansion plan to raise its vehicle capacity to one million vehicles a year.

To make space in the Midlands' factories, all domestic appliance activities would be moved to a new factory to be erected at Kirkby, the post-war new town on the outskirts of Liverpool. Kirkby's range of products would be impressive, for there were Bendix washing-machines for launderettes and homes, refrigerators, spin-driers and sinks in stainless steel and vitreous enamel. Vending-machines and bathroom equipment would be joined by yet more products as Fisher & Ludlow expanded to make ten thousand domestic appliance units a week, of which up to 50 per cent were to be exported. Even before construction began, the directors were musing over the prospects for doubling Kirkby's projected labour force to three thousand. Most of the initial 1,500 workers would be unskilled and semi-skilled men – which was good news in Kirkby which had a preponderance of such residents. Only a few key staff would be imported from Birmingham.

Thirty acres of the fifty acre site were to be developed initially. The factory was big. The production building was 1,020 ft by 300 ft – about the size of five football pitches. The administration offices were separated from the factory, as was the 700-seat canteen.

Fisher & Ludlow had chosen Merseyside because the Government wished to encourage industrial expansion in an area of high and persistent unemployment and had offered the firm loans totalling £2.4 million (which were later repaid) and a £150,000 grant.

It was part of a Government drive to induce firms to move to development districts like Merseyside. Ford at Halewood, Vauxhall at Ellesmere Port, Triumph at Speke were all contemporary consequences of Government persuasions coupled to the inducements of financial aid. It was the golden age of expansionist satellite factories.

In 1961 the Kirkby factory opened and soon began producing domestic appliances along with the Moulton bicycle – the first of the small wheel, independently sprung bicycles. It was hoped that production for Moulton would quickly reach 1,500 per week and demand for appliances was such that the factory was working three shifts round the clock in 1964.

Unfortunately, productivity was low and profits were non-existent, and so BMC was keen to offload the Kirkby factory, which was now called Fisher Bendix. One BMC director also happened to be a director of the successful cooker and gas equipment firm of Parkinson Cowan – which itself wanted to broaden its product base. Parkinson Cowan didn't much like the look of Fisher Bendix but agreed to manage it for BMC whilst holding an option to buy it later.

Despite finding some Kirkby workers playing cards in the afternoon – having finished their stints on the measured day work system – Parkinson Cowan made some initial progress by cutting out some of the worst labour practices, ditching very unprofitable products, raising prices and improving inspection procedures to raise the poor quality of manufacture. The losses were reduced, though due to a fall in demand resulting from deflationary Government economic policy, the improvement was not maintained and, by late 1966, Fisher Bendix was down to two shifts per day. On New Year's Eve it sacked one-third of the factory supervisors. In 1967 the Moulton business was sold to Raleigh.

The first takeover

However, Fisher Bendix's prospects must have looked good because, in July 1968, Parkinson Cowan agreed to buy the Kirkby business from BMC.

In a bouncy mood, Parkinson Cowan pointed to the growth of turnover which would accrue from Fisher Bendix and declared that 'the acquisition of Fisher Bendix should be regarded primarily as a long range corporate opportunity for the group, not as an investment undertaken for short-term financial return'.

Perhaps this was just as well, for Fisher Bendix had been suffering heavy losses. The 1965–7 losses had totalled £1¾ million and a £¾ million loss was anticipated in 1967–8. However, Parkinson Cowan expected Fisher

Bendix to earn a profit in 1969–70 and thereafter to develop into a substantial contributor towards group results. The price for Fisher Bendix was about £4 million.

The plan did not quite work, for there was a continuing recession caused by a Government credit squeeze aimed at reducing consumer demand and the 1968/9 accounts showed that Parkinson Cowan's consumer durables' profits had dropped from £476,000 to just £6,000.

The chairman was notably less confident than at the time of the takeover. There had been a serious reversal of the previously improving tendency at Kirkby. It was not, he said, caused primarily by a shortage of available business but by labour disputes and unforeseen production delays, aggravated by a world-wide shortage of nickel for sinks. The loss should soon reduce, he continued, but if serious doubts continued about the ability of Fisher Bendix to earn a proper return, some radical changes would be made.

Unfortunately, the credit squeeze continued, although Parkinson Cowan did its best to capitalize on the asset of the Bendix name. It increased prices to rectify the underpricing of the undoubtedly good Bendix products and, indeed, redesigned them to take out a lot of unnecessary cost. It wasn't enough.

In January 1970 it was announced that the sink business would close down and that 300 of the 1,900 employees would lose their jobs. Other jobs were to go later.

Parkinson Cowan's next results showed that Fisher Bendix had apparently lost £1.3 million in the year to March 1970. The group's annual profit had dropped from £931,000 to £93,000. Parkinson Cowan soon stopped paying dividends and stated that, whilst prospects for radiators and storage heaters were good, the Bendix washing machine business was not operating profitably.

The Parkinson Cowan board felt that the best solution would be to dispose of the Kirkby operation as a going concern by injecting its Constor night storage heater business into Kirkby and taking the Bendix business away from Kirkby. In February 1971 it was decided to withdraw from washing-machine manufacture and certain plans were made to remove Bendix from Kirkby and create new Bendix manufacture elsewhere. By March 1971 the increasingly desperate board had resolved to sell Kirkby in any way feasible. The firm was in dire trouble.

Thorn makes a bid

However, Parkinson Cowan's excellent position in the gas cooker market made it attractive to other companies and so, aware of the firm's financial difficulties, Thorn Electrical Industries approached Parkinson Cowan with an offer to buy the whole company. Thorn's first private bid was too low for Parkinson Cowan's board but its second approach had to be commended to shareholders, and on 2 April 1971, the Thorn offer was announced.

By 25 May the offer had been so well received by shareholders that it was declared unconditional. Thorn had bought Parkinson Cowan for about £4 million – much the same as Parkinson Cowan, then profitable, had paid for Fisher Bendix alone in 1968. Kirkby's losses had broken Parkinson Cowan.

Thorn hoped to stem the losses and the new acquisition dovetailed in with Thorn's existing activities to the point where a reference to the Monopolies Commission was a distinct possibility, since together Thorn and Parkinson Cowan would control some 32 per cent of the UK cooker market if the two organizations were fully grafted together.

However, surgery rather than grafting seemed to be the chosen method. On 1 June, Parkinson Cowan, now owned by Thorn, announced that 505 of Kirkby's 1,100 employees would lose their jobs. The Kirkby washing-machine business was to close down and work would be concentrated at one end of the factory. But the workers became suspicious and information in the office files led to rumours. The Amalgamated Union of Engineering

Workers (AUEW) expressed fears that Fisher Bendix was seeking to transfer the manufacture of washing-machines abroad. This was denied by Parkinson Cowan which stated that 'No arrangements have been made or are under discussion for the company to manufacture washing-machines outside the UK or to replace all or any part of washing-machine production at Kirkby.'

Connoisseurs of statements can soon pick out the weasel words. Parkinson Cowan did not claim that no discussions had taken place – only that they were not, at present, taking place and that no agreements had, as yet, been reached. Nor did it state that discussions were not about to take place. It indicated that the company would not manufacture outside the UK but, of course, this left it free to get others to do so. Parkinson Cowan restrained itself to mentioning washing-machines when Kirkby was mainly concerned with spin-driers. 'Replace', too, is a vague word if the product is to change.

However, the fact was that much of the denial was a lie. Months of negotiation had already taken place for the transfer of manufacture to Spain. Tools were to be supplied (some had already left Kirkby disguised as scrap), drawings were being exchanged, and assembly parts and Kirkby pressings were to be made available. Parkinson Cowan's denial was a plain act of deceit.

The atmosphere sours

Perhaps the company did not realize that the workers knew more than they had revealed to the management. The press soon tracked down the background story and the Spanish firm of Constructores de Aparatos Refrigeradores SA (CARSA) revealed that it had reached agreement with Fisher Bendix to construct a minimum of twenty thousand spin-driers annually at its Getafe plant outside Madrid.

Harold Wilson (then leader of the Opposition and also the local MP) began to investigate the allegations and approached the workers' leaders. He met the Fisher Bendix convenors of shop stewards, Jack Spriggs (AUEW) and Dick Jenkins of the Transport and General Workers' Union (TGWU), who arrived at the Kirkby Labour club at the head of a four hundred-strong demonstration. Mr Wilson was given what Jack Spriggs described as 'irrefutable' facts and documentation including 'written evidence that Fisher Bendix are moving their washing-machine production to Spain'. The information had come from the Kirkby offices. One of the employees had been involved in the administration of the impending switch of production and had seen the documents. He had been declared redundant as a result of the secret deal with CARSA and this had stretched his loyalty to breaking point. He had informed his union, which had been the source of the story splashed in the *Daily Mail*.

The cat was well and truly out of the bag. It was less than two months after the takeover of Parkinson Cowan. Thorn had made a miserable start to any plan which it might have had to win the hearts and minds of the Fisher Bendix employees.

But did Thorn have any intention of keeping Kirkby going at all? It might claim that recent actions had been initiated by Parkinson Cowan, but Thorn had obtained full control of Parkinson by 25 May. The redundancy announcement of 1 June was on Thorn's shoulders.

The workers suspected that if Thorn succeeded in terminating Bendix manufacture at Kirkby, it would then take radiator manufacture away to its own factories. In fact, Thorn could not speedily do so; for the radiator design would not have fitted on their existing production lines.

Meanwhile, the sour atmosphere persisted at Kirkby where the shop stewards and union officials kept up a dialogue with the local management to try to stave off the redundancies. But Thorn's central management was unyielding. The company insisted that no more negotiations could take place and that all the sackings would go ahead.

It looked quite likely that the company would get its own way too. The Kirkby shop-floor was despondent about the chance of halting the redundancies and was half-inclined to be fatalistic and accept the position. The office staff were divided and some were prepared to take the redundancy money and look for other jobs. On 17 June the redundancy notices were issued.

The shop stewards promptly pulled a flanker. The AUEW convenor, Jack Spriggs, said that they would accept the basic fact of redundancy but that the company had gone too far. The boiler-house staff were to be reduced too much. The boiler-house really needed four men to run it – one more than planned. The management saw their chance. For the sake of one man they thought they could get the stewards to agree to 504 other redundancies. They took the bait.

The stewards called an immediate mass meeting of the employees and told them that the management had relented over the boiler-house manning and were prepared to talk about other jobs as well. The latter point was incorrect; but it had its effect. The employees declared that if the management did not withdraw all the redundancy notices while these negotiations took place, they would strike.

The managers were furious, but they were not beaten yet. Nobody had consulted the night shift and the management sounded them out and found that many of them accepted the redundancy and were not amused at having been left out of the latest turn of events. The management had then written a notice-board letter, which, according to Spriggs, virtually called him a liar and claimed that he had accepted the redundancy situation.

Spriggs was having a quiet drink that night when a message reached the pub that the night shift wanted him up at the factory immediately. When he got there he found that they were fuming. Whilst their pro-redundancy vote would not have tipped the daytime mass meeting, the fact was that they had not been consulted.

However, Spriggs has a characteristic which he shares with the best of Merseyside's political figures. An effective orator in normal circumstances, he gets better when he's hopping mad, and the management's letter had not exactly calmed him. He addressed the night shift and, to the management's disappointment, they backed the strike.

Nine weeks' stoppage

On 25 June 1971, the whole of the Fisher Bendix workforce walked out on unofficial strike.

The problem for the workers, as Spriggs privately pointed out, was that you cannot easily fight redundancies with a strike – you might simply increase the chance of total closure. The workers' choice had been difficult but their gut intuition had inclined them towards immediate risky action. Given the vulnerability of Fisher Bendix, there was no guarantee that the remaining operations would be viable even if the workers accepted the proposed redundancies. Indeed, redundancies could be a way of weakening them, bit by bit, until closure became an irresistible formality. The workers didn't need any training in economics to see the dangers of reducing the range of goods. Like every other large factory with high, fixed overhead costs (such as rates and heating) the Kirkby operation needed the maximum throughput so that the overheads could be spread over as many products as possible. Every time the product range and the workforce were cut, the direct costs dropped, but the largely unchanged overheads had to be covered by the reduced volume of output. It only needed a dip in demand and these remaining products would also become unprofitable – each weighed down by an increased burden of overheads. The factory really needed the unprofitable products to be replaced by other profitable lines if it was to survive securely – but there was no sign that Thorn could, or would, introduce new products to the strife-torn plant.

However, despite the inherent risks of the strike, the

workers were not entirely on their own. The AUEW and the TGWU both declared the strike official, and Harold Wilson was pressing for a full investigation by the Heath Government.

After four weeks, eight hundred workers voted to continue their official strike. It was not their only action. The workers recognized that the strike was risky since it would be easy for the management to decline to reopen the plant. In tactical terms, a more comprehensive strategy was required if they wished to raise the pressure on the company as well as improve their weak bargaining position. The obvious targets were the prosperous parts of the Thorn empire. The obvious weapon was the unquestioning solidarity of a workforce which handled Thorn goods. There was such a workforce close by.

On 12 August Liverpool's dockers agreed to 'black' the products of Thorn, Parkinson Cowan and Fisher Bendix in and out of Liverpool. They hoped to spread the ban to every port in the country. Since the dockers were predominantly members of the TGWU there was also the prospect of blacking by the nation's lorry drivers. London and Southampton docks followed Liverpool's lead. It was a powerful coercive move by the strikers.

There was also the prospect of Thorn's embarrassment. Not only did it face sanctions against movement of its goods and materials, it also risked the possibility that other Thorn workers might take self-protective steps in the face of the Thorn action over Kirkby. The dockers' action had its aspect of luck for the Kirkby strikers. They had found the dockers' organization at its strongest since the dockers were then mobilizing for struggles of their own, which had led to the (far from habitual) situation in which London dock leaders were anxious to demonstrate unity with the Merseyside dock workers.

The Fisher Bendix employees were lucky in another respect. Their strike leaders went to the Midlands to ask the rest of the Parkinson Cowan workers to support the fight against redundancy. The meeting with Parkinson

Cowan's shop stewards was described afterwards by one of the Kirkby representatives as being 'like the Spanish Inquisition'. The Parkinson Cowan stewards described the Kirkby workers as 'a lazy shower' who'd lost money due to their own inadequacies. The Midlands stewards felt that they couldn't sway their men to agree to support strikers a hundred miles away. But the Kirkby stewards asked them to take a gamble and bluff their management by offering seven days' strike notice in support of Kirkby. Reluctantly the Midlands stewards did so and told their management that they were calling their men to a meeting. Privately they were worried that the hollowness of their claim would be revealed to management – and the mass meeting was not initially reassuring. The assembly roasted the stewards for giving the strike notice and said that they had no mandate for such action. However, the Parkinson Cowan stewards stood their ground and, when they threatened to resign if it were not agreed, the meeting accepted their recommendation.

This intensified the pressure on Thorn, which backed down within a few days. The strike finally ended after nine weeks with the waiving of the planned redundancies and reinstatement of those workers who had refused to accept the redundancy payments. The workers were not wholly victorious for it was unquestionable that the remaining jobs would be insecure, since Thorn had already intimated that the whole factory might close in February 1972. The Bendix operation, with its valuable brand name, had already been extracted for Thorn by Parkinson Cowan's Spanish deal. It would not be returned. The surviving workers went back to work with Jack Spriggs saying 'We are all determined to show Thorn that the Kirkby factory is a viable proposition.'

2. Who are Jack Spriggs and Dick Jenkins?

These two leaders play such a critical role in the story that their background really needs to be explained.

Jack Spriggs was born in 1934 into a poor and close-knit Liverpool family. When Jack left Liverpool's St Francis Xavier's school he trained as a french-polisher before doing National Service.

Not long out of the forces, he joined Kraft Foods in Kirkby and was soon a leader of a strike in 1958 which led to the full recognition of the Shop and Distributive Workers Union (USDAW). He had already been in a furniture union (NUFTO) as well as the Transport Union (TGWU) when he had worked as a temporary dock worker on the Liverpool docks. During this time he had taken part in many disputes, though Kraft was his first real taste of industrial struggle.

He stayed at Kraft for a while and helped to develop USDAW in another Liverpool factory, but he was twenty-eight and on the dole when he joined Fisher Bendix (the factory which became KME) in 1963. Spriggs worked as a welder and soon became AUEW shop steward in his section of the factory. The Engineering Workers' Union was the main union at Fisher Bendix and there were enough AUEW stewards for them to have a convenor to lead and represent them.

The AUEW convenor was killed in a car crash, which also injured his deputy convenor and Jack was asked to take over temporarily. He then won the election for the convenor's post, partly because the deputy convenor was still felt to be unfit to cope with the demanding job. Both the management and some of the membership were less than happy with Spriggs' election because there had been many disputes in his section and he had been held responsible for them.

Jack set about uniting the various factory and union groupings. This took time, for the dominant AUEW group and the less numerous TGWU members had never been fully reconciled to each other's presence and an alliance was necessary before unity could be created with the four other unions on the site. It only became practicable to bring the AUEW and TGWU together once Dick Jenkins had become convenor of the TGWU.

Jenkins is fifteen years older than Spriggs and had been on Liverpool docks all his working life. He had been involved, though not prominent, in many struggles on the waterfront, where workers in those days were frequently at odds with their employers. Jenkins had left with some 'compo' (compensation) after an accident. His brother Jimmy worked at Fisher Bendix and was an ASTMS steward. He persuaded Dick to join the Kirkby plant, initially as a storekeeper and, later as a crane driver, which enabled him to move round the factory.

Dick Jenkins became TGWU convenor and, despite its small membership, soon emulated Spriggs so that the two spent a high proportion of their time on union matters. Like many leading shop stewards they did little work on their jobs but remained on the three-shift rotas earning a little overtime.

Spriggs found it difficult to manage, though fortunately he and his wife were in a low-cost council house and then only had one child. Jenkins was in a better position because his compensation had helped to buy their house. (In addition, his wife worked for over thirty years, first at Littlewoods and later at AC-Delco in Kirkby.)

Eventually management agreed to put the two convenors full time on the 7 a.m. – 3 p.m. shift, where afternoon meetings helped their overtime earnings.

The two convenors' jobs were unusual. There are estimated to be only about five thousand legitimately full-time shop stewards in British industry, notably where workforces are large or industrial problems are complicated. At Fisher Bendix, the AUEW had about five hundred members and the TGWU less than two hundred. The two convenors could now work unceasingly on their members' behalf at Fisher Bendix, though from the management's viewpoint, industrial relations remained poor and the factory incident-prone and none too productive.

Once the two main unions had been brought together, the electrician's group (EETPU) – whose convenor already worked on the 7 a.m. – 3 p.m. shift – was soon added, so that virtually all the factory workers were now in an alliance controlled by the joint shop stewards' committee which had been set up under Spriggs' leadership. Inter-sectional rivalries were damped down and so sporadic flare-ups were markedly reduced. However, the management knew that if there were a problem, union action would be coordinated and would have widespread repercussions.

The three staff unions (ASTMS, APEX and TASS) only became more closely associated when Thorn Electrical Industries took over in 1971, but by 1972 Spriggs had welded the whole workforce representation system together under his leadership. Jenkins was effectively his assistant. Policy decisions were taken by mass meetings of the combined union memberships on recommendations from the joint shop stewards' committee – whose joint convenors were Spriggs and Jenkins. The individual unions' power bases had been eroded. Power had been centralized.

Spriggs had joined the Labour Party in 1961 (he lives in Eric Heffer's Walton constituency) and by 1973 was treasurer of Liverpool Trades Council – a fairly left wing body once it had separated from Liverpool Labour Party, thus allowing in other political parties who were no longer barred from membership. Spriggs was a stout Liverpool football supporter. By the time the KME cooperative started, both convenors had been owner-occupiers for several years, Spriggs having bought his house from the council. He has always liked a few pints, but is a committed family man. I have never known 'Big Jack' to swear or tell a doubtful story. In 1981 he still lives in the same house and remains a fanatical Liverpool supporter.

During the story of the cooperative, Spriggs and Jenkins are often referred to as 'the convenors', 'the leaders', 'the directors', 'the worker directors' etc., both to give variety and to show their complex leading roles.

3. The struggle with Thorn: 1971–2

- Sacking the management
- The factory occupation
- Harold Wilson's diplomacy
- In come the money men
- Thorn struggles free

With the nine-week stoppage over, production was resumed at Fisher Bendix, though it was far from clear whether Thorn had changed its mind, or just staged a tactical retreat. There were sound commercial reasons for shifting the manufacture of panel radiators and storage heaters to other Thorn factories. It would get rid of the troublesome and loss-making Kirkby operations, optimize production elsewhere and free the monies tied up in Kirkby. Thorn saw no future in the place and continued to look quietly for a buyer. The workers returned to work knowing that Fisher Bendix might soon close completely. Penniless from the strike, they saw their first task as earning some wages and then preparing for the struggle ahead. But the style of the struggle would have to be different, for going on strike again would be useless. If the management wanted to shut the place, walking out would actually ease their path. On 1 October 1971 the Thorn Group made it clear that closure was necessary because there was insufficient work at Kirkby. Nor, they claimed, was it practicable to transfer work to Kirkby from other Thorn plants. They were willing to talk about the terms of closure.

Three days later came the inaugural meeting of the Thorn combine* shop steward committee which Spriggs

* 'Combine' is a word often used to signify 'group wide, covering the whole enterprise, representing all groups of workers, from all sites'. It may represent all branches of one union in a company (or group)

had initiated by writing round to the senior stewards at all the sites listed in Thorn's directory. This body was unofficial and outside the union/Thorn bargaining arrangements. Its aims were to exchange information about differing pay and conditions in parts of the Thorn empire and to combine together to face what was judged to be the Thorn policy of playing one site off against another.

The Kirkby stewards refused to meet the Fisher Bendix management to discuss the closure, since they did not accept the principle of closure in the first place. Spriggs declared that the workers were considering occupying the factory if the projected redundancies were carried through and that the six unions were working together at factory level on this possibility.

It was the first hint of a new tactic by the workers. By mid-November the workers were talking in terms of a 'work-in'. There was, said a workers' spokesman, no chance of any workers losing their jobs at Fisher Bendix. If Thorn tried to close it the workers would step in and run it – just like the workers at Upper Clyde Shipbuilders – who were to be supported by a Conservative Government made anxious by worrying reports of the social pressure building up on Clydeside.

To improve their strategy the stewards' leaders talked to the people involved in the sit-ins at Upper Clyde Shipbuilders and at the Plessey factory at nearby Alexandria. The UCS experience was not wholly relevant since its workers controlled large amounts of working capital in the form of part-built ships. More significantly there was an order-book of some substance and it was in everyone's interest to complete the ships. Thorn, on the other hand,

---

and can be official. It may, as in the Thorn case, cover all unions involved anywhere in the group and is thus likely to be unofficial, i.e. not constitutionally provided for by the respective unions in their dealings with the group employer. Typically its members are shop stewards of member unions. Such combines may have the blessing, indifference or enmity of union officials and other negotiating bodies.

could manufacture radiators in Newcastle and spin-driers in Spain.

Plessey was a more directly comparable experience. Here the workers had sat in, confronting the management of a firm not unlike Thorn in its product range and multiplicity of manufacturing sites. The Plessey situation, although open to a number of interpretations, had at least shown that resistance via sit-ins was a potentially powerful gambit.

The Kirkby men needed this reassurance, for two miles down the road from Fisher Bendix was an English Electric factory. Following its takeover by GEC, redundancies had been declared and the workers had come within a day of occupying the factory. At the last minute some employees who preferred the redundancy money objected to the proposed occupation and voted down the precarious commitment to sit in.

It was uncertain whether the Kirkby leaders would get sustained backing for a sit-in, although the UCS and Plessey experiences had changed the odds. Not only were workers more aware of the sit-in as a tactical device, but experience was showing that it could succeed where other ploys would fail. Nevertheless, the English Electric incident suggested that if Thorn offered generous redundancy terms, the majority of workers might accept them.

But Thorn didn't. In December 1971 it offered one and a half weeks' pay per year of service, and £75 each because of the loss of jobs in a high unemployment area. The factory would close by May 1972. The offer was not a lot better than statutory redundancy pay, and some firms on Merseyside were then making workers redundant on approximately double Thorn's figures.

The second meeting of the Thorn combine committee agreed to resist unemployment and not allow any movement of machinery out of any Thorn factories, unless sanctioned by the committee. This amounted to an attempt to create veto power for the shop-floor, though it was questionable whether the combine committee could have made its decision stick.

There was a psychological element at work too. The stewards felt that if they could persuade Thorn to defer a definite decision on closure beyond Christmas, the workers would be in a strong position. If the workers were offered good money in the pre-Christmas period, solidarity would crumble. After Christmas, stripped of cash, the workers could be in a fighting mood and ready for anything. The officials appealed (successfully) to Thorn to 'be Christian' and leave it till after Christmas, since people were entitled to peace of mind over the festive season.

But a new twist to the story was about to occur. Early in December it was revealed that a mystery buyer had purchased the Kirkby plant and the whole fifty-acre site for a figure understood to be about £1.5 million. Thorn would not say who was the buyer, but he had been introduced to some Fisher Bendix stewards as 'Mr Gershfield – an economist'. It was his only visit to Kirkby and, hearing of his arrival, the two senior stewards had made it their business to bump into him and had put the case for retaining and running the plant to him. Indeed, Gershfield walked along the main factory aisle ('the golden mile') with Spriggs and Jenkins. He said that the two convenors were the ones he wanted to see and asked them the same question as Thorn's estate agent. 'Would you be prepared to work alongside people in white coats?'. They said 'yes' – not knowing whether it might mean atomic energy or biscuit manufacture. Thorn was annoyed about this casual meeting; for they had expected that Gershfield's visit would have been confidential. Other prospective buyers had toured the plant secretly, disguised as people checking air-conditioning equipment. The atmosphere of unease affected both management and employees.

Although the workers had vague ideas of running the

plant on their own, their main hope was that a new firm would come in to save their jobs and keep the plant running. They presumed that this possibility was being actively considered by the mystery buyer. After all, why else would anyone want to buy the place?

Sacking the management

Thorn made plans to begin moving machinery out of Kirkby on 3 January 1972. None moved. The workers had intimated that they would start a sit-in if any attempt were made to move equipment. The management had said that they would be instructing the maintenance men to begin to dismantle machinery and that anyone refusing to carry out such an order would be dismissed. The stewards replied that if management did embarrass the maintenance workers by ordering anyone to strip the machines, they, the workers, would 'sack' the management.

The next day passed peacefully enough. But 5 January was different. Fisher Bendix's chairman had arranged a meeting at the Kirkby plant between the firm's senior executives and the stewards. The workers feared the worst, and whilst the meeting took place, rumours of imminent closure were developing in the factory. Gradually groups of workers formed to discuss the situation and, almost casually, began to move towards the end of the plant near the administration building.

The original intention had been premeditated, and the workers had been organized by the stewards. Newspaper and TV reporters had also been tipped off. The plan was to demonstrate and chant slogans outside the meeting in order to put pressure on the executives and demonstrate the workers' readiness to act. The groups of workers coalesced and the throng moved erratically towards the administration building chanting 'Thorn, out, Thorn, out'. Many of them had never been inside it. With no clear plan of organization they moved slowly towards the boardroom where, they had deduced, the meeting must be taking place.

They advanced upstairs and after some confusion found the boardroom. The door was shut and nobody was there to report their presence to the meeting's unsuspecting managers. It was an awkward moment. No leader strode confidently forward. The workers were on their own, lacking experience of such situations, intimidated – despite themselves – by the enormity of what they were engaged in, and unsure how, or even whether, to proceed.

But it was difficult to turn back. Who would be first to retreat? As the minutes went by, the feeling of 'now we're here we might as well proceed' strengthened the resolve to act. The pressure from behind caused the front rows of people to move slowly forward. The boardroom door was pushed open and a chair sailed across the room and broke against the wall as the nearest workers were shoved in by the spontaneous surge of those behind. The executives inside were startled observers as a trickle of workers, led by Bernie the Cook*, slowly entered the room and edged round the walls to surround the boardroom table chanting 'We shall not be moved.' There was a pregnant silence from those sitting at the table. The shop stewards were the first to recover – having organized the invasion.

The convenors told the managers that 'as from today, you're redundant' and ordered them to leave the boardroom. The managers immediately offered to leave the factory's machinery undisturbed for four weeks if this would help to facilitate negotiations. They stayed on site for lunch whilst the stewards went back to report to the massed workers, who by now were all gathered together in the canteen. The mass meeting unanimously decided to take immediate control of the factory.

* He wasn't the cook really, but during the 1972 sit-in he was to display considerable culinary skills and the name stuck. While in the boardroom, he became so embarrassed that he passed the time studying form in his copy of *Sporting Life*.

The managers returned from lunch and were disconcerted at being invited by the shop stewards to leave the premises for the second time that day. After a few minutes collecting papers, they left, uttering an urbane 'The best of luck' as they departed. Some senior staff were induced to leave by the news that the gates would soon be locked – with their precious cars inside.

The factory occupation

'We have decided,' said Jack Spriggs, 'that we will not be producing any articles. What will happen is that we will allow all the parts to come into the factory, but nothing at all will be allowed to go out.'

In other words, it would be a sit-in, not a work-in; an occupation to deprive Thorn of the use of its assets. This was an enforced choice since the legal problems of operation and the lack of cash made a work-in look rather forbidding. Who would buy goods from workers lacking the legal title to sell the products?

There was more to come as the workers strove to improve their bargaining position. The next day they took the factories' lorries to nearby Moorgate Road – the site of the Fisher Bendix spares and service operation for the United Kingdom. All the spares were taken back to the occupied factory. Whilst the legality of the sit-in was doubtful, the acquisition of the spares was certainly unlawful, but it was a potent move to improve the workers' position. Without spares, the servicing of Fisher Bendix's existing customers would deteriorate and the workers had calculated that it would have a grave effect on the running of the Fisher Bendix organization, leading quickly to its complete stoppage pending a new spares system being set up from scratch.

At this stage the factory's electricity, telephones, heating oil and gas had not been cut off, although Thorn warned that it would take unspecified steps 'to protect its interests', and the following day – 7 January 1972 – they ordered the Post Office to cut off the telephone.*

A mass meeting voted to continue to sit in. There was only one dissenter and he wanted the redundancy money because he was emigrating.

It was confirmed on 7 January that Harold Wilson would soon be meeting the sit-in leaders to discuss the situation. He had already demanded an inquiry into the running of the factory and, together with the rest of the Merseyside groups of Labour MPs, had tabled an early day motion in the House of Commons which – if accepted by the Government – would be debated when the House re-convened.

However, 10 January 1972 brought a new – if mildly mystifying – development. The secret buyer reappeared.

Thorn announced that it had entered into a contract to sell the Kirkby site for £1·2 million and a London estate agent disclosed that he had bought it as agent for an unnamed third party. The workers promptly tightened security at the plant in case Thorn tried to evict them in order to give the buyer a clear start.

---

* This sit-in had importance beyond Kirkby because it helped to redefine sit-ins at the time when a number of such events were occurring in Manchester engineering factories where workforces were trying to overturn a national wage agreement. (The Manchester sit-ins were unsuccessful since it was one of the rare occasions when the employers showed solidarity too.)

Spriggs later explained that it was publicity which had won the day at Fisher Bendix coupled with thorough organization. 'People don't appreciate the sheer effort that went into that sit-in. Other factories seemed to think that, if you sat there, things would come to you, but you've got to go out and work and search for everything – that's why we produced the Thorn product blacklist so stewards would know what to black, and it gave them an official piece of paper to persuade others. In their conflict, the CAV-Lucas people blacked other Lucas factories and alienated other Lucas workers. You can't blackmail people like that.'

The impact of the Kirkby sit-in was to affect the factory's subsequent reputation, since it became a symbol of industrial struggle for both rank and file movements and for employers.

One problem for the workers was boredom. It was difficult for everyone to come to work to do nothing. Some workers trickled away and accepted the redundancy money. Others were picking up cash driving taxis and doing odd jobs. At weekends the attendance was worse and sometimes the factory was guarded by a handful of men. Had Thorn a mind to move in, the recovery of the factory would, at times, have been easy.

The leaders decided to cultivate the media, be ready with information and encourage the press to attend meetings and to tour the factory. This was a strategic decision of some significance and was markedly different to the secretive posture adopted by workers in disputes at that time. They held an 'open day' for relatives and friends, complete with pop and theatrical groups, plus an address from some Merseyside Labour MPs. Thorn warned that any unauthorized person entering the factory could face prosecution for trespass. It was unclear whether this was directed at the MPs, the relatives, the press or at outside agitators who were rumoured to be running the sit-in.*

There was no substance in the rumours. Some strike committees are prepared to let outside influences into their councils, and there is rarely a shortage of offers.

---

* The search for baleful influences is an occupational hazard for those involved in industrial conflict. In the workers' eyes, the evil manipulators are invisible and usually reside in boardrooms. Their assumed malevolence is increased if they happen to be in the USA or the City. The assumption is that, unknowing and uncaring, they are just proceeding with a cold blooded profit-maximizing strategy.

The management fantasy is usually exercised over the political views of key dispute leaders and much energy is spent hunting for Reds under beds. Such political assumptions are often inconsistent and insulting to the discrimination of the workforce. However, they do provide a comforting cushion against unpalatable facts. As John Garnett of the Industrial Society has said, it is strange how managements talk about their 'loyal employees' when they approve of their behaviour, but call them 'the union members' when they're in dispute – as though they were not the same people. It might be too painful to say that 'our intelligent and skilled employees find our actions so repellent that they have walked out'.

Marxist and Trotskyist organizations offer 'assistance with the struggle'. The International Socialists and the Workers' Revolutionary Party have been the most assiduous campaigners in recent years. However, despite offers of help from Merseyside activists, the stewards said categorically that decisions would only be taken by duly elected representatives from Kirkby's shop-floor. No outsiders would be 'co-opted'.

Harold Wilson's diplomacy

Wilson's agent rang Spriggs to say: 'The boss wants to see you – no one else.' Spriggs demurred and insisted that Dick Jenkins should accompany him – concerned as always to have a witness and a partner beside him. (Avoiding isolation is almost an iron rule for union negotiators.)

On 12 January 1972 the two went, in secret, to the Golden Eagle Hotel in Kirkby to meet Wilson. Jimmy Jenkins also accompanied them as the representative of the staff unions. During the meeting Wilson was telephoned by Sir Jules Thorn, whom he knew well. He called on Thorn to defer closure of the plant and arranged to see Thorn at the House of Commons the following day to obtain more details of the plan to sell the factory.

No statement was issued after the House of Commons meeting. Wilson departed to his Huyton constituency, where he told Spriggs and Jenkins that he would be meeting Thorn executives and representatives of the mystery buyer during the next week. He asked the sit-in leaders to be available to travel to the House of Commons in case it would be helpful for them to join in. He revealed that, at the meeting with Sir Jules Thorn, they had 'exchanged some information and to some extent examined the situation before Thorn took over Fisher Bendix'. He would not be drawn on whether he knew the identity of the mystery purchaser.

Wilson met Thorn executives again at the Commons on

18 January. Prime Minister Heath was asked by Eric Heffer if he would meet the shop stewards when he visited Liverpool during the next month. He would not commit himself and was promptly accused of being 'frightened to meet us' by Jack Spriggs.

On 20 January Wilson caught the Liverpool sleeper to make his third visit to Kirkby in eleven days. He met the Kirkby stewards' leaders, and afterwards Spriggs said that the workers were sticking out for jobs for all at Fisher Bendix. Nothing less would do.

Wilson returned by train to London that afternoon and at Thorn's request again saw Sir Jules Thorn at the Commons.

It had become clear that Wilson was working towards a face-to-face meeting between shop stewards and management. This was encouraging for the workers since it implied that he thought that there was a chance of keeping the factory open and at least saving some of the jobs.

Wilson met Sir Jules yet again, following which Spriggs and the Jenkins brothers went to London for a negotiating meeting on 27 January.

Harold Wilson was host. After brief separate meetings the two groups were brought together in Wilson's Commons room with Harold acting initially as social host. He was quickly invited to chair the meeting. The talks lasted nine hours. The arguments revolved round the management's weary insistence that closure was inevitable and the men's defiant claim that all jobs should be kept intact. At the end of the day Wilson drew up a draft settlement which might lead to a compromise reprieve for Kirkby. He then went to Manchester where he appeared on a TV programme in which a regional MP faces questions from his constituents. He was pressed to amplify the Kirkby situation. He answered warily. Whereas the situation several weeks earlier had 'seemed utterly hopeless' he was now hopeful of an early settlement though there remained 'deep outstanding differences'.

Wilson returned that night to London where the joint

talks resumed at the Commons on the Friday. They lasted for several hours, after which he had to go to an unavoidable engagement in Bradford. But the discussions had made sufficient progress for the three shop stewards to agree to meet the Thorn executives again with Wilson at 9 a.m. the next day, Saturday, 29 January, at Kirkby. Wilson had advised Thorn not to break off negotiations, for if the stewards returned to Kirkby with time to hold a mass meeting, their attitudes would harden and the negotiations could stall. The urgent pace was not wasted, although Spriggs had to miss his beloved visit to watch Liverpool at Anfield. The meeting, once again in the Golden Eagle Hotel, finally reached agreement in mid-afternoon. Wilson timed his call to Anfield so that the agreement could be announced over the Tannoy at half-time.

Under the agreement, the factory would reopen and all 730 employees would be re-employed, although not necessarily permanently. Indeed, Thorn said that the labour force would drop. Half the factory would make radiators and electric storage heaters until at least the end of 1973. Thorn hoped to sell the other half to another industrial firm. It was a triumph of conciliation for Harold Wilson who had taken an initially hopeless case and, by persistence, had won an agreed reprieve for the factory, its workers and its operations.

But what did it really mean? Where was Mr X the mystery buyer? What other firm would take over the remaining half of the factory and what would they do with it? How many employees would *really* have job security to the end of 1973?

The answers were not immediately known since no hint of the negotiations between Thorn and Mr X was leaking out. It was a worry for the workers' leaders, but at least they had bought time. They received a fulsome tribute from Harold Wilson: 'They are constructive, statesman-like and determined to make a success of it . . . If it had not been for Jack Spriggs and his colleagues there would never have been any possibility even that we would have had the negotiations – still less got an agreement. If I could tell the workers one-tenth of what I would like to tell them of the role these three have played, I think they would feel their interests have been very well served.'

Wilson said that two factors had played a major part in his being able to steer the talks to success – his local industrial knowledge and his long-standing friendship with Sir Jules Thorn. Furthermore, he opined, as custodian of the agreement his presence would greatly reduce, if not eliminate, any possible redundancies. The workers accepted the agreement. It was better than they might have hoped even a week earlier.

Nevertheless the atmosphere remained brittle, for mistrust was now the dominant characteristic of relationships between management and workers. The stewards had offered better cooperation in making the factory a more economic and productive organization as part of the agreement, although they feared that radiator and storage heater manufacture alone would not employ seven hundred and thirty people. A joint committee of workers and management was set up to try to reconcile the need for jobs with the need for efficiency but, before it could make any progress, the situation changed dramatically. On 20 March the mystery buyer reappeared – this time with a name.

In come the money men

A great deal had already happened behind the scenes. Six months earlier Thorn had begun private negotiations to sell the Kirkby factory, though it wasn't an easy task – for what leading company would be mad enough to take it on?

Here was a factory which had never paid its way, with a militant workforce which had shown that it could thwart unpalatable plans. All the products were in highly competitive markets and the factory wasn't notably efficient with any product mix. Kirkby had brought the once profitable Parkinson Cowan to its knees. Now Thorn was anxious to get rid of it. Other companies would want to buy Fisher Bendix about as badly as they would want shares in the *Titanic*, and who, in 1971, had the profitable extra products to push into making Fisher Bendix successful – products moreover which they could not make equally well in their existing factories? The answer was – nobody.

The buyer would have to be a small organization, because large companies would be vulnerable to industrial action against their other plants if they tried to cut Kirkby down. The purchaser would also have to be confident of succeeding where others had failed or else believe that, having bought it, he could get out in one piece if the roof fell in. Thorn would have to offer some persuasive inducement to a would-be purchaser. 'We needed,' said Thorn later, 'a cocky mug to take it on.'

It was fair to say that the factory itself was moderately attractive, but the record of business performance and workforce behaviour was distinctly discouraging to any buyer. Nevertheless, property man Joe Hammerson had already entered into a conditional agreement to purchase the whole site just after the nine-week strike had ended. Hammerson undoubtedly wanted the site if Thorn could provide him with an empty factory. But Thorn had been repulsed by the workers in its efforts to sack them, and so the search began for someone to take on the business as well, in partnership with Hammerson, in case Thorn's next attempt to extract the good products and empty the factory also failed.

The man they found was Merseysider Harold King, but the money behind the deal came from December's not-so-secret visitor, Ivor Gershfield. King had met him socially on a ship in late 1971.

The complex activities which led to King becoming managing director of a public company, International Property Development Ltd (IPD), and to IPD buying the

Kirkby business from Thorn, make a story in themselves, but a brief outline will suffice.

Thorn struggles free

Thorn had been so desperate to rid itself of its Kirkby problem that it had quietly offered £500,000 to anyone willing to take the business over. Thorn secretly put this money into a Jersey trust, Harris, whose only director was Ivor Gershfield. Thorn also loaned the trust £600,000 interest-free for the first two years. These monies were then put into a newly formed company called Clohurst, which had King as a director. IPD promptly purchased Clohurst by issuing 5½ million new IPD shares to Harris.

Clohurst had just agreed to buy the Kirkby factory's machinery directly from Thorn for the knock-down price of £50,000 and also purchased all Kirkby's stocks and materials from Thorn for a further £355,000. Clohurst was buying the business from Thorn with Thorn's own money. Furthermore, Thorn agreed to give Clohurst certain indemnities against losses during its first six months of operation at Kirkby.

However IPD, via Clohurst, now owned the equipment and the materials, but not the factory buildings or the fifty acres of land. Thorn sold these for £1.2 million via a property company, Stanbourne, in which Ivor Gershfield's family held an interest. Clohurst had agreed to buy Kirkby's spare twenty acres of the land for £210,000 from Stanbourne and also agreed to purchase the factory buildings and the other thirty acres for £1.8 million or, at its option, to rent them for £207,000 per year. Without anything like enough ready cash to pay the £1.8 million, IPD was on the verge of providing Stanbourne with a handsome profit by purchasing Thorn's £1.2 million site for £2.01 million.

King joined the IPD board and a week later IPD announced that it had bought a loss-making soft drinks business from British Vending Industries, where King was a director. IPD continued to issue shares for cash, including $2^2/_3$ million to a newly registered company which contained only one asset, £595,000 in cash. However, despite those cash-raising deals, Clohurst still did not have the £1.8 million to buy the Kirkby factory from Stanbourne. Nor had its parent company, IPD, whose principal activities had been land and property development – including sugar plantations in Trinidad, on which housing development was scheduled.

These estates were the source of IPD's value. In 1962 the Trinidad land had been revalued from £167,293 to no less than £3,250,000. In 1966 the land was revalued again with a gain of a further £2,188,274.

The problem was IPD's profit and loss account. IPD might be good at profitable land investment, but what else could it do? Since 1964 it had made a loss in every year, bar 1968. In 1970 it lost £256,000 overall and had made a loss before paying interest on its loan stock in every single area in which it operated. In short, its trading record was lousy, and, indeed, one of its directors apparently believed that it could be approaching insolvency.

In May 1972, IPD's chairman resigned and King became chairman and managing director. One of the new board's first actions was to find the money to purchase the Kirkby site, which it did in July 1972 with £2 million borrowed from London & County Securities. (L & C was later to succumb in one of the City's more spectacular crashes.)

The money was borrowed on what were, in those days, penal terms. Not only would IPD have to pay interest at 5 per cent over bank rate, but would also deposit £350,000 with L & C and pay an extraordinarily dear commitment fee of £225,000 to L & C.

The decision to purchase the factory was strange. King explained to his board that 'to take up the lease of the factory could prove costly to the company and adversely affect the profitability of the group'. It was hard to see his reasoning. The factory was available for rent at £207,000 per annum, subject to periodic reviews – less than the interest payment to London & County.

However, IPD focussed its attention on to Kirkby's factory machinery. It was revalued at £1,195,350, compared with the £50,000 which Clohurst had paid for it.

This was all very well but IPD needed to turn its loss-making acquisitions rapidly into profit – if only to pay the interest to L & C. The land and buildings might increase in value, but IPD's purchase price of £1.8 million already assumed vacant possession of the site, and given the history of the workforce, these were risky inflations of the factory's value.

Despite IPD's lack of engineering experience, this was no time for morbid worries and King told shareholders that the Kirkby factory was one of the finest sheet metal plants in the country (this was correct) and would cost £5 million to replace, although the company had paid only £1.85 million for its facilities. He was right, except that nobody in his right mind was likely to replace it.

The Kirkby workers knew nothing of the background or implications of these intricate deals, though the announcement of 20 March had led them to believe that vending-machine production and other domestic appliance lines would be brought to the factory by IPD; but the drinks operation was all that ever arrived.

Their mood was optimistic. They had seen their jobs saved by a bouncy newcomer – King; there was a promise of extra work in the factory; Harold Wilson had given the deal an apparent seal of approval; they had received some financial compensation from Thorn as a transfer fee (about £300 each, based on service – roughly what Thorn had offered the previous July, but now the jobs were safe too) and there was the delicious prospect of expansion of the Kirkby workforce rather than yet more contraction.

Thorn had not done too badly either it seemed. It had

recovered some of its £4 million investment by selling off other Parkinson Cowan subsidiaries and now it had received £1.6 million for the Kirkby enterprise, less the £500,000 and the trading guarantees to Clohurst and less the costs of transferring the Fisher Bendix employees to Clohurst. Meanwhile, Clohurst had taken on some problematical tasks and the workers had lost their stranglehold on Thorn.

However, as the *Liverpool Free Press* concluded in its perceptive analysis* the undisputed winner was Ivor ('Ivor made a million') Gershfield. Apart from the £810,000 Stanbourne profit on the sale of the Kirkby factory and land, Harris had picked up over five million of IPD's shares at a time when their market price was rising strongly – assisted by the allure of the buoyant picture which IPD was painting. Given its desperation, there was considerable logic in Thorn's involving itself in these middlemen's deals, though Thorn later claimed not to know the full position. This may well be so, but they knew it to the extent that Clohurst's £500,000, in addition to the £600,000 loan, had come from Thorn, and the agreement which sold the factory to IPD specifically listed the £1.2 million payable to Thorn and the £810,000 to Stanbourne. The agreement, dated 13 July 1972, was signed by Gershfield for Stanbourne and by Gaston Jack Strowger – managing director of Thorn.

---

* No. 15, May 1974. For stories like the Gershfield exposé, reporter Brian Whittaker won an award from North-Western journalists as 'Reporter of the Year' – the first such award in Britain to an alternative paper.

4. The reign of King: 1972–4

- Success at last
- Behind the scenes
- Britain's three-day week
- Benn begins to help

Perhaps it was just as well that nobody at Kirkby knew anything about these financial manoeuvres for there were enough problems as it was without adding further palpitations.

On the face of it the new deal looked good. None of the 730 workers would lose their jobs, although initially there would be work-sharing while production was being sorted out. Full employment would be provided for all by the end of 1972. The new owners had retained the radiator business and would make Constor electric storage heaters for Thorn. Furthermore, it was reported that Clohurst hoped to bring the manufacture of vending-machines and new domestic appliances to Kirkby.

Harold Wilson was reported to be happy with the arrangements. 'I have met the buyer and I am hopeful that he will be able to make this factory a prosperous one. I am delighted that there has been a successful conclusion to this situation and wish both sides the best of luck.'

King declared that he was no saviour. 'Miracles have nothing to do with getting this factory right. The only way to make a success of it is by bloody hard work.'

All in all, it was not surprising that the workers' leaders were delighted at what Jack Spriggs called 'the best news this factory has had for a long time'. The shop stewards recommended it as the best deal they would get, and the workers backed it unanimously.

Thorn had extricated itself from an apparently intractable situation. It had recovered some monies from Fisher

Bendix, had rid itself of some loss-making activities, had extracted the valuable Bendix business, and, most potently of all, had ensured the removal of any threat to black its other factories, should Kirkby again collapse. The workers were now on their own. Thorn had effectively severed all public links and liabilities.

Clohurst's position was interesting. Clohurst would have to become rapidly profitable, make the half-empty Kirkby factory cover its operating overheads (a feat which had eluded Thorn and Parkinson Cowan even when more products were being made), pay the rent and turn round the drinks operation from loss to profit. It was a daunting task for Harold King.

King himself was not so much an enigma as a puzzle. Ebullient, self-confident, flashy, local-Merseysider-made-good, undoubtedly smart and enterprising, he seemed knowledgeable and competent. His record was not altogether impressive, but beggars could not be choosers. The workers were in a susceptible state. He had agreed to save the jobs and keep the factory running, and this was no time to kick a gift horse in the teeth. The Kirkby people were in no position to rebuff King, nor did they have the knowledge to appraise his competence. They were later to claim that they'd always thought he was a 'no-mark'* but the evidence of the time did not suggest that they had made such a judgement.

Part of the difficulty for the workers in sizing up King was an understandable wish to believe in him. This led to a certain amount of self-delusion. The hunger to show Thorn that the factory could work had carried over from the January sit-in. Now it was, in part, a defiant desire to show Thorn that it had been wrong. The workers wanted to believe in King, so they did – not wholly of course, nor was their faith altogether misplaced.

* Merseyside 'Scouse' phrase for 'a nobody'; 'a poseur'; 'a pretentious person'.

Success at last

King set about reorganizing Kirkby with some gusto. He met the convenors and stewards to discuss plans for the factory on the day after the announcement. He was to address employees for the first time at a mass meeting on 4 April 1972 – the day he officially took over the factory.

The mass meeting was not a total success. Perhaps King had not expected people to ask him how much money there was and what were his operating plans. To compound the difficulties, the workers knew so little about Clohurst that they could neither frame the questions nor judge the answers. They were to recollect that King's overall demeanour was confident but his answers seemed unclear.

King initially negotiated a six-month deal with the shop stewards in which there would be no resistance in principle to reorganization. There would be no restrictive practices nor strikes, although the workers did reserve the right to withdraw their labour if a major point of principle arose. In return for the deal, the workers were to be paid no less than they would be on their normal jobs – even if reorganization meant their sweeping the floor for a while.

The factory, Jack Spriggs opined, would go from strength to strength and was secure for future years.

Six months after Clohurst took control, King told shareholders that there had been a dramatic turnaround. Almost seven hundred employees were now full time, and shift working was being extended. 'The progress the factory is now making is to the credit equally of management, unions and employees, all of whom have combined to prove that a factory on Merseyside can be as reliable, quality-conscious and productive as any in Europe. I do not wish,' King continued, 'to make a forecast at this stage, but, if we maintain the rate of progress which has already been achieved since May of this year, your company should speedily be returned to the dividend list. . .

The surplus manufacturing capacity of your new subsidiary at Kirkby is now being rapidly taken up with a diversity of products which will ensure a continuity that supports my remarks regarding a return to the dividend list.'

The 'diversity of products' was the range of fruit drinks which King now described as 'profitable', together with some contract presswork for steel panels for the motor industry.

King also mentioned that Kirkby's 'new industrial relations philosophy has already shown excellent results in the loyalty and productivity of the workforce employed'. It was a bullish statement, for further acquisitions were forecast for IPD which, together with property development on the company's land, were expected to produce a further profit of £750,000 over the next eighteen months – apart from £200,000 in current property transactions. They were the kind of remarks which would scarcely harm IPD's share price.

A new wage and conditions agreement was then reached between workers and management which would have been excellent had the company been able to afford it. Holidays were extended; wages were raised to £35 and basic hours were cut to 35 by finishing at noon on Friday. (This new 4½-day week was never to change.) One pound an hour basic was an excellent wage at the time. The permanent night-shift workers only worked 26 hours per four-night week because King thought that 'it would be wasting money to work longer and, anyway, I believe that night work is anti-social'. It did not sound convincing. The costs of night work must have been substantial.

But with King labelling them 'the best in Europe' and the company apparently succeeding, the workers were bemused. King amplified his views in April 1973 by saying 'It's a man's basic pay which matters. There aren't many people on Merseyside doing this kind of work who can say they are on £35 basic.' The factory, it was said, was making money. IPD's shares had risen from 10p to 35p.

According to King, much of the success of the factory was due to the open, easy relationship with factory convenor Jack Spriggs. 'It seems,' said King, 'that he and I can talk to each other.' On the anniversary of the takeover they were pictured in the local press posing together over lunch, though no food was in evidence. King looked beautiful with his elegant grooming and clothes. Spriggs was warily clutching a canteen knife.

King's views on unions were disparaging since he claimed that he could do as much good for the workers himself. There were no strikes related to the running of the factory itself though there had been a brief stoppage over a national dispute. It wasn't a bad industrial record, and, whatever King's feelings, IPD's expansion plans for the adjacent twenty acres didn't seem to be affected. Seven factories would be built in the first phase. The development would, when complete, be worth £3 million and bring in a minimum annual rent of £360,000. It could create 1,200 new jobs for the town. It would be, said IPD, 'another development in the success story' of the once troubled Fisher Bendix plant, which itself was to recruit three hundred more workers.

'They have shown that with the right management approach, they are as productive as any in the world. They have put the factory on a profit-making basis for the first time in years.' King had turned round what one commentator was to describe as 'a seemingly hopeless mixture of militant workers and £1 million-a-year losses'. But his rapid recruitment created problems for the future. The three hundred new workers were socially isolated on the new evening twenty eight-hour-a-week 'twilight' shift, and the longer serving workers thought that some of the new recruits were cowboys, even though many of them were relatives of existing employees. There had been no time to take up references, given the speed of recruitment. Much later, the twilight shift was quietly abandoned and the workers absorbed into the two main shifts. Unease about their quality never fully evaporated and the workers' leaders consistently quoted King's recruitment as a mistake.

In July 1973 Clohurst changed its name to IPD (Industrial) Ltd, and claimed a turnover of £5 million a year. In October, IPD's half-year figures showed a profit of £232,000 and assets per share were quoted as being 60p against the market price of 34p. The Trinidad land had been revalued again, this time with an uplift of over £8 million. A Liverpool newspaper reported that 'with every chance of net assets next year reaching £1 a share there should be bags of potential in the current price'. They were breathless times.

Behind the scenes

In fact IPD had been negotiating for a Government loan for months, and the Kirkby operation was severely pressed for cash, with some major suppliers becoming reluctant to continue to trade with IPD (I). IPD had reminded Government of the 'greatly improved industrial relations resulting from Mr King's imaginative and successful productivity deal'. The situation, it said, had improved dramatically. Kirkby had been a disaster before; help was needed soon and IPD could put no more money in.

In February 1973, IPD (I) had been offered an £850,000 loan under Section 7 of the Industry Act. It was dependent on IPD injecting £250,000 and guaranteeing the Government loan. Other conditions were that IPD (I) would not be allowed to purchase shares in other companies and permanent managers (approved by the Secretary of State for Industry) would have to replace the management consultants who were currently running the place for King. Nor could IPD (I) repay the Harris loan without Government permission. IPD declined the loan and instead obtained an overdraft from Barclays Bank. This enabled IPD to repay the Harris loan in November 1973 thus releasing the 5½ million IPD shares which had been used to buy Clohurst and its cash. The circumstances were puzzling. What on earth was IPD doing borrowing money at bank rate plus 2 or 3 per cent from Barclays and then paying off the Harris loan which was still interest-free? Even more pertinent was the cost of the London & County loan at bank rate plus 5 per cent which King had already said IPD might 'repay, or at least very substantially reduce, well in advance of the due date of December 1974'. The Harris loan was cheaper and went on for longer, so that repaying the £600,000 Harris loan – even after allowing for Thorn's £50,000 repayment discount – was twice as expensive to IPD as a repayment of the same sum to L & C. The IPD shares meanwhile were buoyed up by King's talk of dividends, a turnround into profit and the prospects of profits reaching £750,000 for the eighteen months to end 1974. IPD (I) alone had a 1974 profit forecast in excess of £500,000. The £8 million Trinidad revaluation hadn't harmed shareholder sentiment either.

It had been IPD (I)'s hope of a Government loan which had led to the costly repayment of the Harris loan and the release of Harris's 5½ million IPD shares. The hope was not justified for, as IPD (I) deteriorated, Government analysis in early 1974 suggested that up to £1.5 million was by then needed to give IPD (I) enough working capital.

King's family interests had acquired 1½ million IPD shares in late 1972. This purchase did not appear on the circular sent to shareholders on 25 October 1972 – the holding was shown as 20,000 shares. King has repeatedly declined to explain the circumstances of these purchases but, at market price, they would have cost his family interests about £500,000. His father was a retired postman.

Britain's three-day week

The next pressure came from outside. In January 1974 the factory was allocated Thursday, Friday and Saturday as its working days in the three-day week which was the

Heath Government's attempt to deal simultaneously with the oil crisis and with Britain's striking miners.

Since work at the factory stopped at noon on Fridays, half the allocated days were in normal leisure time. The TUC, unsympathetic to attempts to ameliorate the effects of the struggle, had instructed that abnormal working hours should attract the appropriate overtime premiums. Friday afternoon and all Saturday would be 'overtime', despite the idleness of Monday, Tuesday and Wednesday. As loyal trade unionists, the Kirkby men were in a bind. The four hundred drinks workers were exempt from the restrictions. King asked the rest of the employees to work on normal pay for their three days, but they refused.

He gave way and began to pay overtime, regretting that they could not show more loyalty. Jack Spriggs, obviously unhappy, replied that it wasn't a question of showing disloyalty. He realized that it was costly but had to stick to the standard agreement as advised by the trade union movement. The workers would join management in fighting for a change in the allocated days in order to avoid overtime. They were unsuccessful. These extra payments,' said King, 'will obviously affect the future of the company.'

In fact, IPD (I) was already in trouble. The three-day week was not helping, but the indication was that it would never have made it to the end of 1974. The factory was under-used, had a large rent bill and uneconomic working hours. The products were in tough markets which either faced stiff price competition (fruit juice and radiators) or else were stagnating (night storage heaters).

The parent company IPD, was stretched too. It might have all worked if the Trinidad development had accelerated according to schedule and the three-day week not jolted everyone's plans, but they weren't very plausible excuses. The whole enterprise was a precarious affair in which optimistic adjustments were made to the balance sheets while little occurred to relieve the weaknesses of the profit and loss accounts.

Early in 1974, IPD reapplied for a Government loan as the new minority Labour Government took office, but the Department of Industry was far from happy about IPD (I)'s prospects.

On 13 June 1974 the loan story became public. Harold King announced that the new Labour Government – in the shape of Industry Secretary, Tony Benn – had turned down the IPD (I) request for a £1 million loan under the 1972 Industry Act. It had been turned down, said King, because 'IPD (I) did not seem to have a viable future'. He would have no choice but to close down the firm. His statement followed a meeting with Barclays Bank over IPD (I)'s overdraft. What, the bank had asked him, was he going to do about the large sum outstanding? His answer had evidently not found favour. The bank had had enough. Indeed Barclays had already asked insolvency specialists, Cork, Gully, to investigate IPD (I) some months before.

The workers were 'shocked', 'bewildered', and 'stunned'. King was 'sickened'. Dick Jenkins said that the workers had realized some time ago that there were some financial troubles, though there was no evidence that the employees had used the knowledge to change their behaviour or to brace themselves for a shock.

Benn begins to help

Spriggs was on holiday and returned on the Saturday to find a message from his MP, Eric Heffer, who was Benn's Minister of State at the Industry Department. Spriggs was to ring Benn that evening. When he did, Benn told him that if IPD (I) drifted into receivership, the stewards should then come forward with the workers' own proposals. The factory should not be allowed to close, stated Benn. On his return from Brussels on 18 June he would meet the stewards to discuss ways of keeping the plant open.

The weekend over, the stewards' leaders met King and

they emerged in an optimistic mood to tell the 1,200 workers that they were discussing alternative possibilities for avoiding redundancies or closure of the factory.

Spriggs was not alarmed – at least not outwardly. 'I do not believe the Government has made a final decision. I am sure there are still plenty of possibilities. . . Although I am concerned about what Mr King has said, I am not depressed because there is still plenty of hope.' Spriggs was assuming that the £1 million loan was the required liquid working cash. The truth was that the £1 million would have done little to stave off the wretched condition into which IPD (I) had plunged. Wilson and Benn had been advised that it would be better to let IPD (I) go all the way to receivership because £1 million would soon be consumed by the tottering firm without improving the basic situation. Yet Wilson was in a weak position to resist some form of rescue because he had made such a hullaballoo about his triumphant role at Kirkby in IPD's 1972 takeover.

The convenors reached the Department of Industry on 18 June to find Under-Secretary John Lippitt, scotch in hand, watching the World Cup on TV while he waited for Benn to arrive from Brussels. They joined him and settled down to wait.

When Benn arrived the leaders told him that they wanted the factory to be taken over by another company or to be nationalized, because 'they did not want to be run by capitalists'. Benn pointed out that he couldn't force a company to take them over, and did they have any idea of the shape the new scheme should be? They did not, for the convenors felt that it was Government's responsibility to create a solution. The leaders were suspicious of the officials and, initially, of Benn also, feeling that he was being used to put them into a corner to frighten them into a receivership in which they could be allowed to perish. Spriggs believed that it was not possible to recover from a receivership and that suggesting such a route was the officials' method of sinking the business for good.

Nevertheless, the convenors returned to Kirkby in a buoyant mood from their two-hour meeting with Benn. They had been impressed by Benn's evident willingness to try to be helpful and he did give them evidence for his sincerity. It wasn't just the sight of the huge trade union banner behind his desk. His descriptions of his actions to support the *Scottish Daily News* and Meriden motorcycle cooperatives had been persuasive. He had also mentioned UCS.

The significance of the cooperative angle did not register with the convenors. Their central worry was the realization that the onus for an initiative rested on their shoulders and that, if they didn't suggest something, there would be no proposal from the Department. Back at Kirkby they puzzled over the prospects for progress, knowing that nobody but Government would come to their rescue, given the workers' militant reputation.

Two days after their meeting with Benn, the leader's optimism rose further. Robert Kilroy-Silk (the new Labour MP for Ormskirk into which constituency Kirkby had now been shifted) had asked the Prime Minister – or 'Big H' as Spriggs now referred to him – to take an interest in the attempt to create a cooperative. Wilson replied, 'We don't rule out, if necessary, the Government taking over the premises and providing for suitable management.' Both King and the workers' leaders welcomed his statement and Spriggs made it clear that the workers were still backing King. 'We have no complaints about the way he has treated us in the past. He has done a good job at Kirkby and deserves credit for it.' (The problem for Benn and Silk was that of detaching Spriggs and Jenkins from standing shoulder to shoulder with King. It took a while before the penny dropped with the convenors.)

King went with the convenors to meet Benn again and called for the Government to nationalize IPD (I), which was a novel proposition from an industrialist. Benn wasn't interested in helping King, but he and Heffer called for a feasibility study of the plant's long-term prospects, to gauge the likely cost of saving the jobs.

In front of his officials, Benn kept mentioning UCS and Meriden. The convenors took the hint. During a recess they decided to propose a workers' cooperative – perhaps running the place themselves would be better for the workers. They proposed it to Benn and Heffer.

It is worth making clear that the people at Kirkby never consciously set out to establish a cooperative. Their main motive – and that of their leaders – was the saving of jobs. The idea of the cooperative was primarily reactive. It sprang from no deep-felt or widespread ideological commitment. As Spriggs put it later, 'No one would take us on. The people wanted to work no matter what – so we formed the principle of a cooperative and of course the workers accepted it. They didn't think it up. It was nice to become part of history, but it was Hobson's choice.'

Benn was later to say that he was very nervous because he wasn't sure he could deliver via a minority Government and the convenors had been very suspicious of his saying that he *wouldn't* help IPD but *would* wish to save the jobs. Only when they became convinced that he was sincere could progress be made.

Benn had raised the idea of a cooperative, though, as he pointed out, nothing would have come to fruition without the workers' own efforts. It was no use sitting across the table from weak people because he couldn't prop them up if they weren't strong enough to sustain their own case. That's why Spriggs had been such a tower of strength, said Benn, because when the civil servants later tried to break down the workers' case, as they did incessantly, Spriggs just wouldn't have it.

King, meanwhile, was still trying to stave off the collapse of IPD (I) and claimed that the most sensible plan would be for Government to acquire the enterprise because, he stressed, it was facing a cash shortage – not a solvency problem. In fact it *was* a solvency problem and it was scarcely surprising that King wanted the Government to take on the enterprise, particularly since he wanted the takeover price to be related to the value of the plant. (It will be remembered that IPD had bought the machinery for £50,000 and revalued it at £1,195,350.)

King also hinted that he might stay on as chairman, and Spriggs made it clear that the workers would be happy to have him continue as the boss. Despite this apparent air of goodwill, King was fretful over the desperate state of the Kirkby enterprise and the lack of any Government help and so, on 29 June 1974 every employee received a copy of his letter announcing immediate closure of the factory and the redundancy of the entire workforce.

He was swiftly induced to substitute a temporary lay-off so that the employees could claim social security benefits, though some workers were already talking about the possibility of a second sit-in like the 1972 affair.

On 2 July the consultancy firm of Inbucon began the feasibility study proposed by Benn. Uniquely, they were to work jointly for the Government and the Kirkby workers, though Government would pay for it all. King would not be allowed by the Industry Department to take part in the study, for by this stage mutual trust between IPD and Government was at a low ebb. Tony Benn said that he was watching the situation hour by hour.

King again claimed that the £1 million loan would do the trick. 'With £1 million the company can carry on where it left off as a viable enterprise employing over a thousand people in an area that badly needs all the jobs it can get. It could even expand and take on more people. Without the £1 million the company falls, over a thousand lose their jobs and the Government has to pay out millions of pounds of taxpayers' money in unemployment and other benefits. It also loses all the tax revenue from PAYE and all the insurance contributions.'

It was an emotional appeal to a Labour Government which was anxious about unemployment; but the claimed benefit of the £1 million loan was illusory. Even at the end of 1973 the operation was in financial trouble.* Barclays Bank had become increasingly restive about the overdraft and there was little in the way of assets in IPD (I) to reassure them. The £1 million loan would only have staved off the pressure for a while and done little to overcome the basic problems at Fisher Bendix. The Industry Department was even dubious about the viability of the parent company.

But King's style had not changed. He gave an interview to the *Liverpool Daily Post* which reported that King's personal philosophy of business is that it is 'an art form – a creative way of achieving happiness'. King's creative art had been well displayed in his interpretations of IPD's prospects and situation. 'Making money for money's sake without benefiting anyone else is pointless.' In this he had succeeded – certainly to the extent of benefiting Ivor Gershfield. 'This is why I am so concerned about the future of this factory. If ever the day came when I had to close it down permanently, and get rid of all the people who work here it would defeat the whole object of my being in business.' Defeat was a matter of days away, though King was to live to fight another day.

King claimed to have a lot of critics. 'The human being is a very covetous and envious creature. That, I think, is why I probably have so many enemies.' The fact that his critics were mainly concerned about the effectiveness of his business practices seemed to escape him, for all his undoubted smartness.

King's public views included elements of sanctimonious self-delusion and maudlin twaddle.

On 10 July, aid under the Industry Act was refused to

---

* The statement of affairs in the High Court was later to reveal that IPD (Industrial) had lost £220,968 in 1972 after crediting Thorn's £265,000 towards initial trading losses. The net loss of £301,897 in 1973 was achieved after crediting a number of items including £266,800 of deferred and capitalized costs. In the period from 1 January to 11 July 1974, IPD (Industrial) had lost no less than £891,554.

IPD (I) and King told an emergency meeting of his board that he could obtain no more credit. Barclays Bank was informed and on 11 July 1974 it put IPD (I) into receivership. King's reign was over and yet another management had bitten the dust.

5. Birth of the cooperative: 1974

- The consultants show the way
- The workers' business plan
- Structuring the cooperative
- Undermined by Whitehall
- Thumbs down from the Government's advisers
- The receiver's coup
- Political squalls
- A death sentence
- The cooperative sets sail
- The first storm

The receiver, Roger Cork of Cork, Gully, the London firm of solvency specialists, had scarcely arrived at Kirkby before the workers threw him out following his statement, based on Inbucon's figures, that the work in hand would only employ 450 people. The leaders insisted on all 1,100 being employed, and when he refused he was told to leave. Spriggs wouldn't let him address the mass meeting. Cork having gone, the workers welded the gates shut.

Cork went over the leaders' heads and advertised his proposals in the local press, but to no avail, because he wouldn't agree to fund the thumping weekly loss which would result from employing everyone. Heffer, as Minister of State at the Industry Department, wrote to say that Government would consider purchasing the factory if there was a workable scheme to provide lasting employment, but Government would not help IPD (I) because it wasn't possible to have confidence in its prospects.

The first task was to sort out the deadlock with Cork. Spriggs leaked a threat to take the workers down to Barclays main office in Liverpool and sit in there. Indeed there was one invasion by workers pressing for their holiday pay. This alarmed the bank and the leaders were promptly invited to visit Cork at his London office. They worked out a scheme on the train going down, whereby everyone would be re-employed on a flat thirty-five-hour week for four weeks out of six. There would be a rota of layoffs for the other two weeks so that people could obtain social security benefits. This was agreed, thus enabling Inbucon to complete its appraisal of Kirkby's prospects whilst Cork tried to sell the enterprise as a going concern.

The workers accepted the work-sharing deal with some relief, collected their holiday money from Cork and went off on the annual two-week break. Spriggs told them that the Cabinet was then meeting in London with Benn's recommendation of Government takeover as the last item on its agenda.

Work resumed under Cork's management after the holiday and the number of workers on the books soon fell because Cork was willing to organize redundancy for anyone who wanted it. The stewards agreed to let volunteers go, and, over the autumn, upwards of 250 people departed. The rest worked as hard as trading conditions would allow. The principal job was fixing the leaks in the stock of radiators, for, as the King era was ending, the production and inspection quality had fallen in the factory. As Spriggs put it, 'We have to show everyone how well we can operate. It is vital to make the best of the work-sharing and show a cooperative and united front.' He told reporters that 'we have had enough uncertainty about our jobs to last a lifetime. This time Government has to produce a solution which will take away this abnormal worry. It is a terrible strain having to fight for our jobs every two years.'

The Inbucon study continued as Government pondered alternative ways of coping with the problem. Was it worth helping at all? If the business was to be saved, was it better to buy it from the receiver as a going concern or let it go all the way and pick up the bits cheaply from the defunct business?

Cork was drawing a blank in his search for a buyer.

One or two companies were interested, but walked away when they found that the workers wanted everyone to be re-employed. The employees, said Cork later, just wouldn't accept that with everyone restored to the payroll, the plant would be permanently unprofitable. Other firms were approached with offers of Government support, but they didn't want the Kirkby problem coming anywhere near their own factories. Nobody had really thought through the way in which a Government-sponsored reconstruction would work. King seemed to think that Government would invite him back to run the Kirkby operation which was, as he put it, 'an undoubted success; if you like, my little brain-child brought to life'.

On 2 September all the parties gathered at Benn's office – Spriggs, Jenkins, Cork, King, Inbucon. Cork reported that he could not find a buyer for Kirkby as a going concern and wanted a definite solution in sight if he were to continue beyond the end of the month. Otherwise he would have to auction off what remained. Benn said that if the stewards prepared a detailed and sensible scheme for a workers' cooperative he would give it full consideration. The leaders should report back to him after discussing a price for the factory and its contents with the receiver. Meanwhile, Government would support the receiver for a limited period with up to £27,500 per week of temporary assistance.

The consultants show the way

By now the leaders had been in touch with Meriden and had also received – as had Benn's department – the Inbucon report. The fifty-five-page document was quite clear in its conclusions. If the factory carried on with 1,100 people and its previous volume of business, up to £2 million a year could be lost. The drinks operation should be discontinued since it was doubtful that it could ever become viable and might not even recover its direct costs before paying for any overheads. On the other hand, the engineering activities could be developed to reach break-even – or better – though this was likely to take up to a year. The revised business would provide employment for 590 people, including 150 indirect workers and 130 in administration, though further profitable work would be needed to generate enough profit to secure the business in the long term.

Inbucon gauged that the depressed radiator market would not recover to 1973 levels for at least two years and that industry over-capacity would lead to severe competition within one year. Kirkby's understaffed sales force would be poorly placed to hold its market share of 8 per cent, and a competent management team should be recruited as well as a strengthened marketing group. There was also the prospect of some market trends towards high efficiency radiators, which then accounted for an insignificant segment of the market. The prospects for Constor night storage heaters were reasonably good and profit margins might improve.

Kirkby could also service the extremely large demand for contract presswork where the prospects for expansion in the long term were excellent, provided that the marketing activity was developed to match the level and expertise of the manufacturing competence. Kirkby's quality and delivery performance was considered to be of a high standard. The only criticism Inbucon had heard was that IPD's presswork was somewhat overpriced. However, there was a good base for competing successfully and substantially increasing this activity. A new work, pay and productivity scheme was needed to raise performance appreciably and rapidly and to reduce the excessive costs of the twilight and night shifts.

It was a crisp, professional, even-handed analysis of Kirkby's operations and prospects.

The workers' leaders now had to prepare a case for Government aid, relying on Inbucon's report and their own limited knowledge of business. They had little skill and no experience in preparing either a financial case or a business plan. They already felt that an experienced outside manager would be needed to run their cooperative on a day-to-day basis. Meanwhile, Inbucon agreed that its consultants would assist the stewards informally to develop a three-year business plan as part of the workers' submission for Government aid, though Inbucon made it clear that it did not necessarily agree with the stewards' assumptions about the Kirkby enterprise.

The workers' business plan

The employees' leaders were under great pressure. Not only did they have to grapple with unfamiliar considerations, but time was of the essence. The general election campaign was already under way, and there was no guarantee that the Labour Government would still be in office after 10 October 1974.

Benn visited the factory on 6 September and told the workers of his 'deep personal commitment'. They had 'earned the right to find a new structure for the factory . . . I am anxious,' he said, 'to promote your proposals inside the Government.'

On 13 September 1974 the two leaders, Spriggs and Jenkins, submitted the workers' application for a grant of £3,901,000 under Section 7 of the 1972 Industry Act. The proposal, which the Industry Department termed 'the convenors' considered plan', would enable the workers to buy the whole business at Kirkby, excluding the factory building and land, which they would rent from IPD. The grant would provide working capital to run the business and cover any initial losses. It also included £500,000 for investment in new machinery.

There was one major snag. As the Industry Department soon deduced, the application was hopelessly insufficient even on the applicants' assumptions, let alone on the more cautious basis of the Department's analysis. The cooperators had asked for some £850,000 too little for their requirements in the first year alone. The leaders had originally wanted this extra sum plus about £1.75 million to buy the factory from IPD. Officials had pointed out that the less the workers asked for, the easier it would be to support the application, and so the leaders had deleted the site purchase and whittled down their other plans. As later events were to show, this economy was to determine the cooperative's likely destiny before it could even start trading and made Inbucon's objective difficult to achieve.*

However, the convenors' submission did incorporate a number of Inbucon's proposals. The twilight shift would not return, management would be strengthened from outside and strict financial controls would be needed. It was intended to introduce a range of profitable new products to complement or replace low-margin activities such as drinks. The main focus would be on engineering products, and so the high level of adaptability in the workforce – arising from all the different products which they had made over the years – would be underpinned by a strengthened expertise in product development. Presswork business would be expanded rapidly using a new, full-time sales organization.

It was all good stuff, but there was one major deviation from Inbucon's requirements. The convenors proposed to employ 913 people rather than the consultant's 590. The drinks business would be retained and developed, though its viability would be reviewed critically and quickly. The leaders felt that the drinks market could become profitable once divorced from its erratic history under King. Furthermore they saw a more rapid upturn in the radiator market than had Inbucon. Storage heater sales would recover from the impact of electricity price rises and the

---

* It is worth noting that everybody involved at Kirkby thought that the application had to be below £5 million or else it would have to be approved by the House of Commons. This wasn't true – there was no such limit on Section 7 assistance – but it was certainly believed to be true at the critical time.

new sales organization would swiftly expand presswork business.

Inbucon had been particularly flattering about Kirkby's presswork reputation and the prospects for gaining new business. Nevertheless, the convenors' optimism was worrying, particularly over the drinks business. But one of the objectives was to save the maximum number of jobs, and it could prove difficult to ditch people who had hung on through all the struggles. Sacking people was the last thing the convenors wanted to do and besides, they could claim that they were already showing the necessary commitment to efficiency by letting natural wastage take the workforce below 913. Despite this legitimate argument, the retention of the drinks business and its personnel was to offer a powerful obstacle which was to be well exploited by Benn's opponents.

Structuring the cooperative

There was also a question mark over the way the cooperative would be organized. Consideration had been given to establishing the enterprise under the aegis of the Industrial and Provident Societies Act (1965), but it was dropped – partly because the Industry Department officials insisted that the cooperative would need a limited liability company as the trading vehicle and so only a separate cooperative could be registered as a society.[*]

The convenors' submission visualized a company in which all shares would be held in trust for its workers (or else by Government if that was a condition of financial support). The mechanism for actually running the busi-

[*] This is not a criticism of either workers or officials. Only with hindsight did the cooperative's framework assume a greater significance than was realized at the time. The assumption in 1974 was that the enterprise could be arranged to work effectively as a result of enthusiastic goodwill and the growth of experience. People in the cooperative movement were later to claim that if the cooperative had registered under the IPS Act it would have been better able to succeed.

ness was unclear, which was scarcely surprising in view of the haste of the submission's development. The Inbucon report had only been available for a few weeks and it was a mere three months since King's shock announcement of closure.

The convenors had already asked local solicitors to set up a limited liability company, initially under the name of Merseyside Manufacturing Industries Ltd, with Spriggs and Jenkins as directors, together with four stewards who would represent the other four unions. Apart from this proposed board for MMI Ltd – a name which was soon changed to Kirkby Manufacturing and Engineering Company Ltd (KME) because the name MMI Ltd was found to be already registered by another company – the proposed organization system had two central features (see Figure 1 overleaf).

The objectives and policies of the enterprise would be determined by a management board of managers and workforce representatives. It would include the four most senior managers (managing director and the finance/administration, marketing and works directors), who would manage the business day to day. They would not be directors of KME Ltd, though they would be recruited 'at board level' – whatever that meant. Three of the six worker directors of KME Ltd would also be on the management board which would have three further outside 'directors' who would not be on the board of KME Ltd, one of whom might be invited to become chairman of the management board.

Secondly, there would be an implementation review group. This non-executive body would enable a larger number of shop-floor workers to make detailed reviews of progress towards the achievement of company objectives. It could monitor progress at first hand through formal discussion of action plans.

The structure was intended to give workers 'extensive oversight' over the company's development, though day-to-day operation would be the responsibility of managers

Figure 1 The workers' proposed company structure,
September 1974

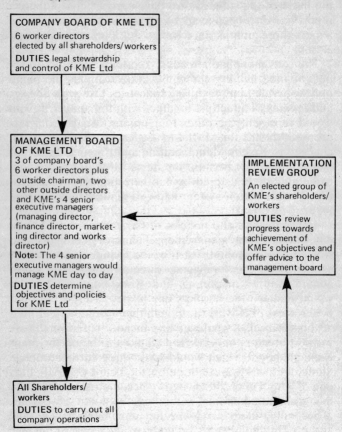

COMPANY BOARD OF KME LTD
6 worker directors
elected by all shareholders/workers
DUTIES legal stewardship
and control of KME Ltd

MANAGEMENT BOARD
OF KME LTD
3 of company board's
6 worker directors plus
outside chairman, two
other outside directors
and KME's 4 senior
executive managers
(managing director,
finance director, market-
ing director and works
director)
Note: The 4 senior
executive managers would
manage KME day to day
DUTIES determine
objectives and policies
for KME Ltd

IMPLEMENTATION
REVIEW GROUP
An elected group of
KME's shareholders/
workers
DUTIES review
progress towards
achievement of
KME's objectives and
offer advice to the
management board

All Shareholders/
workers
DUTIES to carry out all
company operations

Note
The cooperative itself was expected to arise as a separate structure. The overall
structure of the complete enterprise was unclear at this time — even to the
leaders — as the proposals continued to evolve.

'designated with specific tasks'. Workers' representatives on the management board would 'have a major influence over the determination of all aspects of company policy', whilst relying on other directors for professional advice on key matters.

While it is fair to emphasize the speed with which the application had been prepared and note that it did recognize the uncertainties by saying that the structure allowed flexibility and suited initial needs 'as far as they can be foreseen at the present time', the proposal did beg one crucial question. Who would actually carry out the policy?

There would be a management board determining policy and a review group monitoring its progress, but who was to turn policy into progress? The managers would run the business day to day, but to whom were they accountable? Legal responsibility for the company would rest with the six worker directors, three of whom would be on the management board as well. The managers would presumably be responsible to the company shareholders – the workers themselves. Each worker director would probably be selected by his union members so that the AUEW director would represent hundreds of workers and the ASTMS director only a handful.

It wasn't clear whether there would be a cooperative separate from the trading company or who would 'designate specific tasks' to the managers. There was no mention of the Kirkby shop stewards' committee. Perhaps everything would all fall into place so that control and accountability could be securely defined and a workable structure developed. It was, after all, an experiment, and these were all prospective problems. The first step would be to induce Government to cough up the money.

Undermined by Whitehall

This was a daunting task, for the Industry Department's Industrial Development Unit (IDU) produced a damning report on the workers' application which concluded that the proposed enterprise was not viable even if Government made good the £850,000 underfunding and provided finance to buy the factory. Benn had, most unusually, given the IDU report to the cooperators as part of his persistent concern for open government. The IDU could scarcely have expected him to do this and its document was an eye-opener.

It repeatedly misrepresented Inbucon's conclusions. For example, on presswork Inbucon had painted a bright picture of prospects and had written:

- presswork would be plentiful and could provide consistently profitable business for efficient firms
- the scope of facilities at IPD (I) were highly regarded in the car industry and were surpassed by only a few of the large presswork companies
- in the short term, existing customers could rapidly provide sufficient business to raise presswork utilization substantially
- the presswork market had the greatest potential of all current IPD (I) activities to achieve both profitable involvement and steady growth
- full capacity work by IPD (I) could be achieved with less than one per cent of the current UK market and
- the prospects for expansion and diversification in the long term were excellent

Not one of these statements appeared in the IDU analysis. The analysis merely repeated Inbucon's remark that most of the previous work had been 'low-volume pressing for minor, obsolete and pre-production [car] models'.

The IDU claimed that, in order to develop the presswork business in the longer term, the cooperative would need to invest substantially in new presses and tool-room facilities. This was quite untrue. Press shop capacity was substantial and tool-room facilities would only be needed if the cooperative went into the original equipment business and if it could not use existing local tool-making firms to build tools.

The IDU stated that current designs of radiator would

become obsolete within two to three years. This was patently wrong. (It still is, over six years later.) The IDU's concern was over microbore systems and finned radiators. The adaptation to microbore systems requires only that the metal boss which is welded into the radiator ends should have a different hole in it – it would probably have taken one man-day to organize the change at Kirkby. The other development – still relatively uncommon in 1981 – is a high output design to increase heat transmission. It is usually effected by welding a shaped metal fin to the back of the existing radiator design – again not a difficult problem and well within the cooperative's proposed capital investment figure. (It is worth noting that the cooperative's radiator was no low-grade job. It was the Potterton design of the smoother premium round-top type and made from thicker steel than some of its rivals.)

A further distortion came from the IDU incorporating the consequences of the cooperative falling short of its sales targets but not reducing the cooperative's overheads at all (which wasn't even consistent with their own views on the matter).* Nor did the IDU incorporate the submission's one quantified cost variation – the ditching of the drinks operation.

The convenors had said that employing 913 wasn't immutable and a substantial reduction would be considered if necessary. Natural wastage would help – then running at 300 per year as Cork's redundancy scheme continued. Worksharing was possible and drastic measures might be needed to reduce manning without loss of output. They stated, quite firmly, that the drinks

---

* 'All overheads, including labour, have been treated as fixed, although many are variable and will increase in line with production.' How convenient it was for the IDU team to forget that variable costs also *decrease* in line with *reduced* production. They had reduced the cooperative's projected sales by 10 and 20 per cent and had taken not a penny off the overheads which they had said were variable. There is a word to describe their omission – incompetence.

operation would be terminated if it weren't profitable within six months.

'It is clear,' said the IDU, 'that early implementation of these modifications to the convenors' proposals would reduce the losses likely to be made by the company . . . However,' they went on, 'we have not been in a position to evaluate, in financial terms, the effects of these possible adaptations. Our appraisal therefore relates to the proposals as originally submitted.' This was odd, for the IDU team weren't fools. The evaluation which they could not make would have taken them about half an hour.

The relevant facts about the drinks operation were laid out in the application, but naturally, since a loss was forecast, extracting them improved the cooperative's prospects. The removal of the drinks operation and 141 people improved the forecast results by £128,000 in year one and £158,000 in year two. This assumed no savings whatsoever on overheads, and while the IDU was quite prepared to speculate on the financial effects of the cooperative being 10 and 20 per cent under its sales forecasts, it was apparently beyond it to speculate similarly on the consequent reduction of overheads such as electricity, heating oil, maintenance, protective clothing, or even depreciation on the idle machinery. It would not have been unreasonable to reduce overheads by 5 per cent for every 10 per cent shortfall in sales – particularly since the elimination of drinks could have brought a major reduction in the factory's rates. The IDU could also have considered the value of further manpower reductions resulting from rising efficiency or from sales shortfalls. But it did none of these things.

(It wasn't just the misrepresentations of the IDU report which made it reprehensible; its whole style was bitchy. It couldn't bring itself to say that the convenors' forecast for radiator sales was reasonable, but instead said that it 'does not seem, prima facie, implausible'.

Six years later I find it hard to suppress my contempt

for the IDU.) The analysis was biased to the point of being deplorable. These are not reflections of hindsight. My own analysis of the cooperative's prospects was carried out for the convenors over Christmas 1974 using the workers' submission and the IDU report. My conclusions were as follows:

The IDU appraisal states that it is an appraisal of your *submission*, not your *situation*. Even so, it is a puzzling document for the following reasons:

1 It is not so much an appraisal as a critique.
2 It seems principally orientated towards discrediting your submissions.
3 Only downside risks are incorporated in the analysis.
4 The consequences of guesses about sales shortfalls have been incorporated but the only quantified detailed variance (that of major labour saving) has been omitted. (I have rectified this curious omission later in these observations.)
5 It contains no helpful or constructive suggestions for developing the business.
6 I judge that the IDU team were briefed to produce the most unappealing view of KME's prospects. They have succeeded.

Nevertheless, there was agreement on the overall picture, for my analysis continued, 'Unfortunately, these criticisms of the IDU report's displeasing style do not destroy their central conclusions. The cooperative, as proposed, *is* overmanned, *is* overburdened with overheads, *is* underfunded, and *is* unlikely to reach its sales growth targets.' At that time, I was scarcely aware of the mounting hostility between Benn and his officials.

Years later, one of the IDU report's authors said that the cooperative idea had been nonsensical and that protecting factories against international competition was wrong if Britain was ever to become competitive. The balance of payments didn't matter. The comical feature of his assault was that he was then working for a company which sold equipment to British public enterprises at much better than international prices – protected by just the kind of balance of payment and job protection considerations that he was condemning for the cooperative.

Surely, he was asked, the cooperative had demonstrated skill in selling many more radiators than had been forecast? But he couldn't even give them that. 'They had a couple of pieces of luck,' he observed. Given this antagonism in 1979, what it must have been like in the Industry Department in 1974 scarcely bears thinking about.

Thumbs down from the Government's advisers

The workers' submission and the IDU report were then put to the Industrial Development Advisory Board (IDAB) for its recommendation. This body had been set up to advise the Secretary of State on the exercise of his powers under Sections 7 and 8 of the Industry Act. Composed almost exclusively of industrialists and City men, the Board had only one trade union member (Harry Urwin of the TGWU) when it considered the cooperative on 22 October 1974.

IDAB did not receive the Inbucon report nor, under its normal procedures, did Benn – or any politician – debate with it. Nor could Inbucon or the cooperators give evidence to it or answer any questions. The people there were Industry Department officials – including members of the IDU. The presentation and amplification of the case were wholly in the hands of civil servants. IDAB turned the application down.

The workers' proposal, it said, fell far short of overcoming serious shortcomings. There weren't enough profitable activities; storage heater demand was low; drinks were unprofitable; very good management was needed to succeed with contract presswork so that there wasn't a stable product base with a ready market; there was major overmanning and over-capacity in the uneconomically large factory.

Despite the earlier criticisms of the IDU, it was now possible that in presenting the case to IDAB, the officials had rectified their misrepresentations, but the IDAB statement was revealing in mentioning the lack of a stable product base. The Board didn't even mention the cooperative's largest product line – radiators – nor the excellent prospects for presswork. It looked as though IDAB had been misled.

'The support of such ventures raised crucial issues about the proper employment of taxpayers' money.' It certainly did. It also raised the question about the proper employment of analysts and advisers. There was no hint that either the IDU or IDAB had suggested that the convenors be asked to put forward a more realistic proposal which would improve the chance of success, or that Government should consider offering funds only if the cooperators agreed to carry out actions to improve viability – such as ditching the drinks operation. There is no sign that, having shown the inadequacy of the money requested in the submission, either the IDU or IDAB had suggested that Government should improve the cooperative's chance of success (and hence improve the justification for any funding and any protection of public funds) by increasing the grant from £3.9 million to the £4.75 million which the analysts had concluded was necessary. Indeed, the IDU had suggested that provision for the cooperators' original request for £6.5 million should be used when determining the total costs of financing the company. (In other words, the cooperative proposal should be *judged* as though it were costing as much as £6.5 million, but it should only get £3.9 million and it should be criticized for asking for too little, although no effort should be made to increase it.)

The Industry Department had received an amateurish proposition, left it unchanged and apparently undermined it. It is hard to avoid the conclusion that the cooperative was being set up in a way which maximized the chance of its failure. The kindest thing one can say about the IDU in this matter is that it had temporarily mislaid its integrity.

It is worth remembering the climate at that time. The outgoing minority Labour Government had been returned with an overall majority of four. Labour had improved its position, even though its overall vote had declined slightly (the Opposition's vote declined more and Labour's share of the vote rose from 37 to 39 per cent). Its mandate to govern had improved, and Labour's manifesto had said that the people would judge it not only on policies and records, but on the calibre and experience of those responsible for carrying out these policies. Benn and Heffer were reappointed to their posts at the Department of Industry.

Benn's later view about his reappointment was that the Prime Minister didn't want him on the loose during the campaign leading to the forthcoming EEC referendum. It should be remembered that Benn had Wilson's backing for a post in the Cabinet in February 1974. Wilson wrote in his memoirs* '[The Shadow Cabinet including Benn were] the very ones I would have chosen – indeed I had voted for them'. Yet Wilson had become so alarmed at the way things were going that by May 1974 he had taken over the Industrial Cabinet Committee himself. Benn was never allowed to chair a committee.†

* *Final Term* (Weidenfeld & Nicolson, 1979), p. 12.
† Author's note: A Department doesn't like the relevant Cabinet Committee to be chaired by its own Minister – though Varley later took over EI – because its best advocate is then impartially in the chair, having not only the Department's brief, but unlike other Committee members, the Cabinet Office's wider brief. So he cannot just put a Departmental view and, if ambitious, would be likely to back the Cabinet Office and Treasury line, since, as it was put to me, 'The Prime Minister would see how young Varley was shaping up and whether he could be considered for promotion.' The more I learn about Cabinet Committee mechanisms, the more I comprehend why Prime Ministers relish the system. It gives them and their most senior civil servants an immense centralized control over the substance and outcome of ministerial meetings.

There was to be much public discussion about the right of the Labour Government to govern – given its bare Parliamentary majority and its minority of popular votes. Resentment sprang from disgruntled opponents and thwarted coalitionists, but the fact was that no other group had any significant right to usurp the Government's position – nor was there any alternative alliance. Of course there will always be those who claim to speak for the 'silent majority', despite the risks of such presumption, but the people had confirmed the Labour administration in office and Labour's position had been reinforced both in Parliament and in the country.

Benn now had to decide. It was, he told his officials, a worthwhile experiment. Wilson and Heffer were in favour. Benn commended the convenors' scheme to his Cabinet colleagues and they endorsed it. The Cabinet members had known of IDAB's opposition. Some of the Cabinet had been opposed, too, to the point where Wilson had leant on them to support the proposal.

On 1 November 1974 Benn announced that the Government had decided to provide a grant of the £3.9 million requested, on the clear understanding that this Government aid would be strictly 'once and for all'. The decision had been reached against IDAB's advice, but Government had been greatly influenced by the resolution and determination of the workers in a high unemployment area 'who have demonstrated their readiness to take responsibility for their own affairs and to see to it that the cooperative is a success, an experiment in industrial organization of great potential significance'.

Government would not have an equity stake, nor would it be a preferential creditor if the cooperative failed. The £3.9 million grant would become repayable if any assets were disposed of, or the project changed without Government consent, or if the project's future became in jeopardy. KME would have to consult the Secretary of State for Industry before agreeing any general increase in wage rates or paying any dividends to members. The cooperative couldn't borrow against its assets and would have to provide monthly performance information to the Industry Department.

On the same day, Benn announced backing for the Meriden motorcycle cooperative and aid for the Herbert machine tool company. He had already offered conditional aid to the *Scottish Daily News* cooperative. A fair-sized public row ensued, with Benn being attacked by the Conservative Opposition.

Spriggs was 'over the moon'. 'It will make people see that they don't have to surrender just because their company has problems.' After giving the workers the good news he told them, 'You will have to work like you've never worked before.' The ten-minute mass meeting had been strangely silent. As one worker said afterwards, 'It was a dead cert all the way along the line. Actually it's a bit of an anti-climax after the excitement of the last couple of years.' In contrast, Spriggs himself had been far from sure that political pressure would overcome 'the hostility of the officials'.

It was a tribute to the convenors that the workers had harboured few doubts about the outcome. Not for the last time the leaders were carrying the load of the workers' expectations whilst stifling their own doubts in order to avoid demoralizing people or risking adverse publicity. The cooperative had answers to some of IDAB's strictures. It was already selling far more than the forecast number of radiators. There were only 863 people on the site – not 913 – and natural wastage would soon take this down to 750. They would review the foods operation by March and shut it down if necessary, though ditching yet more jobs would be difficult. It wasn't in the spirit of the cooperative, and those who would go would include veterans of the 1971/2 struggles. With luck there would be an upsurge of trade which would justify retaining everyone.

Meanwhile Spriggs was making all the right noises. He had no wish to become the 'Mr Big'. 'The first stage is to elect an executive committee which will be responsible for major policy decisions . . . we want to run a business not a holiday camp. Everyone now realizes that they are responsible for what happens in the factory and there won't be room for anyone to swing the lead.' The present management and a new managing director would run the business day to day. 'We have always accepted the need for experts,' said Spriggs. The managers would be paid the market rate for their jobs. 'The Government has not given us money merely to pay wages for the next couple of years. We have to invest in new equipment for new products.' It all sounded highly competent.

The receiver's coup

However, the cooperators weren't yet home and dry. They still had to deal with the receiver, who wanted £1.8 million for the collapsed business. It was an excellent price – for him.

The convenors hoped to pay less and so improve their working capital position. It was a question of whose nerves and bargaining position were the stronger. The receiver knew that the cooperators were the only people likely to buy the plant as a going concern. The auction value of the installed machinery would have been substantially lower – the whole business was worth little more than £1 million in a forced sale.

However, Cork was friendly with the Industry Department officials, who thought that the £3.9 million grant was a dead loss. He knew of the earmarked £1.8 million, and wouldn't budge on the price which he had agreed with the leaders in July, even though, during the autumn, he had run down the stocks and used up virtually all the steel. Furthermore, the officials were hinting that unless everything was signed up quickly there could be a change of heart. Both Cork and King were later to agree that the parties were pushed by the officials, who were apparently fearful that Tory opposition could upset the agreement to give the grant. The High Court had already adjourned a petition for winding up IPD (I) on the understanding that the factory sale should be progressed quickly. KME was being pushed too. The officials had insisted on the £1.8 million being shown as a separate figure in the application. When the leaders tried to beat Cork down, he replied, 'I've been told that £1.8 million is set aside . . . After all,' he continued, 'I got you the business.' The cooperators, anxious to get on with the job before even more damage was done to the floundering business, and with the officials' warning of withdrawal ringing in their ears, gave way. It had, Cork said later, been £400,000 too much.* KME would be left badly underfunded in an extremely difficult period. Yet it was Cork's duty to obtain the best price for IPD (I)'s creditors.

Political squalls

Christmas was approaching but matters became somewhat unseasonal as Parliament rose for the recess. IDAB was evidently incensed about its treatment at Benn's hands and invoked Section 9(4) of the Industry Act for the first time and requested that a statement about KME be laid before Parliament.

Benn lodged the statement in the Commons' vote office in the afternoon of Friday, 20 December when almost all MPs had left for Christmas. The Opposition was furious. Michael Heseltine described it as 'a flagrant abuse of Parliament'.† There had been repeated Conservative

---

* Author's note: In my view, £800,000 too much.
† There is a certain symmetry in politics. Six years later, on 13 November 1980, the Conservative Environment Secretary, Michael Heseltine, tried to tuck away an announcement of increased council house rents by attaching it quietly to a written Commons answer in the dying hours of the 1979–80 session. There were furious scenes in the Commons over what Roy Hattersley termed 'this scandalous denial of the rights of the House'.

complaints that Benn was spurning the views of the Board, which had been advertised at the time of the Conservative's Industry Bill as a brake on any Secretary of State who was tempted to waste taxpayers' money.

The statement gave the Board's objections, together with their view that 'it appears regrettable that such a large sum of the taxpayers' money should be advanced on a project which holds out little prospect of yielding long-term employment. In any event, if the Government's conclusion is that the venture should be supported in spite of IDAB's opinion, it would not be right to provide the assistance by way of a grant (free gift) which would leave this small body of workers with all the benefit of nearly £4 million of capital provided by the general body of taxpayers.'

In the statement the Government commented that the grant would help overcome the risks which IDAB had identified, and there were conditions included in the grant to satisfy public accountability.

Heseltine commented that 'Mr Benn has made what amounts to a free gift of taxpayers' money to electors in a part of Britain associated with the Prime Minister and the Minister of State in his own department.'

Spriggs responded, 'We have already shown that the Advisory Board did not fully understand the situation because to date we have sold five times as many radiators as they believed possible,' and pointed out that Government had been presented with a very full report by the consultants after several weeks of study, whereas the IDU had 'written KME off after only five hours at the factory'.

Benn and the IDAB Chairman, Robert Clark, clashed on a radio programme. The £3.9 million would not be enough, said Clark, to safeguard the jobs of the people at the Kirkby factory because 'the thing is simply not viable' and had no real hope of commercial success. The chances of KME asking for more money were very great indeed. There was overmanning, continued Clark. Benn retorted, 'The greatest overmanning in Britain at the mo-

ment is overmanning in the unemployment register . . .
In a democratic society ministers have to decide for themselves, not advisors appointed by a previous Government.
The Opposition would rather see these men sacked. Even
if the workers of IPD were unemployed they would still
be given a Government grant to do nothing.' The controversy had only blown up, said Benn, because the Government was giving money to workers rather than
shareholders.

Heseltine had already anticipated Benn's argument
over job subsidies. 'Every worker made redundant from
now on is entitled to ask why he, too, cannot be given
taxpayer's money by Mr Benn to start or continue a business, no matter how scant the prospects of commercial
success.'

Clark was right about the need for more money. The
way KME's application had been handled had indeed
reduced the chance of the taxpayer getting value for
money, since it increased the chance of failure of the
assisted enterprise. It didn't even seem to make sense on
non-commercial grounds. If these lame ducks were social
experiments, what was the point of ensuring that their
lameness continued? Wasn't the experiment supposed to
indicate the conditions for success rather than failure? It
only made sense if the aim was to kill the whole idea
dead.

A death sentence

The year 1975 began with a *Times* report that Peter Carey
(now Sir Peter Carey), the second Permanent Secretary
at the Industry Department (under Permanent Secretary
Sir Anthony Part), had placed on file his objections to the
KME grant. His reservations had been recorded because
he might be answerable to the Public Accounts Committee for his administration of the Department. (Carey's
action was part of a system used sparingly by a civil
servant to protect himself in the event of being held res-

ponsible for a decision with which he strongly disagreed. Civil Service rules permit him to place a formal written objection on file if he believes that a minister's act is illegal or does not conform with policy or is an imprudent use of public funds.) *The Times* (7 January 1975) commented on the 'difficult position that Mr Benn appears to be creating for his civil servants – on the one hand, the job of a civil servant is to interpret the political wishes of his minister, on the other he has to observe the administrative proprieties'.* Following the *Times* report, by that evening, Part had produced a minute detailing Benn's errors. Benn realized that it was meant to be a sentence of death but was able to demonstrate that in each case where there had been an official's warning, he had changed his policy. Then, alleged Benn, the Department briefed Fleet Street.

Whatever Wilson's motives, Benn had been reaffirmed as the Prime Minister's choice to hold the seals of office in the Industry Department, despite the breakdown of relationships with his department's civil servants. It was for his civil servants to serve Benn loyally, since their primary task was to serve the minister's political will.

* It was the second attempt to raise public criticism of Benn. The first had occurred on 13 December in a fulminating article by Sam Brittan in the *Financial Times*, of the type to which Brittan is prone when his anti-union, right-wing proclivities get the better of him. Writing of the Government's 'cavalier attitude to breaches of the law' and of 'illegal occupation', Brittan hinted darkly, 'Many of the workers live in the Huyton constituency' (i.e. Wilson's seat). Complaining that taxpayers were being forced to devote money to activities which they wouldn't support voluntarily (which might also characterize some of the expenditure on the Civil Service itself), Brittan claimed that 'before 1974, direct aid was given to companies only if there was hope – however slender, long-term and half-hearted – that the enterprise could become profitable again. One change brought about by Mr Benn has been the abandonment of this criterion.' The claim was abusively unfair. The article revealed that a Permanent Secretary was believed to have put a note of dissent on file in one of the cooperative cases. Perhaps because of its intemperate tone, the article had little impact.

They had no mandate to presume otherwise, nor any legitimation to arrogate to themselves the definition of a contrary policy. Their problem was that Benn was being undermined via other ministers and ministries, but there is a limit to the value of that as an excuse for disloyalty to their own minister.

As the *Sunday Times* put it, 'Obviously these are difficult times to get any business under way, and the co-operative will face a stiff test initially. Its credibility has already been damaged by IDAB's unusual step of laying its objections before the Commons; and the intervention of Peter Carey.' Some were not sorry about such damage. The Prime Minister ordered an inquiry by Sir Douglas Allen into the accuracy of reports of Carey's objections and the way the material might have reached the press. The leak inquiry got nowhere. Benn told Allen where he thought the leak had occurred. Allen's inquiries petered out. As Benn pointed out 'Why should I have leaked that story? It was directly against my interests to do so.'

It was believed that Carey had also objected to Meriden and the *Scottish Daily News*. The media were buzzing with objections to KME and the source of some information could only be the Industry Department. The publicity from them and the actions of IDAB were isolating Benn – who had just announced the first Government injection of money into British Leyland, then tottering feebly into the State's arms. The publicity suggested that Benn was just aiding a few madcap enterprises, but in the eleven months following the March 1974 election no less than 1,241 companies had applied for Industry Act support. As Benn complained, he was fed up with being abused by industrialists one day and finding a queue of them begging on his doorstep the next.

The cooperative sets sail

Heffer addressed a mass meeting at KME on 8 January. He was anxious to dispel the impression that he and Tony Benn had cooked up the KME aid between them. It had, he said, been a collective Cabinet decision. It was a useful reminder of Benn's isolated position. His Cabinet colleagues had remained silent during the row, even though they were party to – indeed collectively responsible for – the granting of the £3.9 million.

Heffer's second message was equally clear but directed at the workers. They would stand or fall by their own efforts. 'People have the impression that other money will be available, but the Government cannot provide any other money. We decided to help, but it was a once-and-for-all grant.' Heffer privately pointed out that if he and Benn hadn't agreed to the 'once-and-for-all' condition, the grant would never have gone through at all.

The cooperators' negotiating troubles weren't over yet. The landlord, King, eventually agreed to assign the lease to the cooperative after failing to get the Industry Department to guarantee it. But King did have some backing for the lease. A clause had been inserted which was later to cause recrimination between the convenors and the Department of Industry. Spriggs and Jenkins were to be held personally responsible for the thirty-five-year lease. In the event of the cooperative's failure they would have to pay £207,000 a year rent between them. Spriggs, Jenkins and their solicitor were to claim that the Department of Industry had leant on them to sign up quickly or risk losing the grant. KME's solicitor later wrote saying that the Department had made it clear that, unless the convenors guaranteed the lease and all its covenants, the lease transfer could not occur and 'it was upon this ultimatum that the cooperative's directors agreed to sign'. The Department could find no record of this conversation. There is no suggestion that the Department knew of the offending clause. Spriggs insists that Lippitt, as Department Under-Secretary, was adamant that they sign all the necessary documents, which they did without reading them line by line. It had been virtually on Christmas Eve – after Heseltine had raised the roof over Benn's IDAB statement.

On 15 January 1975 the cooperative started trading. Its legal status was in doubt since the workers had only just received the lawyers' draft of the cooperative constitution, which they rejected. The cooperative was intended to be separate from the company and would hold in trust all the cooperators' shares in KME as well as appointing a ten-man executive committee to control the company's affairs. In the meantime, the management board was no longer part of the proposed company structure and the idea of having six worker directors had also disappeared. Spriggs and Jenkins, meanwhile, had been appointed the only directors of KME Company Ltd and held the only two £1 shares which had been issued. This led to a news story claiming that the two convenors had become 'instant millionaires' because the cooperative's constitution wasn't settled.

The first storm

Spriggs stated, 'We have a management team and we are making sure that KME gets off the ground rapidly.' The problem was that there wasn't a complete management team. They had no chief executive, nor any commercial manager. Silk, the local MP, had suggested Len Collinson as a prospective chief executive, a decision backed also by Arthur Ward, the regional industrial director of the Industry Department. Collinson had a good reputation, but he soon fell out with KME's convenors and had departed before Christmas 1974.

This was a great pity, for Collinson's track record was ideal for this situation. He had been with the Bristol Retail Cooperative Society first as a training officer, then as personnel officer. Unusually, he had also worked on the producer side in the Cooperative Wholesale Society as national personnel manager and then deputy group manager of their bakery division. From 1966 to 1970 he had been director of manpower at Plessey Telecommunications which had 25,000 employees. He had declined the job of managing director of Plessey's International Group and left to set up a management consultancy firm (Collinson, Grant). As if this wasn't enough, he had been a trade union education officer and Collinson, Grant had surveyed the Kirkby factory for a prospective buyer before Thorn had acquired it. Collinson, Grant had gained a reputation for being committed to Merseyside and had taken in two of its largest independent inward investment firms, as well as turning a Merseyside business round from receivership – ownership of which Collinson was returning steadily to the people who worked in it. It would have been difficult to find a better man to straddle the conflicting requirements. The Industry Department could see him as a competent businessman; the cooperative could see him as a committed leftie.

Everyone outside warned Collinson not to touch it – except his father, an old socialist warhorse. Collinson looked at the cooperative, realized that it was possible to make it work under certain conditions, and decided to have a go. Silk offered his support whilst making it clear that he wasn't going to get too near to the hot potato bequeathed to him by Wilson. Collinson's colleagues in Collinson, Grant agreed to carry him while he did the part-time chief executive job at the cooperative without pay. Collinson realized that it would take all his emotional capacity and would be a sapping experience. It was sapping too, but not for long.

The convenors set him up in the administration building, but Collinson insisted on moving to the factory offices to be cheek-by-jowl with the workers so as to create a busy community with good communications. But it quickly began to go wrong. Collinson found that the management disciplines were appalling and managers went out as and when they pleased, so he discussed the situation with them and duplicated a location sheet on which executives could fill in their week's travel schedule. The sheet included Spriggs and Jenkins.

Collinson also proposed to meet senior managers and supervisors in groups together with shop stewards, who would observe the discussions. He wanted to meet employees in small groups too, his view being that involving people would build understanding and commitment. The senior managers also indicated that they needed protection from Jack Spriggs' dominance if they were to do their executive jobs properly. Collinson began to draw up action plans and a schedule of review meetings and began to pull out accounting and production figures to identify the problem issues. He presented the convenors with an outline of their responsibilities as directors which specified that they should control the company's affairs via reports submitted by the chief executive who would be empowered to interpret the board's policy into effective executive action 'for the fulfilment of which he is answerable to the board'.

The proposals were logical; they were relevant; they were doomed. Through the union, Spriggs instructed Ellen Gallagher (who became his personal secretary and the cooperative's receptionist) not to type or issue the location sheet. It was, said Spriggs, 'a gross interference with personal liberty'.

Spriggs instructed that no documents would be issued without consultations with them as directors, though he and Jenkins were not acting as directors, he claimed confusingly as he struggled to define the leadership role. The stewards should be partners in discussions, not observers, said Spriggs, adding that the chief executive would never meet with the cooperators but would instead meet the stewards who would decide themselves what to say to their members. The cooperators, Collinson complained to Heffer, would be instructed by Spriggs and Jenkins not to attend meetings with the chief executive even with the directors present, though Collinson could address a mass meeting if the stewards agreed. Heffer was also told that Spriggs refused even to read the discussion document on the board of directors and that Spriggs had told Collinson that all he needed to know was that 'the trade unions are paramount'.

Indeed, Spriggs admitted to Collinson that he had wanted a private takeover rather than a cooperative so that the trade unions could perform their traditional role, but Benn had indicated that he would only provide support via a cooperative. This was discouraging for Collinson, though Heffer persuaded him to hang on and try to improve matters. Arthur Ward was also trying to support Collinson, who did not realize that Civil Service protocol ensured that his conversations with Ward would be noted and fed back into the Civil Service.

By the time the convenors and Collinson met Heffer on 16 December, Spriggs was fuming. He had dragged the factory through thick and thin to a cooperative and though Spriggs later claimed that Collinson wasn't a strong personality, he was far from happy about Collinson's robust initiatives, which hinted at a return to traditional management powers. Collinson, for his part, resented Spriggs pontificating to him when he'd spent twice as long in the Labour Party, nine years in cooperatives and had managed businesses successfully.

The meeting with Heffer only confirmed what was already inevitable. According to Spriggs, Eric had said that 'either Collinson runs the place and turns it round as a business or the convenors go on their merry way. Whatever happens, it's been formed as a cooperative and so the convenors have to decide.' Spriggs accused Collinson of 'looking for a way out', though a search for an exit seemed superfluous. Collinson told Heffer privately that someone had to break through the convenor's resistance to a competent control structure for the business. Eric had reacted that it was Benn's job to tell the convenors.

The trouble was that Benn was off on something else by this stage and, said Eric, he thinks he's dealt with it.

The following day Collinson wrote to Spriggs rejecting the proposal that he become KME's designate chief executive. 'I am persuaded that success is unlikely with the present attitudes. It is saddening to realize that I am eliciting the responses usually reserved for a nineteenth century mill owner.' There was a real opportunity for success, wrote Collinson, because effective and coordinated action could make the business viable. (Collinson stoutly maintained this five years later. There *was* a business there. There was no doubt that it could have worked, he asserted, for there were lots of good people there.) 'It really is important that you think out the role you wish management to have in KME,' he continued, for time was precious since on present performance cash would run out in about eight months, and even if KME could borrow against its assets, they would still be dissipated in eighteen months.

The letter, Collinson told Heffer, gave him a real sense of failure. The task was worthwhile but the gap between Jack's stated intentions and his behaviour was beyond solution in the time available. KME's collapse or a request for further funds was inevitable.

Collinson had seen other facets of the problem. He had helped to organize a display of KME's products at a London Hotel a few yards away from the Labour Party Conference held after the October 1974 election. The cooperative had hoped to influence delegates to press local authorities to consider KME radiators and heaters. It wasn't to induce them to favour KME (in the wake of the Poulson corruption trial, everyone would have run a mile from that), but to match what many suppliers do by making people aware of what was on offer. Every delegate received a leaflet. Three people turned up. The Labour Party's support was merely intellectual.

Still, it was better than the trade union movement which was relatively hostile. It wasn't just that the Kirkby workers had built up enemies as well as friends over the years, but Benn had bypassed the whole of the union structure in dealing directly and solely with the Kirkby stewards and Spriggs had publicly declared 'I am convinced that the national leadership of the unions is terrified of workers' control.'

Collinson knew that Spriggs had threatened to ring Benn at 7 a.m. on a Sunday and get Lippitt 'sacked' if Lippitt insisted on a cash flow prediction from KME. Collinson also believed that there had been a sniff of an offer of well over £1 million for KME's canteen and administration block from a leisure group which wanted the canteen for a bingo hall. Jack had apparently rejected it, though it would have bought KME some vital cash even if IPD had taken its cut as landlord.

The phrase about 'a nineteenth-century mill owner' reverberated round Whitehall. It was still being quoted by ex-Industry Department people in 1980. Collinson's withdrawal was probably the last straw for the strongly anti-KME Peter Carey.

In the end the convenor directors did the simple thing – they appointed the ex-IPD production director, Bob Lewis as general manager. He had been at the factory since 1962, initially as a foreman. He knew the plant and the people intimately, he was prepared to stick with the cooperative and he had been running the factory on a day-to-day basis under King. The disadvantages of his appointment were major, though none of these were his fault. He had no commercial experience, had spent all of his management career working at the consistently unprofitable factory under a succession of rotten managements (there had been five owners and fourteen managers in fifteen years), and was also well known to the workers and disliked by some. He had no experience of working in a competent, successful management team and could bring no mystery, no charisma, no expert power to bear on the situation. His enthusiasm would have to make up for these deficiencies. He was not appointed to the board.

Most observers thought that Lewis was a poor appointment for a daunting task. KME had chosen the easy, inadequate way out. Indeed there was more than a suspicion that the cooperators had appointed the manager they had walked all over already, in order to maintain the convenors' dominance. Admittedly, their choice had been difficult. How would they get on with a stranger? Who would come and what would his motives be? How long would it take to find someone, and how could they judge his competence before appointing him? Could the leaders keep him under control? – a worry that had been behind the rejection of Collinson. Might the Industry Department suggest a nonentity as part of its campaign to sink the cooperative? It is easy to see why KME appointed Lewis, but it was a poor omen for an enterprise crying out for commercial experience and desperately needing speedy success. It was all very well to talk of democracy and cooperation, but KME had been born in a hostile commercial climate in a mainly capitalist economy. If it didn't survive in the market as a competent business there was no discernible future for it at all.

6. Early days: 1975

- Plans, performance and wages
- The place of power
- Some outside help
- Power and the advisory council
- Smashing the council
- Workers and mobility
- Mounting pressures
- Benn is moved
- Trade up – losses down: the business improves

The business problems were appalling. Drinks sales had halved as customers had fled to more reliable suppliers; radiators had been sold cheaply for months as the receiver had tried to liberate cash for creditors; indeed it took low prices to shift them, since KME's goods had looked like the remnants of a dying product range.

The suspicion and uncertainty about KME's prospects extended to its suppliers and few would provide materials on normal trade credit. Many wanted cash and some even tried to get KME to shoulder the trade debts of the collapsed IPD (I). British Steel Corporation was to prove the most resistant to supplying on credit, having been the biggest unsecured creditor of IPD (I).* KME had to go to Holland for glass bottles and Germany for steel. This wasn't cheap and the cooperators were promptly accused of squandering tax payers' money abroad.

The cooperators themselves were in a poor state even though some of them were exhilarated by the challenge which they had been given. They were still work-sharing, hadn't had a wage rise since 1973 and inflation was run-

---

* So much for the charge by Benn's critics that he would order BSC to help since it was accountable to him.

ning at 20 per cent. The bulk of the factory workers were
on £37.40 for a thirty five-hour week compared with £35
back in 1972. Craftsmen were getting £42 and the few
unskilled workers £35. There was no incentive scheme.
Night work was paid at one and one-third normal pay;
week-day overtime at one and a half normal pay and
weekend overtime at double pay.

KME's women workers were not on equal pay. The
staff remained in several pay grades which, like the works
grades, had all been inherited from IPD. Sectional jeal-
ousies might have been exacerbated by any attempt to
change the pay structure. Lewis was the highest paid at
£6,000 a year.

Managers were not paid overtime, though staff were in
a sick pay scheme which paid for thirteen weeks' sickness.
The workers had no scheme. The two convenor directors
received the basic semi-skilled rate, even though they
intermittently worked long hours.

The cooperative continued the IPD practice of finishing
at noon on Friday and so carrying on with its thirty five-
hour week, whilst most firms worked a basic forty hours.
It was an expensive decision, but like several initial
choices it avoided disturbance to existing habits, for there
was enough flux at KME without adding unnecessary
complications.

That was the kinder interpretation. The alternative was
to see it as a failure to face up to reality – in this case an
unwillingness to give up the nice custom of a free afternoon. It would, the leaders thought, be easier to concentrate on other methods of increasing productivity and so
avoid provoking resistance straight away. In hindsight this
looks complacent, perhaps, but nobody could be sure
what the trading situation would be once the cooperative
had settled down. KME hoped that its performance would
silence the economic Cassandras. It was not to be that
easy.

The operating and financial control systems varied from
non-existent to second-rate. There were few managers of

any great experience. Apart from Lewis, the only senior manager was the financial controller, John Bandell. He had been the office manager at Fisher Bendix and, although not a chartered accountant, was widely respected at KME for his integrity, though Ward and Collinson both felt that he was primarily a functionary and was unwilling, and possibly unable, to interpret the figures he produced or to put them into a management action plan. This was unfair to Bandell, though he certainly wasn't strongly assertive. Lewis, Bandell, Spriggs and Jenkins were the four key figures. There was no marketing or commercial director. KME had nobody of senior business experience to get to grips with the product costs and margins, the marketing strategy or the commercial negotiations which were critical if contract presswork sales were to be doubled.

There were other managers of course. John Watts headed the fruit juice sales operation. Frank Mills was in charge of selling radiators and Constor. Lewis would take on the commercial role of contract negotiations and new product development. There was a works manager, John Davis, under Lewis.

Meanwhile, the media were buzzing round and the *Money Programme* came to do their version of *Animal Farm* and wasted a lot of film trying to show that workers would behave viciously with each other. *This Week* sought to demonstrate that the 'Old Pals Act' was at work with Benn, Heffer and Wilson all involved in a none too reputable rescue. However, *This Week* did commission an analysis of KME's position which still stood up five years later. The drinks operation, it said, held out the prospect only of ever-increasing losses, but radiator sales could be doubled so that the factory could make a small profit.

Overall, the media oscillated between portraying the workers as heroic underdogs fighting for the dignity of useful work and as a group of undeserving beggars who had blackmailed a credulous minister. Much play was made of KME's product mix and the workers soon grew

weary of jokes about selling radiators filled with orange
juice. Some of the jeering came from a mindless search
for a cheap story; other criticism was based on antipathy
towards what many saw as an economic nonsense.

Plans, performance and wages

Against this background KME started trading. It was
losing over £25,000 per week, and since the cooperative
couldn't borrow against its assets under the terms of the
grant and if losses continued on this scale, KME would
be insolvent by June 1976 at the latest.

Yet the leaders were calm, though it was hard to tell
whether this resulted from steely nerves, relief at the
success of the application, confidence that transformation
could be achieved or ignorance of their dodgy situation.
Certainly the point about underfunding had not fully
registered during 1974 and there was little evidence that
the convenors shared the outside analysts' views about
the urgent need for painful decisions if the cooperative
was to survive.

However, if one set aside the analysts' reservations
about the drinks operation and the workforce size, the
central business priorities were agreed by all.

1 Win back business by keeping prices low initially.
2 Extra sales were needed urgently so that the fixed costs
of the factory could be spread over more goods so reducing the cost of each unit of output.
3 Pay cash if necessary but quickly re-establish normal
trade credit from suppliers.
4 Raise prices to market levels as fast as KME's perma-
nence could be established. (Note: At no stage during the
life of the cooperative was serious consideration given to
keeping prices down as a benefit to consumers or as a
question of business ethics. KME's aim was always to
charge what the market would bear. The wish to maximize
sales revenue and profit margin was as strong at KME as

in any capitalist organization. KME was just less competent at it.)

5 Introduce profitable new engineering products to increase turnover and to replace the fruit juice operation if it couldn't make a profit. The cooperative would only introduce new lines which used the skills of the people and the existing type of factory equipment. There would be no fanciful diversions into unknown areas.

6 KME would not retail any products. Radiators would continue to be sold to builders merchants and installers; Constor heaters to the electricity boards; drinks to wholesalers and grocery chains; and presswork would still be contract work. This would keep down sales overheads since the sales force would be small and the advertising budget negligible. This was an eminently sensible decision, given the financial situation and the lack of marketing experience.

The emphasis would be on 'realistic' plans. The leaders had seen enough of 'pie in the sky expansion plans' under King. The priorities were KME's version of 'a dash for growth'.

During its first three months KME lost £345,000. Drinks sales had trebled from the pre-Christmas level. Spriggs was delighted and wanted to put more money into the drinks activities, but KME's prices were at rock bottom in a desperately competitive market. For all the brave talk about 'now buying the raw materials at the right price' the drinks operation was a touch short of covering its direct material and labour costs – let alone the indirect workers' wages or any overheads such as electricity, maintenance or selling and administration costs.

Sales of storage heaters remained poor in the wake of electricity price rises coupled with a squeeze on living standards. There was no marketing drive from the electricity boards.

Contract presswork was proving difficult to find. Due to the recession, presswork was being taken back into companies' own factories rather than farmed out and, despite the services of a temporary consultant, KME was just marking time.

The main success story was radiators. KME was selling far more than it had expected. The first year's scheduled output was 5,600 units per week, compared with sales of 1,500 to 5,000 per week during the receivership. In its first six months KME sold an average of 6,400 radiators per week. (In the second half of the year the average was over 7,000.) It was the best possible answer to the IDU's denigrations of KME's radiator prospects.

The other 'success' story was that the workforce had, as predicted by Spriggs and Jenkins, come down to 750 by mid-July 1975. They had not discouraged some people from leaving under Cork's scheme in 1974, nor had they dissuaded others from leaving in the cooperative's early days. (This amused Cork, since the leaders had previously insisted on 1,100 being employed by any new employer, but were now ditching people themselves.) It wasn't exactly a success to shed labour but it showed that the cooperators were serious about making a secure business out of the enterprise. They hoped to recruit people again when the sales volume grew and new products were introduced. As the number of employees declined, worksharing stopped, and on 1 April the workers received their first pay rise for two years.

The wage rise hadn't been originated by the shop stewards. Lewis, Bandell, Spriggs and Jenkins had sat down and worked out what the cooperative could afford and still make what Spriggs described as 'a profit on its budget'. Something 'had to be given' because everyone had already missed out on the previous anniversary of their regular wage rise. The quartet felt that KME could afford to pay £5.75 more per week to everyone. It was 'a bit revolutionary because we believed that we'd reached the Garden of Eden', said the convenor directors – who presented it to the stewards as a *fait accompli*. It was accepted.

The skilled men were not too happy to receive the same as everyone else but, since it was a new situation, they agreed to show goodwill and not argue about percentages and differentials.

The rest of the problems remained.

The leaders had said that they would review the drinks operation within three months and shut it down if necessary. It continued its heavy losses, but they kept it on – hoping that more effort would create extra sales and pull it through. Besides, they had a problem. How could they sack 141 people who had stuck with them through the struggles? The trouble was that every single analyst who had looked at the drinks operation had recommended its closure – everyone without exception saw it as a major haemorrhage of KME's precious cash.

The place of power

KME had not recruited a single senior manager. Lewis, as general manager, was trying to be the commercial manager as well, and it was patently too much for one man, even if his commercial experience had been adequate. Furthermore, the cooperative constitution had not been settled and only Jenkins and Spriggs had been appointed to the board. There were no plans to spread power to other cooperators.

The convenors claimed that they weren't managing the business, though there was no doubt that the two of them were in control. The managers didn't feel free to create policy and it wasn't even clear that the managers had a secure mandate to carry out policies on behalf of the convenors. Lewis felt that, if there were shop-floor objections to his implementation of the convenors' instructions, they would be just as likely to back the shop-floor as to back him.

The supervisors had listened, appalled, as Spriggs had announced that no one would be sacked while he was there, thus undermining the ultimate form of discipline

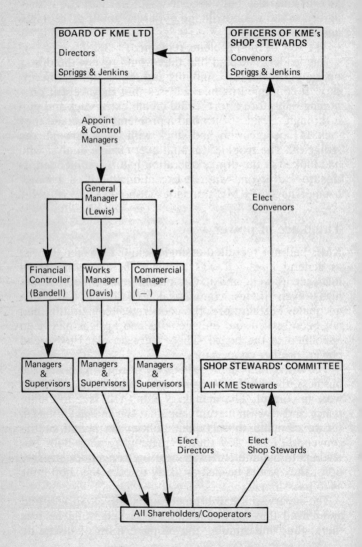

Figure 2 Showing Spriggs and Jenkins at the head of both management and trade union structures

BOARD OF KME LTD

Directors

Spriggs & Jenkins

OFFICERS OF KME's SHOP STEWARDS

Convenors

Spriggs & Jenkins

Appoint & Control Managers

General Manager (Lewis)

Financial Controller (Bandell)

Works Manager (Davis)

Commercial Manager (—)

Elect Convenors

Managers & Supervisors

Managers & Supervisors

Managers & Supervisors

SHOP STEWARDS' COMMITTEE

All KME Stewards

Elect Directors

Elect Shop Stewards

All Shareholders/Cooperators

from the start. The two convenor directors were now at the apex of both the management and worker power hierarchies. As Figure 2 on p. 106 shows, any cooperator who wanted action, either via his steward or his manager, sooner or later came to the power of Spriggs and Jenkins. Given that the workforce were the shareholders, the managers were powerless. They had no source of power, for they were accountable to the convenor directors who, inside the factory, could only do what the shop-floor would allow, but, given the shop-floor's trust in the leadership, all the power was effectively in the leaders' hands.

The workers were still working to a 'score'. This stint system (where you work to an unvarying target then stop, regardless of the time of day) was prevalent in a number of Merseyside factories, as it is elsewhere. Under some of the previous managements, work standards had been so low that it had been known for some workers to have finished their day's work by 10 a.m. The idea of doing so much and no more was deeply ingrained at KME.

Fortunately for KME's few friends, they didn't then know about this problem or they would have been even more depressed. Admittedly, the cooperative had made strides towards economic operation. Sales had gone up, surplus people had gone, market confidence was returning, suppliers and customers were stabilizing, prices could begin to be raised, wages were more attractive and experience was being accumulated.

Yet management was inadequate, the financial controls were not being improved, the drinks operation was continuing on its dreary path, workers weren't being educated into responsibility and people had been given a wage rise and were keeping their thirty five-hour week when money was leaking out of the cooperative at a rate of £40 per man per week. As things stood in mid-1975, they would barely have broken even if everyone worked for nothing. Heseltine visited the factory and found a level of enthusiasm 'which many industrialists would like to harness in their factories'; but the enthusiasm was not reflected in the trading performance. Lewis seemed cheery enough. 'We know we're going to lose a million pounds this year,' he stated. It wasn't clear how he thought the cooperative would survive into 1976 if that were the case.

In the first six months the cooperative lost £750,000. It had been losing between £3 and £4 on every £10 worth of goods sold.

KME was carrying on with IPD's unusual policy of announcing a radiator price increase and then taking orders at the old price until the date of the new price list. Naturally, it created a flood of orders which were then delivered – sometimes months later – at the old price. It was one way of gaining orders and losing profit margins. All KME's competitors followed the normal trade practice that 'invoices will be at the price ruling at date of dispatch'. KME was being silly – though it felt that the trade would turn away from the cooperative if it changed this policy – not that anyone had analysed the position.*

KME had raised its targets, with 1975 sales now at £6.7 million and the budget loss increased to £703,000 in the first half of 1975, and £247,000 in the second six months. The sales to June 1975 were actually £2 million, 24 per cent below budget. Radiator and drinks sales were roughly on target both in sales and losses, but Constor and presswork were dragging the enterprise down with sales roughly half the projected level so that overall losses were greater than expected. The row about electricity prices was hammering Constor and contract presswork results were poor, but the cooperative believed that time and marketing effort should improve them both.

It seemed that some targets were attainable on the revised, more realistic budget. Perhaps drinks *would* pull through if the volume could be increased further. Radiator sales were going well with a rising sales trend.

---

* It wasn't until 1978 that the policy was brought into line with the industry. There wasn't a squeak from the trade, though admittedly the market in 1978 was more buoyant than it had been in 1975 – but it had been buoyant since 1976.

Some outside help

The convenors took Lewis, Watts and Mills with them to Manchester Business School to receive a presentation from twenty five senior executives attending a course there who had analysed KME's position using the Inbucon and IDU reports – together with KME's aid submission and the author's analysis. The MBS executives concluded that KME was desperately short of cash and needed a rapid improvement in its sales and efficiency. Good managers were needed immediately – particularly in marketing of contract presswork. Financial and management controls needed strengthening and the drinks business should be shut down and its workers sacked. The KME party expressed interest, but no action ensued. This was understandable over the sacking of the drinks workers, for that business was displaying the odd sign of hope, but the inaction over the other suggestions was dispiriting to those who, like the MBS executives, recognized that KME had been given a rotten deal and wanted to see it overcome its handicaps.

Instead, the cooperative found another source of hope. KME had been asked by a small Midlands firm to manufacture a new type of ventilator for offices and homes. It was designed for use where double glazing was installed to combat noise near motorways and airports. Local authorities wanted the heavily insulated fan and exhaust unit to install in outside walls so that air could be let in but not noise.

The Accadiair unit, as it was called, was technically ahead of its rivals and sales were beginning to boom for the marketing company which owned the product rights. KME undertook to manufacture the units and sell them to the marketing company. KME would help to develop the product in a deal expected to be worth up to £2 million a year of additional turnover. KME could also sell the product overseas. It was precisely the kind of work which all Kirkby's analysts and critics had maintained was essential for the factory's viability. Commercially, things were looking up.

Power and the advisory council

So far as the cooperative structure and worker behaviour were concerned, little progress was being made. The draft constitutional rules had changed significantly by June 1975. The cooperative's projected 'executive committee' of ten people had been changed to a seven-man 'cooperative council'. Its members would still be elected by ballot at the cooperative's annual meeting but would now consist of one member of each of the six unions and a representative of management.

No longer would six of the executive committee's ten members become directors of the company, but only 'two shareholders of the company and members of the cooperative'. This gave anyone with one year's service the chance to become a director of KME. It actually meant that Spriggs and Jenkins would continue as KME's sole directors.

The revised rules also made it clearer that all the power would rest with the company and that its directors would be responsible for its management (as must be the case under the Companies Act), though they would be accountable to the worker shareholders for their running of KME. The cooperative council could not have a controlling role in the limited liability company of KME Limited. KME's directors held such power. Consequently, the cooperative council's powers had been emasculated despite the constitution's brave words. Indeed it was no longer clear that the council would have any significant role, except as an advisory body to the directors of KME. The council could recommend the appointment of the general manager, though the directors would have sole responsibility for his appointment. It could recommend the hiring and dismissal of employees, though the company would decide such matters. The council was also to obtain from the company, twice yearly, a full statement of the workings of the company, audited accounts, and any financial statements required by the Industry Department. These would be presented to the cooperative's members at the first available general meeting of the cooperative. The council never managed to obtain the statements – nor were they presented to any cooperative meeting. Only the statutory accounts were made available at the company AGM. The council did not even have enough power to insist on carrying out its specified tasks. All power became concentrated into the hands of KME's two worker directors. The cooperative council became downgraded further and retitled the 'advisory council'.

It was reported that 'when the constitution is fully operational, soon, the council will monitor and scrutinize the progress of the cooperative under directors elected by the workers'. Well, the council certainly tried.

Six workers were elected to the council and its introductory meeting was held with the two worker directors also present. The constitution was accepted in principle, pending a ballot of the membership. Further discussions would be held on the company's product and financial position when Bandell supplied more information. The council endorsed a management proposal to discontinue the press shop night shift until business picked up. Spare labour should be moved to other jobs and there should be a reserve pool of the vital radiator welders; the factory shop shouldn't sell cheap soft drinks outside break times and the IPD discipline code should remain in force pending review. The council requested a management chart showing areas of responsibility.

It was all eminently sensible stuff as a start to the council's work – and it should have spread knowledge and ownership of the cooperative's problems and progress beyond the few managers, the two directors and the twenty-six shop stewards. But there were already tensions about the council's role. It had begun by meeting frequently – sometimes on consecutive days. The directors were very wary of its actions, since it could form an alternative power base to their own. The stewards and directors were not at all sure that they could rely on the sense of the council members. They expressed concern that the council was running off with the idea that it was an executive body. Other people saw it somewhat differently, since its pell-mell opening actions could also be explained as the initial release of pent-up emotions and of desires to take responsibility and to become involved.

After all, the years of struggle had forced dissent underground and had concentrated power into the hands of a few people who often had plenipotentiary powers of initiative and negotiation. Solidarity had a cost. The council could have been seen as a necessary and welcome safety valve, but, like so many traditional company managements, the directors and the general manager were concerned that active participation could run amok. None of them were members of the council. The general manager had no hold over it and the director convenors could only directly control the shop stewards' committee (and the management). The leaders saw the council as a Trojan horse in their midst.

When the general manager attended the second formal council meeting on 5 July, he answered many of its queries by saying that management were reviewing the matters. The requested management structure was not available, but he did promise to give them a report on company cars. This was a vexed subject. When the company had bought four Marina estate cars, there had almost been a march on the administration building by cooperators who suspected that the cars were for the two directors, the general manager and Spriggs' close friend the transport manager. In fact, the cars were for the four Constor field service engineers.

The general manager also reminded the council that the contents of their constitution must be strictly adhered to. Lewis was thus lining himself up with the directors, though whether this was wise was questionable in view of the management's powerlessness in the face of the directors' control. Pressing for a systematic management mandate might have been in management's better interests, assuming that it actually wanted to have power and responsibility.

By the third formal meeting on 4 September the council was complaining that the management chart was still not available; nor was the car report. The general manager's answer about stocks was 'not satisfactory'. The council was raising issues about the disciplinary code, pass-outs, unassigned labour times, cash transactions over pallets, purchase of diesel fuel, security, progress reports on product development, labour loading in certain departments and the boundary between production and product development. All were related to the efficiency of the enterprise. All were concerned with clarification and seemed legitimate and sane, though they were also matters for the management.

The convenors were contemptuous of the council. 'What does it do? The stewards' committee does the most good because it keeps us on our toes. What the council says has no bearing at this time. What they're talking about is too futuristic for the needs of the cooperative now. We've been getting academics on the council – no disrespect to you Tony – who've been exercising their brains on matters that they don't know about.'

Spriggs and Jenkins were right about the council's limited knowledge. It was being starved of information and was being treated in an increasingly offhand way. The leaders saw the council members as amateurs. The shop stewards' movement, by contrast, was described as 'professional'. 'We've been given the experience by events. The shop stewards' committee makes the operating decisions via the management.' 'The council wanted to inform people by putting information on the notice-boards' but, said the leaders, 'it's difficult to be accurate and there's been shop-floor reaction.' In fact, one councillor had started typing up council minutes and had put the first set on the notice-boards to show the actions of the council and to demonstrate its accountability to the co-operators. Jenkins ripped them down and told the council it had no permission to display them. Spriggs insisted that he must approve any minutes – even if he hadn't been at the meeting.

The leaders preferred to keep information to themselves. Most cooperators knew little of the company's position. Tremendous trust and affection were placed on the directors, although reservations about Lewis were widespread. Spriggs had induced them to accept Lewis by embarrassing a mass meeting by asking for objections to Lewis's appointment. There had been silence.

The leaders were finding that, on the terms in which they were prepared to offer participation, few cooperators wanted to participate actively in the running of the factory. The convenors felt that it would be quite a time before the shop-floor could absorb and understand fully the problems of running a business. Meanwhile there would continue to be information which should not, in the interests of the enterprise, be disclosed to the work people. Hence the row with the council. If knowledge was power, then it was also a way of centralizing power. They were troubled by this problem but it did not result in their making any deep or sustained attempts to be frank with the cooperators.

They had reason to be cautious about the wish of people to become involved. The arguments within the council were one source of worry; another was the depressing fact that there had been only three nominations for the four trustee positions on the cooperative itself even though the jobs entailed little work or responsibility.

Smashing the council

An assault was then mounted on the puny, alternative power base of the council. Despite the leaders' wish to keep roles clearly separate by having no stewards on the council, the TGWU had appointed a shop steward as its council representative. He soon resigned from the council and the TGWU refused to replace him because the smaller, white-collar unions were unfairly over-represented on the council – a view which had considerable support from the shop-floor. Other council members began to feel weary over their exposed and discouraging role and, bit by bit, the council fell to pieces. 'The directors were right,' said Lewis, 'it had to be smashed.' Many shop stewards had been hostile to the council as a threat to their own power. The cooperators had been turned against the council and its hapless members found no support for their undermined role. They gave every impression of not knowing quite why they'd been clobbered and they mounted no counter-attack on the directors' centralized power.

Whatever the original intention or wishes might have been for people to become involved in running their own working lives, Spriggs and Jenkins were now in control of all four power bases. They were KME's only directors, the leaders of the stewards' committee, Spriggs had acquired the role of chairman of the cooperative and they were *de facto* managers of the enterprise. KME's survival chances rested on their powers of leadership.

Workers and mobility

Survival for KME meant not only trading more effectively but weathering a series of internal and external pressures. The most serious pressure came from inside. Since early in the King regime, the workforce had agreed to full labour mobility if labour priorities required it. Those who moved would not lose money and would be paid the higher rate if their new job was in a higher grade. Such labour transfers would be temporary pending further work being available in people's original jobs.

There were sixteen tool setters at the factory – all skilled AUEW men. They had enjoyed extensive overtime during the early months because contract presswork had demanded a lot of tool changing. Recently, the Accadiair introduction had meant more overtime. Now these jobs were almost finished and there was work for only nine setters. The others refused to move to fill gaps on the semi-skilled production lines. Spriggs was in a slightly awkward situation because he was the AUEW convenor but not a skilled craftsman. (Only those familiar with factory-floor attitudes will fully appreciate the subtlety with which craft workers sustain their status in the face of the semi-skilled and dilutees.)

The stewards' committee agreed that the men should move. The setters refused again, and Spriggs wouldn't initially implement the mobility agreement. The setters downed tools for two days, sat tight and wouldn't work on their jobs. The radiator shop rapidly ran down and press shop people complained that they had nothing to do. The stewards' committee became argumentative and three night-shift stewards walked out of the meeting. The management then tried to give the setters notice of termination, but the mass meeting on 11 July voted to allow some of the setters to be laid off without pay rather than work on the production lines. It was a major test of a key component of the cooperative's supposed advantages – a committed, enterprise-backing workforce. A group from the press shop had voted against the layoff plan saying 'work or go'. They could see, like the directors, that if the setters were allowed to avoid mobility, everyone else could refuse to move in future.

Jack told the setters that work-sharing could last eighteen months, given the recession in the motor industry. They would be better off reducing their number, and so seven should go – preferably into other work in the cooperative – leaving the nine men to get on with the job. Spriggs told the next mass meeting that the seven would go.

However, the setters changed their minds (if indeed it was ever exactly sure that they had agreed). Jack felt foolish and told them that they were making him look a liar. Lewis and Spriggs decided that the seven shortest-service men would have to be sacked. The problem with this hallowed union practice of 'last in, first out' was that it wasn't the short-service men who were most resistant to moving. The setters appealed to the AUEW, which looked at the work agreement and repeated the cooper-ative's instruction for their members to move.

A split then appeared, with the nine retained setters agreeing that the other seven should go. It was an un-pleasant episode in which the nine senior people had agreed to the sacking of their mates rather than to their own mobility. In one sense, the incident had proved little about mobility one way or the other. The seven men left with about £200 each in lieu of notice because KME didn't want to give redundancy pay, since the cooperative was against the whole principle of redundancy and said that it wouldn't be party to it! The seven later took the com-pany to a tribunal alleging unfair dismissal but lost their case. Even if they had stayed and agreed to move, there could have been a problem. One steward had made it plain that if a skilled setter worked alongside him on a skilled rate, he and his semi-skilled members would want that extra rate too. So much for cooperation on the shop-floor.

Mounting pressures

Another incident was just as inconclusive but equally serious in its implication. A worker had been caught clocking his mate off work, but his mate's card didn't register properly and just left a red smudge – '. . . not enough for a forensic test,' said Spriggs, and so nothing was done. Yet a few weeks earlier one of the radiator men had been sacked for clocking on and going missing for the day. Clearly the disciplinary code was going to break down if it were not endorsed and applied consistently.

Everything was quiet for a week, but on 17 July a night shop steward was waiting for Spriggs when he came into work. There was bad news. A foreman had found seventeen people playing football on the back road at 6 a.m. Their argument was that they'd finished their target score for the night and their leisure time was their own. Indeed, they claimed, Spriggs and the management should set out a pitch and some proper sports facilities so they could enjoy the game better. Spriggs pondered the problem and recommended that Lewis do nothing because of adverse publicity.

There was a real problem for the leaders. The cooperative leaked like a sieve whenever there was news. Not everyone liked the leadership, and people would ring up the papers if there was a story. Given the row about funding the derelict enterprise, a story about cooperators playing football during working hours at the loss-making plant would have been seized on by the press. It was a reason for letting such incidents slide and was also used repeatedly by the leadership as a justification for not spreading trading information among the workforce – either directly, via the stewards or via the council. People in the dark couldn't spread stories. Unfortunately, they could spread suppositions. Spriggs was worried. 'There's been many an occasion when we've got to this point of dissent, but we've always managed to keep it steady.'

The leaders were under pressure from outside also. In July 1975 the Department of Industry's Peter Carey told the Public Accounts Committee that special monitoring arrangements had been set up for KME and a 'very senior monitoring officer' (John Lippitt) had been allocated in addition to the Department taking 'very detailed steps to see that the grant is used for the purpose for which it was provided and that it is being effective'. Monitoring generally was being tightened, though it seemed as though KME was the subject of a particularly tough scrutiny. It may have been the case that 'detailed steps' were being taken by the Department but there was little evidence that the Department took any practical steps to ensure that the aid was 'effective'. Perhaps they couldn't, for officials argue that once money has been granted, there is very little which can be done to intervene in the recipient's affairs.

Benn is moved

KME's tiny band of political supporters was dwindling rapidly and the campaign of vilification against Benn was an unedifying spectacle as well as a millstone round KME's neck. His policies had become a symbol of the struggles over industrial policy, and hostile civil servants quoted the opposition of his colleagues as justification for their own behaviour towards Benn, who had been able to make little progress in the face of widespread resistance. He had managed to change IDAB's guidelines and appoint some new members who might be more sympathetic than the bankers and accountants who dominated it, and Lord Wilfred Brown, John Hughes of Ruskin College and George Doughty of AUEW/TASS were added. It was to make little difference. Between 1972 and 1980 there were only five appointees who could be construed as potentially socialist. In contrast there were four bankers, three accountants and nine industrialists. Capitalism was under no threat from IDAB.

Benn's position at the Industry Department was now highly precarious and Wilson was only biding his time before action would have to be taken to restore confidence in Labour's industrial policy. The moment came on 5 June 1975. On that day over twenty four million British electors took part in an historic referendum and voted two to one in favour of staying in the Common Market. Five days later, the anti-market Benn was removed from his post and swapped with Eric Varley from the Energy Department. Benn agreed to move when Wilson told him that it wouldn't change the industrial policy 'even though,' said Benn, 'I knew differently. . . But I then had no reason to refuse to move,' he concluded oddly. Wilson also told him that if he had declined to move he, Wilson, would have taken over Industry himself – as he had done briefly in 1974. Benn was to sit quietly at Chequers in November 1975, when the Cabinet reversed the whole basis of its industrial strategy. Planning agreements, nationalization and massive intervention were all scrapped in favour of selective 'picking winners' support for industries and industrialists. It was a much more emollient policy.

Heffer had already gone in April, having spoken against the Government EEC recommendations in the Commons debate, in defiance of the Prime Minister's ruling. Wilson sacked him immediately. This may have been a relief to Eric who had been under increasing criticism from his Tribune group colleagues, who disliked his saying that he was really with them in spirit whilst he remained in the Government and was thus associated with the policies which the Tribune group was fighting.

KME had now lost its chief sponsor, though the links with the Industry Department continued as Lippitt carried out his monitoring role. In August he asked KME about directors' fees at the cooperative. The company explained that at a KME board meeting on 9 July, Spriggs and Jenkins had authorized the payment of directors' fees to themselves. They had worked the first three months on their flat rate of £37.40, even though they were working unpaid overtime too. They could scarcely clock on when on the phone at home. In July 1975 they decided that, backdated from April, they should each be paid a director's fee of £3,000 per year in addition to the semi-skilled rate (now £43.15 per week). The reason given was 'added responsibilities'.

The leaders had already checked with the stewards' committee and there had been no reaction to the proposal, which put the directors' income below Lewis's £6,000 but at 'executive level' like Bandell. (These directors' fees were to be quoted by some critics as showing the elitism and anti-egalitarianism of KME's leaders, but it wasn't clear why they should be paid virtually the lowest male rate for taking so much responsibility and working such intermittently long hours. Some people inside and outside KME felt that the extra money was fully justified.)

Trade up – losses down: the business improves

To try to counter the persistent criticism of the cooperative, KME publicized the licensing of another new product called Canespa. They were using their well-honed flair with the press to try to overcome the adverse publicity which seemed to flow their way too often. Canespa was to turn out a flop. It was an electrically conducting, painted material which was supposed to be able to replace pig lights and calf heaters and even be used for radiant wall heating. Sadly the device could never be induced to pass its electrical safety tests and KME wouldn't sign the licence from its German inventors. It was a prospective £1 million of turnover which never came to anything, but at least KME was trying to expand its operations in its field of expertise – just as it said it should.

The orange juice operation was reported as 'running profitably'. Indeed KME's losses were coming down. Turnover had gone up 25 per cent in the period July–September 1975. KME's overall loss was declining slightly, and the decline was set to continue as turnover rose.

The problem was that the Government grant was being eaten up in funding the losses and the working capital requirements of the expanding business. In fact the drinks operation was still highly *un*profitable and KME was selling drinks at prices so low, the trade was suspicious. Corona's drinks salesmen were told by their management, 'Don't follow them down in price, they're fanatics.'

In addition to the £1.8 million paid to the IPD receiver, some £1.2 million had been lost on trading in nine months. There was only £350,000 of the Government grant still to be drawn, and KME would be running out of cash by early 1976. The crunch could be deferred by running down stock levels, delaying payments to creditors and pressing customers for early payment in order to squeeze cash into the business. None of these would be painless.

Running down stocks would interrupt production as raw material supplies became hand to mouth. Low stocks of products would risk dissatisfied customers receiving only part of their orders. Creditors read the newspapers and, knowing that KME was underfunded, would smell a rat if the cooperative began paying late. KME was finding increasing willingness to supply on normal commercial terms ('We haven't found anyone who'll stand on his dignity if he's got something to sell'), but it's easier said than done to induce customers to pay quickly and owe less – particularly if they are buying more and more goods. As the problems mounted, the Kirkby leaders and managers were becoming more thoughtful.

They were still trying to introduce new products whilst minimizing the investment cost of these new ventures. Talks were held with the US Kaiser-Sherer group about the production of steel laboratory cabinets. The convenors visited them in Michigan, but it all came to nought. A contract was signed to produce humidifiers for another company and there were still hopes for the German Canespa heating product. The contract presswork side of KME's business was also declining, but at least the radiator sales were booming.

KME sold 25 per cent more radiators in the last quarter of 1975 than in the third quarter, and production was some 40 per cent up with 116,000 radiators being produced despite the Christmas break.

However, Lippitt knew that KME would need more money and Jenkins had told him in October 1975 that it would be about £2 million. The October loss figure was down to £30,000. Spriggs and Jenkins drafted a seven-page letter to Varley asking for further aid, supported now by the November trading loss of only £47,000. The leaders worked throughout the Christmas break and on 29 December sent an application to Varley and Wilson for £2 million to rectify the original underfunding and to secure a future for the growing business.

7. The new loan application: 1976

- Varley shows his colours
- Stresses inside
- Advice ignored
- Searching for friends
- The action plan
- Help from the bank
- Another wage rise

The Government now had an awkward problem. It could try to shelter behind Benn's 'once-and-for-all' statement and refuse further aid, but nearly every political decision is provisional and previous statements can be over-written if the stakes are raised and Government is prepared to brazen out a row. Unemployment had already risen above one million.

However, Varley would want to reassure industry, then grappling with high inflation and reduced output. He had been put into the Department to reverse the effects of Benn's tenure, and how politically appealing it could be to let one of Benn's brain-children expire whilst blaming it all on Benn himself.

However, the Department knew that the original rescue had been backed by the Cabinet and by the Prime Minister. There was also the embarrassing publicity which had been given to the original underfunding.

KME capitalized on this in its letter of application to Varley. 'We were induced to accept a proposal for £3.9 million.' The Department, wrote KME, knew of the £850,000 deficiency. 'We do not know with what vigour this point was pressed upon your predecessor but, regrettably, our proposal was not adjusted. Had that partial restoration occurred, we might well have avoided this further application for funds.' KME insinuated that it had been forced to pay well over the odds for the assets (a point later emphasized by the Public Accounts Committee) because the receiver 'had learned' of the earmarked £1.8 million and had refused to budge. KME was unshakeably convinced that the civil servants had told Cork.

KME also explained the 'catastrophic' consequences of a receivership on stock levels and supplier and customer relations. This and the inadequate grant have, the cooperative said, 'placed us in a catch-22 situation'.

- customers would only buy at low prices, but we needed higher prices to survive
- we needed to raise output, but this would only occur with low prices, which would cause losses
- we needed to absorb losses whilst demonstrating our durability, but couldn't survive with persistent losses
- we needed to invest in new products without spare cash to invest

KME had attempted to break out of this unsatisfactory state. Progress had been mixed. 'When viewed against the gruesome situation which KME inherited,' said the application, 'some major strides have been made despite the unpromising climate of 1975.'

The application pointed to the growth in turnover and reduction of loss. KME freely admitted that turnover had grown more slowly than anticipated.

However, KME claimed, the cooperative had rectified the worst features which it had inherited, but the shortage of working capital would soon ruin the opportunity to sustain the improvement. 'The drive towards profitability is now at risk because of the original underfunding.' The irony would be that a solvent business with £2.5 million in assets would then go under, at a likely cost to Government which would be three times as large as the £2 million application.

The letter finished with a thinly disguised thrust at Varley's ambivalence towards socialist objectives: 'We believe that further support from your Department is justified to bring the cooperative to a successful position which will be a source of pride to those who believe that, ultimately, workers can and should be responsible for their own enterprises.'

The argument over the cost of closure was of considerable concern to Government. KME had assumed that if the cooperative closed, its trade would be taken over by other British factories and that the Kirkby factory would lie idle, both reasonable assumptions in 1975. Indeed, one of the arguments against the original grant had been that saving employment at Kirkby would simply displace unemployment to other parts of Britain. This argument was becoming irrelevant, for there was now a shortage of radiators. KME also assumed that all 750 cooperators would remain unemployed, so adding to Kirkby's existing 20 per cent unemployment.

The loss to the public purse could be £6 million over three years by virtue of lost income tax, graduated insurance, unemployment pay, social security benefits and local rates. Even if one struck out the income tax and insurance costs on the grounds that other workers would pay these from making KME's output elsewhere, the figure was still £4 million. Of course, if KME's production was to be replaced by imports the cost to the nation would be considerably higher. It was an argument later used to justify both the Chrysler rescue and an increase in the temporary employment job subsidy.*

The political problem was tricky. KME's closure could be made to look like an act of spite against Benn and a

---

* Comparison between job subsidies and unemployment costs creates argument. It can be used to justify individual interventions but, as a general proposition, the implications are worrying. It could be claimed to justify paying every threatened firm a subsidy equal to unemployment pay. Not only would this be impracticable, it could lead to even greater resistance to industrial restructuring and change and great reluctance to raise unemployment pay. It was scarcely surprising that Government was wary of approving any general direct employment subsidy, even though KME might save the nation money.

triumph for the Civil Service over ministers. It would add to unemployment in an already truculent area and one, moreover, which was a Labour stronghold following the Parliamentary gains of 1964.

Nevertheless, the civil servants had something to support their concern. KME *had* missed its targets, even though there were good reasons for so doing. It had *not* stiffened its meagre management or shut down the loss-making drinks operation and nor had it put in any effective operational controls. The 1976 forecast was optimistic, with turnover anticipated to rise by over 80 per cent compared with 1975's £4.8 million. The unproven humidifier and Canespa products were both expected to show a profit in their first year and without them only the sale of scrap would keep the rest in bare profit. The budgeted profit of £334,000 would still require radiator sales to rise by 50 per cent, Constor sales to double, presswork sales to rise from £180,000 to £450,000 and food sales to jump 70 per cent.

Some of it was possible – even given KME's problems. Contract presswork could be obtained if only there was the commercial management to seek it. The radiator market was picking up rapidly and KME's budget hadn't included price rises, which should have been readily obtainable from KME's underpriced position. The cooperative hadn't fallen to pieces as critics had forecast. Given the appalling economic climate and the underfunding which had hampered KME, the trading figures were not too bad. The management accounts sent to Government monthly had shown what had been achieved in KME's first year. Turnover was up; the loss was down; all the trends were moving in the right direction (see Figure 3, p. 128), and civil servants couldn't just rubbish the proposal. Breakeven was a distinct possibility within a few months.

Discussions were held with the Industry Department in January 1976 but they just gave more ammunition to KME's critics. Two more new products had been added

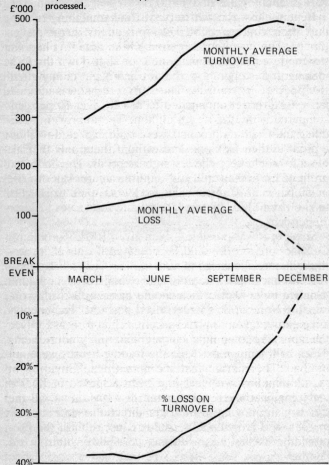

Figure 3 KME's 1975 performance. These graphs accompanied the loan application to Varley. The dotted lines show the further month's results which were sent to the Industry Department while the application was being processed.

£'000

500 —

400 —

MONTHLY AVERAGE
TURNOVER

300 —

200 —

100 —

MONTHLY AVERAGE
LOSS

BREAK
EVEN

MARCH   JUNE   SEPTEMBER   DECEMBER

10% —

20% —

30% —

% LOSS ON
TURNOVER

40% —

Note
The figures are monthly averages of 3 months moving figures and were sent in this form to iron out the effects of holidays and of 4- and 5-week months.

to the budget. 'Transglobe' was a self-lifting, hydraulic device for shifting large containers on and off commercial trucks. It was designed for use where no lifting equipment was available and had military as well as commercial potential. (It was never to come to anything. After some half-hearted attempts to develop it at KME, the project ended. The inventor later sued KME, who should never have offered to develop a prototype in two months.) The other product was a domestic, infra-red cooking grill which KME could make under licence but which would have taken the cooperative's small sales organization into a new and competitive market. The new forecast included the grill at an exuberant £1.25 million of turnover and £284,000 in net profit after allowing for no sales or distribution overheads. KME's forecast profit for 1976 had become an implausible £719,000 on a turnover of £10.3 million. Another version showed £943,000 profit on £11.3 million turnover.

Varley shows his colours

Despite these hostages to fortune there was some outside support for KME. The Electricity Council told Lewis that Constor sales should exceed the forecast 225 units per week. Silk reported that Varley was in KME's camp. The cooperative's accounts had shown a £2,000 profit for December 1975, aided by some year-end stock adjustments. None of it mattered.

On 2 February, Varley's committee turned down KME's application. He had, he wrote, taken account of all the points KME had made, the views of IDAB and 'particularly the categoric statement to Parliament by my predecessor Tony Benn that the assistance of £3.9 million was on a once-and-for-all basis'. Instead of offering aid, Varley waived some of the restrictions in the original grant conditions so that KME could borrow against its assets and issue extra shares if it chose. His letter reminded KME's directors of their responsibilities under

Section 332 of the Companies Act, the section on fraudulent trading which holds directors personally responsible for debts incurred by the company when there is no reasonable prospect of the debts being paid. Varley also mentioned Benn's statement that the Government wouldn't accept responsibility for KME's debts and that those who trade with the cooperative must do so without Government guarantees. It was a dangerous letter for KME. If Varley published it, the cooperative's trade reputation could evaporate overnight at the mention of trade risks and section 332.* The letter was also disappointing, as well as angering to KME, in view of the original underfunding and the progress KME had made. The leaders requested an immediate meeting with Varley.

It was a tense occasion. This wasn't surprising, for it was a dirty game which was being played. Jenkins told Varley that his 'job as Secretary of State should be safe if the Government changes to Conservative. Mrs Thatcher will be well satisfied with your performance.' Varley took it calmly. Like most politicians he was used to insults. The Industry Secretary rested virtually all his case on Benn's 'once-and-for-all' statement. The Government couldn't give more assistance.†

* Varley later agreed that KME was not in a Section 332 state, which was scarcely surprising given the £2.5 million of assets. He was told that KME was taking legal advice and were his letter to be published – as the leaders suspected it might be, to embarrass them – it would seek to remedy the adverse effects of the Secretary of State's insinuations. It wasn't published.

† Blaming it all on Benn had its bizarre implications. Varley was engaged in a naive tactic by claiming that Benn's statement prevented aid, because it implied the end of Parliamentary democracy. If all a minister had to do to override the provisions of an Act of Parliament – in this case the Industry Act – was to stand up and announce a new policy, then it would save any nonsense about passing Bills and winning votes in the House. The Chief Whip would have been able to sleep peacefully at night, having shed any worries about the problems of governing via a minority Government.

During the meeting Varley and the officials wouldn't say how many companies were barred from Industry Act assistance. They eventually

Varley said during the meeting that he had supported the original application for £3.9 million (since it was backed by his political benefactor, Harold Wilson, this wasn't too surprising) but that he had now withdrawn his support. He pointed out that IDAB had been unanimously against the new aid with only Harry Urwin of the TGWU absent. The absence of IDAB support for KME was a good weapon for Varley. But what had IDAB been told?

The Cabinet committee dealing with industry affairs (codenamed IDV and later called EI) had also been unanimously against KME. Its composition was secret but KME knew that Benn was a member and that he hadn't been at the meeting. Nobody on the committee, said Varley, had objected to the decision to refuse further aid. He was implying that Benn had gone along with the committee papers.* Varley was indicating that KME had no real political support. Also, he challenged, the cooperators hadn't put any money into KME as had both workers and unions at the *Scottish Daily News*. Varley suggested that the leaders go to their bank and borrow against their trading prospects. (After the meeting he told Silk that they wouldn't be able to get bank money and that KME would be finished in two weeks.) He angered Spriggs by wondering aloud whether the KME workers were really backing the worker directors. Varley wasn't alone in wondering about Spriggs' position. Silk was unsure of it too.

---

told Silk that the answer was three – the three Benn cooperatives. Varley backtracked the next day when KME asked him how a ministerial statement, such as Benn's, could override an Act of Parliament which had been debated and passed in both Chambers and which had received the royal assent. The wonder was why Varley thought he could get away with such a ploy. Perhaps it was just to get through the meeting with minimum trouble whilst trying to turn the convenors' venom against Benn.

* Benn was later to say that he had stopped going to the committee after he was moved to the Department of Energy because 'I didn't think it fair to breathe down the neck of my successor.' Even so, he could have objected, but did not do so.

The meeting ended with Varley offering to consider KME's wish to see the IDU analysis of the cooperative's application. This was the key to the whole affair. After all, if the IDU had produced an analysis which was as disreputably hostile as it had been in 1974, then no wonder IDAB had turned the aid down. Varley had indicated that he had put in a neutral, or even negative, paper to the Cabinet committee. If there had been an inter-divisional and Treasury Civil Service committee which had preceded and shadowed the Cabinet committee, it was sure to have been against KME. Out of a derogatory IDU report which concentrated on the cooperative's losses, rather than its prospects and its progress, all the rejections of KME's application would naturally flow. Cabinet committee members would take their briefs from the IDU analysis and from their own officials' views. There were no important political power blocks to placate, and if the minister in the department concerned wouldn't back it, then the signals were all red, weren't they? KME had been boxed off.

After the meeting the convenors went to the House and had tea with Heffer. Eric was gloomy, believing that KME would be ditched to embarrass himself and Benn and to placate the City.

But the cooperators weren't the only ones with problems. The civil servants had seen enough of Spriggs and Jenkins to know that they were resourceful and ruthless. Nor could they predict what the cornered cooperators might do. In fact, the leaders neither panicked nor blustered. There *had* to be a way round if only they could think calmly about it.

The next day was difficult for the convenors. Back at the factory, everyone wanted to know what was happening. The leaders wouldn't say, while they worked out the next moves. Varley was telexed with a request for the release of the IDU analysis. There was, KME telegraphed, no problem of precedence, since they had received the earlier one from Benn, and, whilst a summary of IDAB's conclusions would be of some use, 'the valuable part of the information would be the argument and reasoning which led to the conclusions . . . so that we could obtain your Department's best advice.' Varley sent them only IDAB's uninformative conclusions. He refused to give them the IDU analysis.

They weren't surprised. The civil servants wouldn't want the embarrassment of any IDU inadequacies being revealed and their concern was valid in one respect. Publication of confidential advice would inhibit choices and make candour unlikely. Nevertheless, Varley could have offered them some insights – perhaps orally – into the analysis of KME's business needs, but that would have helped KME, and Varley wasn't in the business of offering help.

Elsewhere, KME was trying to find anybody who could be remotely sympathetic and who could serve as an ally. Little progress was made with the TUC; Wilson told Silk that the cooperative was a matter for Varley and he didn't particularly want to meet anyone. Silk wanted to set the story off on the floor of the House but was persuaded that publicity would ruin the business by causing suppliers and customers to run away. The racket would just help the Tories to rub everyone's noses in it. After all, KME had already been granted £4 million of public money.

Spriggs rang Lippitt to ask if Varley would consider waiving all the grant conditions. What paragraphs in particular did KME want waived? 'Nothing in particular,' he was told, 'but since you and Varley don't want to know us we thought it best if you were detached completely. Meanwhile, said Spriggs, 'we are asking for £100,000 temporary assistance while we sort out our position.' Lippitt seemed relieved, reported Spriggs, that KME wasn't going to do anything rash and had advised the cooperative to try to obtain temporary overdraft facilities.

This was exactly what KME had in mind, coupled to another source of money. The cooperative would also apply for the £10 per week which could be obtained under

the temporary employment subsidy scheme (TES). This
could last for twelve months for every threatened full-
time worker – which meant virtually everyone at KME.
But there was a snag. The company had to demonstrate
that the subsidy should lead to a permanent saving of the
jobs when the year was up. The yardstick of viability
would be the bank's willingness to lend to KME. In other
words, if Varley was right and the bank wouldn't lend,
the Employment Minister probably couldn't grant the
subsidy – or else he, like Benn, might wind up having
civil service complaints being lodged and leaked.

Stresses inside

The KME stewards meeting on 9 February was a solemn
affair. Spriggs told them that Varley didn't want to pay
a penny. Chrysler, Spriggs said, had only been saved by
some heavy politics behind Varley's back (a reference to
Varley's unfortunate role in being bypassed and overruled
by more senior Cabinet colleagues).

Spriggs then took a line he had been considering over
the weekend. He tried to turn Varley's waiving of some
of the grant conditions into a positive success, saying that
it was a lot more than the *Scottish Daily News* ever got.
KME could, he said, make political capital out of it 'but
we've got to keep everything very quiet; we can't afford
more publicity'. He explained the asset position and how
the money was tied up in stocks and working capital, but
the expressions on people's faces suggested that he was
accidentally blinding them with science. He went on to
complain about the factory activities. 'There's been too
much complacency on the shop-floor – people think we
can just go on for ever'. . . 'The trouble is, when I've said
things on television to keep the outside world at bay,
those inside believe what I say'. . . 'We've got over fifty
thousand radiators in stock and yet we are sending out
incomplete orders . . . it's been easy for foremen and
some men to produce simple radiators, not the ones we

need. There's even the welt* being worked – we couldn't get people to a mass meeting at eleven-thirty rather than eleven because it would cut into their own time'. . . 'The time of doing it by consent is over . . . we've offered to resign and perhaps we might have to have a hard man. If we'd left it to Collinson, this factory might have been in profit. . . We said the losses wouldn't happen with us. But they have. It's the same few backing the cooperative as in the sit-in. The others want it while it works and if it goes, well it goes. We've been a burden on ourselves and we could have done much more about it. . . Members have said we can do anything we like, we're a cooperative. We haven't been strong enough with ourselves. Even now some members don't see the writing on the wall. I know that some people believe that this meeting is over the next wage rise and that we've got the money and we're just talking over the conditions.'

The stewards realized that if KME didn't now get a bank loan, the cooperative was finished. 'It's not that I'm despondent,' said EETPU steward Archie Bredon, 'but when you look back over the year we've initially gone for democracy and ended with no production†. . . Perhaps we need direction. You and Dick are doing well commercially. It's inside that we've got the problems of production. We need deeper, stronger shop-steward involvement and you two perhaps have to come back and look at it inside. We're definitely flagging. Some of the faults are obvious before we begin a job. I'm beginning to change my ideas about industrial democracy as a result.'

What Bredon was implying was that only Jack and Dick

* A Liverpool word for unauthorized breaks and spells in which part of a group rests while the remainder does the work.

† This wasn't true. Radiator outputs had risen steadily over the year, but as experience was gained, Archie saw how the initial confusion had not been replaced by commitment and efficiency. There was a growing gap between production and the self-evident potential for output.

had the power and the reputation to change things inside. The managers, foremen and shop stewards needed them. It was a point taken up defensively by steward Fred Gleaves. 'If it's our union policy to defend our members, we'll do so. We're throwing ourselves on to Jack and Dick. We need direction.' Gleaves was implying that the stewards could only behave as traditional representatives and that the convenors would have to shoulder the contradictions of control. Other stewards joined in. 'In our section overtime is overmanned because, if one worker's needed, everyone is brought in regardless, even if they sit around all day. There's a war between us and the supervisors. They're backing the men and giving everyone overtime and we're saying it's overmanned. . . The foremen are dodging it and leaving it to the shop stewards and the result is that we are not exactly mistrusted, but we are being watched.'

Spriggs replied that 'some people will do what they want and they'll use the stewards. The bloke we sacked for going missing and running a market stall every Tuesday – the day he was sacked he said, "But I can do it. It's a cooperative. I can do anything I please," and he meant it. He really meant it!'

The mass meeting later that morning revealed all the problems of communication, direction and control from which KME was suffering. Spriggs spoke clearly, but what was the average cooperator to make of the words? 'I told you at the half year that the rate of loss was as bad as it had ever been [bad]. I warned you that we had to meet the programme so we could then go round and congratulate people on performance [good]. Our loss dropped to as little as £8,000 a week [good], now it's back up to £24,000 [bad]. I said if we went on we'd run out of money [bad]. We could analyse and criticize each other. You have to take action – only *you* can, not a workers' council, or the shop stewards, but *you*. We had to start off struggling to sell goods cheaply and pay more for materials

because we're a coop [bad], but now we've got the freedom of the park [good]. There's a rosy future if we put
it right [good], but without cash we have no chance whatever [bad]. . . If we don't pay a bill the red lights will go
on and our creditors will immediately be alerted [bad].
I'm glad to say that we have no cash flow problem [good],
but we've reached the point we knew we'd reach over
money. . . Varley is prepared to let companies close down
[bad]. Our application was a profit forecast [good]. It was
a conservative approach [good], but we're dealing with
hostiles [bad]. They're the same people who obstructed
us in 1974. But Varley's said we can seek extra capital
and so we want you to give us permission to approach our
bank to get a temporary overdraft and further long-term
loans [good].'

Spriggs was telling them contradictory things as he tried
to galvanize them into action without alarming them. It
looked as though a bank loan would give a rosy future
without people changing their habits. Under questioning
he even made it worse over the target scores. 'Are you
telling us that we've got to raise outputs?' he was asked.
'No. Just make what we have on budget.'* Spriggs revealed that the place could close in a week without loans.

But there was a persistent undercurrent of frustration
from the floor. 'It's ridiculous to pay people overtime to
lean on machines when we've got no money.' 'We talk
about efficiency. There are lots of people in this room
who've nodded their heads but who'll go back and do
nothing.'

* Author's note: I could have kicked his teeth in. People were asking
if extra performance would help and he was pretending it wouldn't.
The loss rate was running at £30 per person per week. Spriggs did
have one argument on his side. Extra output had to be sold and he
didn't necessarily want extra drinks and extra Constor. My argument
had been that this didn't prevent radiator output and sales being
raised and that extra performance would lower cost by cutting the
overtime requirement. The leaders didn't find these arguments attractive, though they did cut down on overtime for a while.

The vote to support the directors' approach to the bank was unanimous. Varley could stop asking if the leaders had the workforce's backing; whether it was comprehending support was another matter.

Varley was now saying that Government was not prepared to give further selective assistance and that he would not agree to any request for selective assistance because that would breach the once-and-for-all qualification. In other words, Government was debarring KME from further *selective* aid. Under further pressure Varley denied this. In the end it was hard to know what Varley was even trying to say, but it seemed to be that KME would be refused any selective assistance, but wasn't debarred from it. His squirming didn't upset the leaders. They had an extremely low opinion of him in the first place. In other words, Benn's once-and-for-all statement had no statutory force; it was being used to justify governmental discretion. Varley was claiming that the rejection wasn't solely due to the Benn statement, but that it would be a breach of Benn's undertaking if Government gave selective assistance to maintain the same jobs for which the £3.9 million had already been provided. The convenors then neatly reversed the impact of this by pointing out to the bank that nobody had questioned KME's 1976 forecast and that it was really Benn's statement which was stopping Government supporting the co-operative. The local bank manager was sympathetic, but an overdraft would have to be approved at a higher level in National Westminster.

Advice ignored

Factory overtime was chopped temporarily to save cash and to try to push people into being more productive in normal hours. Sadly, other ideas were not followed up. The convenors were advised, yet again, to straighten up the drinks operation or else close it down now that its manager had left. Stock levels should be cut, indirect workers sacked, a commercial director hired and a big price rise introduced on radiators. KME knew that its radiators were some 14 per cent below market price and competitors were complaining that KME was restricting their own price levels. Radiator demand was rising and delivery delays were widespread – just the market to accept price rises and suck in imports. KME raised its radiator prices by 10 per cent and ignored the other suggestions. The author pressed the urgent need for a commercial director on to the leaders. 'How much would we need to pay him?' they asked.

'About £8,000,' was the answer.

'But we're only paying Lewis £6,000,' they protested. 'Then you could tell Lewis that you can't pay him more due to the incomes policy and point out that he'll be no worse off and that you'll make it up to him later. Otherwise you can do what any other firm would do and re-define his duties to get round the incomes policy.'

'If we did that, what would we have to pay Lewis?'

'About £11,000,' came the response.

'If we had to pay that, we wouldn't want Lewis!' said Spriggs.

The easiest way to dissolve this dilemma was simple. It was to do nothing; and although there was a desultory search for an experienced manager, that's exactly what they did. No commercial director was ever appointed.

As usual, the cooperative was relying on its political symbolism to guarantee support, but the climate was unpromising following the change of industrial strategy. The Merseyside firm of Bear Brand was being allowed to go into receivership less than a year after receiving a Government loan. 'Few will regret the change of policy,' wrote the *Financial Times*.

Searching for friends

KME's leaders approached the National Enterprise Board's regional office – set up as a modest sop to a hard-hit area, since all major decisions had to be referred to headquarters. Its regional director Arthur Ward was an ex-Department of Industry man who would be unlikely to cause the Department great aggravation. He didn't seem too pleased to receive a request to invest £1.75 million in exchange for 30 per cent of KME's equity. KME's goal had changed. 'We had a goal of profit before the money ran out,' said the leaders privately. 'We failed. Now our goal is to be part of a large organization. The NEB would be ideal.'

The next month was a trying time for those affected by KME's plight. National Westminster turned down the cooperative's request for a £500,000 overdraft. The bank wanted a Department of Industry guarantee before it would offer any money. National Westminster was playing an elegant game. It would be bad politics to turn down aid to a worker cooperative. After all, nationalization of the banks was intermittently on the Labour Party's agenda and it wouldn't help the bank to provoke Labour's left wing by treating a cooperative less favourably than a normal company. Even their banking rivals wouldn't thank them for such unwelcome publicity. On the other hand, there was no reason to accept the exploding parcel that Varley had handed to them. So they were handing it back.

National Westminster then met KME at its Lothbury office in the shadow of the Bank of England. National Westminster explained that it wouldn't gamble with depositors' money and wouldn't go into any situation where it would have to liquidate the assets to get its money back. 'We all accept that it's a most unusual problem. Mind you, we've got customers of long standing with liquidity problems. It's going to be very tricky in 1976, and it's difficult to know when to go in and when not.' KME pressed the bankers. 'Are you saying that you wouldn't permit one pound of overdraft?' Well, the bank wasn't saying that. They wouldn't refuse to pay cheques if it went to £50,000 – to buy steel to keep the place going. They ended up talking themselves into offering a £250,000 overdraft. The convenors could scarcely have expected this, but they took it coolly.

Yet all the parties were still looking at each other. The bank would only lend if the Government gave some sign of help; TES would only become available from Government if the bank would demonstrate KME's viability by lending it money, and KME was trying to square the circle. Varley was being cautious about guarantees and KME was getting nowhere with the NEB.

It wasn't proving easy to get a fresh meeting with Varley, so Lippitt was told that the leaders were prepared to camp outside the Industry Department, bring television news teams along and hold a board meeting on the pavement, at which they would resign and hand over the assets to the Secretary of State. They couldn't do that, said the Department. What's stopping us? asked KME. Silk told Varley that KME would most likely carry out its threat. A meeting was agreed.

At the meeting, Varley was told that Government would have to make it crystal clear that the State was a totally subordinated creditor so that the bank could not be exposed if the roof fell in and it then found that Government wanted the £3.9 million grant back. Spriggs told Varley that the convenors were prepared to hand over KME to him in the hope that he could protect the workers' jobs better than they could presently do. Varley agreed to consider having the Department monitor the cooperative and tell the bank if KME approached insolvency. (The bank could then blame the Department for pulling the plug on KME.) Everyone was trying to get someone else to carry the can.

Meanwhile, the political climate was disturbed at the highest level. On 16 March Harold Wilson announced his resignation. The struggle for the succession started, which made it difficult to get any attention from ministers, although Varley was trying to clear up the misunderstandings about guarantees and the status of the grant *vis-à-vis* creditors.

The bank asked accountants Peat, Marwick & Mitchell to run their slide-rule over KME whilst the cooperative was conserving cash by axing the night shift and running down its stocks to liberate money.

The action plan

Ward, the NEB regional director, visited the factory but was clearly unenthusiastic about a liaison. The NEB had told him to deal with the problem locally. Ward expressed pleasure at KME's new 'action plan' and said that it should all have been done long ago. He was right. Lewis had drawn up a scheme for change. Overmanning was to be removed, outputs raised, discipline tackled, commercial management strengthened. It was all encouraging – if it ever happened. Ward was worried about the new product projections – since they were all unproven prototypes – but at least he agreed to consider KME's application, although the leaders felt that the NEB wouldn't want to touch the cooperative with a barge pole.

Wilson expressed regret that the Government 'was not in a position to put forward a solution'. The tone of KME's political contacts was that people would like to help if it didn't give them any difficulty.

Help from the bank

Fortunately for KME, the bank received a favourable report from Peat, Marwick & Mitchell who could find no significant fault with KME's accounting procedures, though they were concerned that Accadiair owed the cooperative £233,000 and was being financed only by its creditors at no cost to itself. The bank agreed that, in view of the way KME had been established and operated, past performance couldn't be used to assess the future. That was a relief to KME.

The bank agreed that £320,000 of overdraft would see KME through to July 1976 when a clearer picture would have emerged about viability. If the July review was negative KME would either pay off the borrowing or it would ask the bank to appoint a receiver. In other words, in the likely event that KME couldn't re-finance the overdraft, the cooperative would agree to pull the plug on itself. The leaders accepted. After all, what would happen at the end of July could be a different story, and with TES, the July deadline shouldn't be the end of the road. Once the bank had agreed, Employment Minister Albert Booth was able to show his support for KME. TES was made available.

The leaders were also dealing with two other fronts. The NEB expressed grave reservations about the under-manned management team being able to turn a £1.2 million loss into a £943,000 profit in one year. Expanding the marketing effort would be taxing and having to do that whilst developing new products, cutting costs, de-manning and raising factory productivity was an excessively tall order, said Ward. KME should not take on new developments until it had created a sound base for its current operations. It was unlikely that this would occur before the end of 1976.

The message was clear and the convenors quickly withdrew their application to the NEB so that nobody could say that they had been turned down.

The other front was internal. A mass meeting had already backed the 'action plan' in principle. Unfortunately the shop stewards were running into heavy weather over the scheme to raise factory efficiency and so an ad-hoc committee of workers was set up, under Lewis's chairmanship, to finalize the proposals.

Another wage rise

Against clear advice from outside, the convenors then threw away a strong card.

The wage rise anniversary was 1 April. There was an incomes policy flat rate limit of £6 per week. It didn't mean that you had to pay everyone the same wage rise – or any wage rise at all for that matter – but £6 per week was the top allowable figure.

KME had started off 1976 by losing £35 per head per week. By March this had fallen to £13 per head. Target scores were not being met regularly, and when they were, the workers stopped for the day despite a backlog of orders for radiators. KME was strongly advised to offer a wage rise only against improvements in both targets and performance. The leaders disagreed and paid everyone the full £6 per week – for nothing. Their first argument was that the action plan would raise efficiency through demanning, though it wasn't clear why people would lift their work rate to maintain output and, besides, it was *more* output which was needed. 'Would some surplus people go without compensation or agree to any layoffs without pay – after all, it would preserve their business?' the leaders were asked. 'They don't believe it's their business and some would agitate to pull the whole place down in order to get compensation,' concluded the leaders.

Their other argument was different and reflected shop stewards' notion of reward. It was people's *right* to be compensated for cost of living increases, and if the Government had decreed that £6 per week was fair, then that was what people should receive. If you wanted more performance out of them, then that would have to be a separate negotiation and you would have to pay extra for extra output. The two arguments were not wholly consistent, but there was no doubting the sincerity of their belief that workers had a right to be compensated for the ravages of inflation – more or less regardless of economic circumstance. The leadership could also point to the declining losses as evidence of some justification for hope. Sadly, this improvement was not sustained and by April the loss had worsened to £26 per head per week.

There were some brighter signs of resolution. The cooperative's constitution had been settled and lodged in the House of Commons library. Over seven hundred cooperators now held one share each in KME. KME had bought a new paint booth to raise the quality of paint finish being achieved on their ancient and breakdown-prone plant. Their thermal brick supplier had declined to go on making the storage heater bricks and so they had bought his equipment and installed it at Kirkby. A Dutch distributor was interested in their new air curtain. Servotomic were about to order between 70,000 and 100,000 stove enamelled radiators – though goodness knows how KME would supply them if outputs couldn't be raised. The works manager visited Germany to inspect the automatic welding of radiators and KME was taking on extra welders to replace wastage in its young radiator workforce.

Spriggs was beginning to wonder if the drinks business could be hived off to a low overhead building – perhaps a Government factory. It all looked active and resolute.

The Department of Employment rang up to say that they couldn't pay TES; the bank's overdraft offer wasn't conclusive enough. Spriggs told them that a Government decision had been made and KME wanted no more chat and put the phone down. It was consistent with the leaders' contempt for the officials' habits. It wasn't that they felt that the officials were personally inept; more that the whole bureaucratic system would be a nuisance, and political decisions were the ones which counted. Perhaps it was also accompanied by the feeling that if you embarrassed, threatened, cajoled or offered political capital to a Labour Government, a way would always be found to support employment. So far the leaders had been right.

8. Troubles at the mill: 1976

- **More advice ignored**
- **Optimism and gloom**
- **Fruitless meetings**
- **Problems, problems**

Inside KME, Lewis's action plan had been difficult to agree with the newly established ad-hoc committee which, the leaders felt, had gone in, feet first, with a mandate from various sections to negate the demanning and mobility proposals. Particularly irate were those who were going to have to move their jobs.

The demanning exercise should have released fifty-six people, including some maintenance workers, for reallocation to other work. The resistive maintenance craftsmen had held a series of inconclusive meetings because there was, as always with maintenance work, some genuine fluctuation in work load so that it wasn't possible to be exact about labour needs. None of the maintenance section's shop stewards stepped in and took hold of the situation. Under pressure, Lewis agreed to leave the maintenance staff untouched so that they could work on new products, when these turned up. This reduced the fifty-six movers to twenty-six – which wouldn't do a lot for efficiency.

The stewards had discussed and agreed the original plans by twenty-five to one. They were later to say that they knew that the plans wouldn't work, though they would try to push them through. The modified plan was launched on Monday 17 April, and it worked in the drinks section. It even worked in the press shop for four hours.

Problems rose first on the radiator multi-welding equipment. Nine people were asked to move to different work without loss of pay. When they refused, Lewis said that people would have to go back to square one and all fifty-six should move. They were given fifteen minutes to consider it. When that had no effect, the supervisors were told to sack those concerned. This was odd, for the managers had no authority to take such action. People began to walk out, section by section, accompanied by their shop stewards, most of whom had supported the plan against which the workers were taking action. Nearly half the workforce went out on the cooperative's first (and virtually only) strike. Dick and Jack had already left for a London conference without knowing that there was a problem or that their trip would have a comical aspect.

They were to speak at an Industrial Society conference on industrial democracy! Quickly alerted to the action plan's débâcle, they returned from London as soon as they could leave without arousing curiosity, and roasted the stewards' committee, charging that by walking out, stewards had acted against their own decision. The stewards' mandate was gone. It was hideously embarrassing, Spriggs told them, the media was round his neck, and if the strike weren't stifled and the workers brought back inside quickly, the cooperative would become a laughing stock. The stewards' committee was contrite and defiant simultaneously. Although apologetic about the mess, the committee felt that the whole thing had been bungled by the management. A few stewards didn't seem to think that the chaos was anything to do with themselves.

In some ways it would have been braver and more honourable if the stewards had all resigned, but there wasn't another group to come forward. The incident could be seen as a case of worker representatives being unable to broaden their role and take unpalatable decisions in the aid of the well-being of job security, when faced with the distaste of their members. Under the load of these contradictory pressures, they had reverted to their traditional role as workforce representatives. To be fair, not every section was out and some stewards had not reneged

on their backing for the action plan, but it was an evoc-
ative incident. Most stewards felt that they would have
been brushed aside if they hadn't gone along with the
strikers. As it was, workers were still coming to the stewards for leadership. There was no other focus through
which the cooperators could concentrate their concerns.

By the time the stewards had resolved that the demanning exercise should start again from scratch, the strike
was three days old. Thursday's mass meeting went the
usual way when the directors said that they would step
aside if they weren't believed to be doing well, and what
suggestions did the people have as an alternative? There
weren't any. The stewards agreed to get together with the
staff and management to see what the job loadings should
be, although there was still a lot of aggravation between
the stewards. The TGWU stewards had appeared to want
to man the barricades, though against whom was never
clear. The TASS representatives had their own festering
agenda over wage relativities and rates. The ASTMS
supervisors were divided among themselves. The shop
stewards were worried that they had lost the confidence
of the membership.

Nevertheless, the stewards showed unity at the mass
meeting and the platform was given complete powers to
look at labour loading in principle and negotiate the new
schemes with the shop-floor. Most people were glad to
get back to work. KME's only significant strike was over.

The inquest began among the stewards. Some of the
trouble stemmed from the fact that, despite all the agreements about mobility, there had never been a skilled man
going into production. The surplus tool setters had left
rather than do it. It was only the semi-skilled people
who'd worked the mobility agreement, said Spriggs
reproachfully.

Electrician Ralph Peacock intervened. 'There's eight of
us willing to move from maintenance to production.'
Spriggs warmed to the idea, warily. 'If we could set an
example it would be a good precedent. But not today.

There could be a problem if we just leave a right-wing maintenance shop.'

The discussion broadened out. 'We don't want this dispute to become a red herring,' said Spriggs. 'It's only one part of the problem. We've got an absenteeism problem. Some staff are working the sick scheme, that's how militant they are for their jobs. We're thirty thousand radiators in arrears to our customers already. My priority is that the production programmes be met.'

Bredon was cautionary. 'Just be careful on absenteeism – it should be a mass decision.'

Someone suggested a way of improving outputs. 'It's ridiculous to stop when the score is done. If a radiator welder puts his torch down, there should be someone else competent to pick it up.' But it wasn't a steward who said it, it was one of KME's advisers. He also suggested that a taskforce should be formed of versatile people who could fill holes in the production teams to keep work going. There should be local discussions in every department on why things were going wrong and what the department should do to straighten things out. None of these suggestions was taken up.

Instead, a toolmakers' steward suggested that some of those present should go out selling to Ford. Bandell was, unusually, at the meeting. His reply was succinct. 'Last year our problem was to get the business. Now it's getting the production. Some sections like Constor assembly can do it, but with the press shop it's a different story. I'll only be convinced we're efficient when I can go round the factory and see people working and not groups sitting around. There's work to be had from Ford and Leyland. Radiator sales are going well. We want to accept more orders, but we're afraid that you won't be able to meet them.'

The meeting ended with the ritual decision that the stewards should go back and talk to their members and explain the problems to them. Sadly, there was no precision, no clear task, no report back or decision date.

There was no sign that there would be any response to Bandell's bleak challenge. Nobody was going to pick up the threads of effective control of the production process.*

More advice ignored

The message was rubbed in yet again when Bandell and two stewards visited another MBS project on KME. The MBS executives told them:

- sell the drinks business
- increase radiator prices
- sort out some proper management control information
- make to standard cost because production variances were appalling and this made reliance on new products unacceptable
- viability would have to come from existing products and so production problems *must* be overcome
- recruit marketing and commercial managers to attack markets competently

The central problem, the executives continued, was that the development of the *business* and the development of the *organization* had become out of phase. It was important to give workers an effective form of control at the top. Good managers should be hired at the going rate and allowed to manage within a policy framework created

---

* Author's note: In my view, this strike and its aftermath was one of the key incidents in KME's development. The leaders had seen, yet again, how thin was the commitment to commercial success, how fragile were the stewards when exposed to conflicting pressures and how nearly the stewards had lost the mandate to lead. Never again was the leadership to really try to lead from the front and to take risks with the membership's feelings. The leaders had attempted to take people towards the goal of business efficiency, even if they had done it in amateurish fashion – but they had lost.

The stewards would not risk being rebuffed in case it totally destroyed their mandate. Managers don't mind so much – they're not being rejected by their own people, so it doesn't reflect so much on them. Nor does it destroy the basis of their power.

through the leaders. The advisory council was important and the key need was to broaden the basis of responsibility and accountability. If people couldn't take responsibility for their own actions, then there was no hope of efficiency, for the leadership had no power to impose. It was exactly what KME's advisers were saying, again and again.

The MBS executives might as well have saved their breath. Bandell understood the problem well enough, though it wasn't clear that Lewis did. The stewards could see the dilemma – well, most of them could – but were in no state to propose or carry through the necessary changes.

Spriggs and Jenkins were the obstacle to change. They wouldn't risk being rebuffed by trying to use their authority and position to organize a new climate at KME. They wouldn't give out much information to help cooperators in case it leaked. They wouldn't share power with other people and they would neither accept the role of joint managing directors (which *de facto* they were) or give Lewis the job. They were in a defensive position but, unlike good football defenders, they wouldn't use their size and weight. Instead, they were worried that their hold on events was precarious and would be lost if others were brought in to share the burden. And, to be fair, there was evidence that ignorance was a barrier to understanding for too many shop stewards – ignorance which was the inevitable result of centralized control. The stewards did not attempt to reduce the leaders' tight control, which wasn't really precarious at all. In fact it was all-enveloping, so that it was only too cosy for the stewards to remain ignorant and let the convenors carry the burden of responsibility. The leaders were advised yet again to open up the worries to more people in a way which would prevent the situation from going out of control. The shop stewards and the sections *had* to become more involved. But nothing happened.

Optimism and gloom

On Friday 4 June 1976, KME's first annual general meeting was held, just before the lunchtime finishing hour. Of the 707 cooperator shareholders, 259 attended.

'This is a historic meeting,' said Spriggs, 'the first AGM where the shareholders happen to be workers in the company.' [Not quite true, but it was a proud moment.] 'For all the tribulations, we have arrived at a point which a lot of outside people said we would never reach. Some of our critics gave us only till June last year, but after a burst of amateurism we have settled down professionally to conserve capital.'

It was the usual mixture of public relations flannel and fact which led Spriggs into using words which were enigmatic if not accidentally misleading.

'Sales, except for Constor, have never been better,' said Spriggs, 'and we're even in arrears to customers. We hope that we'll soon be satisfying our customers and getting more orders. . . We have a bank loan of £320,000 and we've nearly completed negotiations with Government for TES – free money if you like . . . I'm convinced that with the help of the production workers, we'll soon be close to breakeven . . . If we don't make this money work there won't be another AGM. We'll soon have to make last year's £1.2 million loss public. I hope to be able to make a statement in the next few weeks which will put those losses into the background.'

The auditors then explained that they would need more time to give the figures the proper treatment and the AGM was adjourned for seven weeks. Perhaps the 448 non-attenders had been telepathic.

The bank was pleased with the reduction in loss, said the leaders privately afterwards, and it was prepared to wait until September for the review. Nevertheless the strain was still considerable and Spriggs went into hospital for a check-up. On his return, the worries of the enterprise's efficiency were discussed yet again. It was no use bemoaning people's behaviour, KME was told, if steps were not going to be taken to diffuse information, to create more commitment and to get people involved in deciding which way they wanted the cooperative to go. The £6 wage rise had been given – and for what? There was little mutual trust between sections and levels.

The leaders were gloomy. It was absenteeism which was killing the output, and that was an international problem let alone a feature of Kirkby. Only two people had offered to leave maintenance and go into production. The ad-hoc committee had seemed to think they'd been elected to run the company. It was the same accusation which had been levelled at the council. Spriggs accused the *ad hoc* committee of becoming 'Stalinist', which had its aspects of irony, given his own behaviour.

The action plan had created a tizzy, said the two directors, and the stewards had been told that their members should work to the production programmes and not to the 'scores'. It was two thousand extra radiators a week which were required, said the leaders; but the new targets hadn't been negotiated with the shop-floor and so the stewards were helpless. There was no mechanism to break the log jam, unless the leaders stepped forward. They didn't. Nor did the dwindling band of managers.

John Davis, the works manager, was leaving to go to a new job in Canada, though the leaders were not too sorry. He was, said Spriggs, a 'woolly back* – a disappointment really. Like Lewis, he became officized.' The convenors had this odd habit of criticizing KME's few managers, whilst being reliant on their work and totally unable to replace them. The leaders were strangely sanguine about such departures.

Lewis had several times told them that he was turning down lucrative job offers, but they didn't believe him. Dick said that he and Jack would make Lewis a director, but, given his history, could they get it voted through by

* A sheep – derogatory Liverpool patois for a country yokel.

the cooperators? There was never to be an answer to this, for it was never tried and never seriously considered. Lewis was not well regarded by the leaders. He was never invited on to the mass meeting platform and not allowed to have meetings with his management group, the supervisors, shop stewards or the shop-floor. There was no evidence, apart from their occasional assertions, that Spriggs and Jenkins ever intended to give Lewis any real power.

The leaders and, to an extent, Lewis himself, had been against the plethora of meetings which had been held in King's reign. The convenors had now gone to the other extreme. No wonder Lewis seemed powerless. All the signs were that he was not the head of the enterprise in any meaningful way. In part, it fitted his own working style. He didn't show much enthusiasm for going to sort out problems on the shop-floor or for making decisions, and his favourite phrase was 'leave it with me'. He became known as 'The Pawnbroker'.

Fruitless meetings

Out of the run of play, the supervisors were called to a meeting which, they claimed, was the first time they had been brought together in the life of the cooperative. It was at the instigation of the author – perhaps to humour him – and was part of his campaign to share information, spread responsibility, build group commitment, create work group autonomy, face up to dilemmas of power and help the leaders and shop stewards to cope with their contradictory roles. It was preceded by a shop stewards' meeting and followed by the only joint stewards' and supervisors' meeting which KME ever held. The meetings weren't bad, but the effect was nil.

Spriggs opened the stewards' meeting, pointed out the need to get out of the present unsatisfactory situation and withdrew to leave the stewards to speak their minds.

The stewards agreed the logic of changing work practices as put forward by the ad-hoc committee, but they had no plan to effect the changes and complained that the people on the floor didn't fully comprehend the trading problems. Further, some stewards observed, the stewards' committee had got out of touch with representing the members. 'At the time of the strike we knew what needed doing, but when the shop-floor were adamant, we had no one to turn to.'

(It was painful to hear. The vacuum of leadership was rendering them impotent as guardians of the enterprise. Lewis had some position power, some expert power, but no authority power and no political power. Spriggs and Jenkins had all these powers, but wouldn't use them. They weren't prepared to risk their authority. It was clear that they felt that the only legitimation of their position was the populist support of the cooperators and they couldn't risk having specific plans in case they were rebuffed. Then nobody would be left to lead. It all suggested that KME would have a low common denominator of agreed action – to the point of being unable to move, which was, of course, exactly the position.)

The supervisors in their meeting said that the shop-floor felt that the stewards were ganging up on the workers and that was why stewards were being changed.

'The problem is that a steward can understand the problem and agree with the supervisor. The supervisor can stand back, but the steward has to actually work with the people.'

'We could try rooting out the problem people.'

'We need the whole factory to know the state of play.'

'Most of all we need localized department by department communication to solve the problems day by day. We need proper information and each section to pull its own weight.'

The supervisors had never had a meeting with Jack. The gloom was pervasive. 'It's going to close down anyway. I'm getting my holidays in.'

The joint stewards' and supervisors' meeting which followed also seemed to agree on the diagnosis of KME's central problems. The conflict between management and worker shouldn't be exaggerated, they decided. However, the communication problem was large and it was difficult for the stewards to accept, let alone handle, their dual role, and their workers wouldn't really accept it. The only way was to have the business situation spelled out clearly to everyone. 'We should lose an hour's production talking to each section,' said Freda Staples. 'The platform still won't say much,' said Jimmy O'Neill. Another steward was worried that too many people were looking at each other and not doing enough themselves. The meeting ended with an exhortation for the stewards and supervisors in each section to try to jointly involve the section's people in solving problems and putting their own section right in a harmonious manner.

The effect, if anything, was negative. The shop-floor had sussed out the purpose of the meeting and there was a reaction from one or two areas – with stewards being told in no uncertain terms to look after the section's interests and not get ensnared in business problems.

'At least we've got a response,' said Spriggs, with more optimism than conviction. Yet Lewis and the leaders weren't keen on the specific proposals which were being advised. They didn't like to extend the responsibility base. 'Wouldn't the shop stewards turn over every few days?' Lewis felt that management had to rectify its own problems on manning and organization before it could ask people for more. All the evidence showed that the management couldn't and wouldn't sort out these problems.

There was no joy over the proposal to hold a monthly review meeting of the stewards, council and supervisors under Lewis as chairman, nor over the idea of splitting the policy-making role of the cooperators from the executive role of management. The concept of having the power group decide the policy and then give managers a mandate for action was just not acceptable. Indeed, it wasn't clear that the basis for the proposal was even understood. Nobody was prepared to take the risk of change. Besides it would have modified the leaders' power and removed the managers' excuses. Given that it was the leaders and managers who would have to agree, it was easy to see their political objections to the proposal. Yet the existing situation was a mess. People were confused, resentful and feeling helpless in the face of events beyond their apparent control. One worried supervisor later told the author, 'that meeting you had jointly with us and the stewards and without Jack and Dick – it was made to fail by the leadership'.

Problems, problems

A dispute about design engineers' wages had been intensified. TASS was preventing recruitment and local officials were taking an increasingly stern line with KME.

Spriggs was resentful. 'TASS is trying to starve us out of labour and grind us into the ground.' The extent of KME's uncompetitiveness on wage rates wasn't clear and not belonging to employers' associations, it wasn't easy to find out. The draughtsmen and design engineers had been levelled up in pay when King arrived in 1972. Several mass meetings at KME had mandated the leaders to have across-the-board increases only. If Spriggs changed this, he felt that he'd 'have the five other unions bounce me'. The incomes policy limit would prevent any further rises unless KME followed private industry's practice of restructuring the wage system to give more money than existing jobs would permit. The leaders didn't want to play that game. They felt it was deceitful and risky.

It was exactly the kind of problem faced all the time by any management. There'll be trouble from one group if you don't do this, and trouble from the rest if you do. It showed that administrative dilemmas were not just the consequence of capitalism.

The leaders were depressed. 'Have we struggled for two years to throw it all in a heap now?' TASS was putting on pressure. There are only a few of them, said the local official, ignoring the knock-on possibilities. 'Never let it be said that the union brought down KME,' he told Spriggs. 'KME will bring itself down by mistreating TASS.'

This problem was never solved. KME wouldn't change its rates; TASS prevented recruitment and so the number of design staff was allowed to run down.

Meanwhile the leaders were making no inroads into KME's production problems. The maintenance workers were still rejecting the principle of mobility.

Spriggs was receiving more and more abusive anonymous telephone calls and was becoming cynical of workers' motives. 'There's a rumour that we're dealing with long-term absentees by pushing them into the medical scheme. Two absentees turned up and asked for light work just in case they would be fingered. They'd been off for months and they'd only been back a few hours before they were asking what industrial action we were going to take about two drivers who've just been sacked from the docks.' It was just the kind of nonsense to disgust the leadership as they worked out how best to handle the publication of KME's trading accounts.

Another Friday was chosen for the meeting. Not only could it be held without much interruption of production, but it minimized press interest. There were only 211 co-operators there to hear Spriggs gloss over the £1.5 million loss of the first fifteen months and claim that the cooperative was now making a small profit. Spriggs had been forewarned that there would be some nastiness, but nobody questioned the leaders' actions or their directors' fees, and the cooperators didn't just adopt the report and accounts – they applauded them.

The press was given a tour of the factory and the reporting was highly positive. 'Cooperative in black' said the *Guardian*, 'Worker's Coop "healthy" despite £1.5 million losses' said the *Telegraph*. 'We gave them open house,' said Spriggs, 'but they went away with nothing.

Friday is an ideal day. It's flat on Saturday; dead by Monday.'

He was right. There was no follow-up; no campaign of abuse or derision. It was just as well, because KME had its hands full with output problems caused by demand for radiators far outstripping its ability to supply. The company had raised its prices again, though it soon found that its rivals had promptly raised theirs too. Given the cooperative's old habit of letting people continue to order at the old price for four weeks, it was no surprise that more than forty thousand radiators were overdue.

The radiator sales manager presented the directors with a fiercely worded report. 'We do not possess *a single contented customer* . . . The sales force have been defending the company – we are running out of tricks.'
The past year figures were shown:

	1975	1976
Radiator order		
intake	189,000	305,000
Production	194,000	209,000

Sales were up 60 per cent, production only 8 per cent. The market was screaming for radiators which KME was not producing.

'Ten thousand radiators per week is now not enough,' he continued. 'Customers are now reintroducing rival brands of radiator . . . We need 14,800 radiators per week for the rest of 1976 even if we don't rebuild our depleted stocks . . . We have slipped deeper and deeper into the availability mire, in fact we are now up to our nostrils, stood on one toe on a brick in this particular cess pit.'

The sales manager also reported the loss of Constor orders due to non-availability and unacceptable delivery dates – and this on a grossly under-employed product line.

In response, overtime was increased again. The rest of the year was to show production running well ahead of order intake, mainly because orders were being throttled

by the inability to deliver. Nevertheless, in September
and October a total of 98,000 radiators were produced
against orders of 53,000. The drop in orders reflected the
order lull after KME's price increase had finally come
into effect. The industry had been complaining about
KME's under-pricing and a well-informed attack on the
cooperative appeared in the *Investors Chronicle* of 13
August 1976. The magazine had apparently been briefed
by the Industry Department as well as the radiator industry, since it claimed that KME had not adhered to specific
purposes of Benn's grant (a reference to the £500,000
capital investment sum), raised the question of TES and
was able to state the exact trading position of each of the
cooperative's products. None of this information was public knowledge, nor had the key points come from KME.

Whilst these strictures on KME's behaviour may have
been justified, the assumption that it was KME's deliber-
ate policy was wide of the mark. It hadn't been KME's
intention to be under-priced except to stabilize sales. The
problem was one of commercial information. Not being
a member of the radiator trade association, MARC, the
cooperators had few accurate facts on sales and prices.
The industry's habit of giving discounts of up to 60 per
cent off list price made a nonsense of price lists, and
something of a nonsense of the *Investors Chronicle*'s price
comparisons. Fortunately, the article had little impact,
though it was used by KME's advisers to press the cooperative towards a more aggressive pricing policy.

Meanwhile, discussions were taking place within the
leadership group about the way ahead for KME. Despite
the rebuff over mobility Spriggs was trying hard to push
up production by getting commitment from the shop-
floor, but he was only intending to do it via the stewards'
committee, mass meetings and, perhaps, some regular
meetings with the management and shop stewards. There
would be no departmental meetings, nor any real worker
participation. He was fretful about the likely response to
any suggestions. Would it be possible to do anything with

the agreement of the people? The problem was creating uncertainty in the factory and the membership must decide what to do.

He was again advised to create a policy-making committee which would give the managers a clear mandate to act, backed by the workforce via the new policy-making committee and the stewards' committee. The question of scores, mobility, attendance and performance *had* to be faced. The thirty-five-hour week might have to go in favour of a forty-hour-week. Spriggs was unenthusiastic. 'Once you've won something, you don't give it up – and the people probably wouldn't give such a thing to the cooperative.' 'How do you know what people will do, if they don't know the seriousness of the position?' he was asked. The leaders claimed that the people did know, but there was no evidence that they did. Who *was* going to turn the company round? they were asked. There was no ready answer.

Spriggs was trying though. 'The question,' he asked the stewards, 'is whether we're in a position to control matters or will we simply chug along until we grind to a halt?'

'Why don't we let the people decide?' the stewards replied.

'But we *are* the people here this morning, we're the government, so to speak,' reacted Spriggs. 'If you want to be involved, then involve yourselves.'

The discussion then diverted to the need for more labour, which was evading the issue of the performance of existing cooperators, even if absenteeism and mobility did create problems, for as one steward grumbled: 'We've got daft problems like the two Stacca-truck drivers on the big press. One won't work without the other.'

Jenkins sounded a warning note. 'Remember. We made a recommendation about mobility. We had to eat it dry.'

'We have to work the hours, not the scores,' said Spriggs. 'We've got to get on with it and not just look at each other.'

'The trouble is that you get abandoned,' came the reply.

'You look like the fellow outside Lewis's.'[*]

The stewards agreed that they were having difficulty getting the problems over to their members. 'They know the problems generally, but it's like Belfast. They just don't hear you any more.'

The author suggested monthly meetings between stewards, supervisors and management. Spriggs rejected the idea. 'It's not a problem of communication, but one that we won't face the antidote. The stewards should assess whether the membership do or do not want anything to be done. If not, we're wasting our time. You the stewards, have got to exhibit leadership and be resolute in sticking with it. There're no more rabbits to be pulled out of the hat. Why are we, the leadership, appealing to you to appeal to the shop-floor? Why isn't it the other way round?'

The meeting ended with the usual decision for the stewards to sound out the membership. It would have been the normal thing to do in a normal company when considering, say, a management proposal. There the analogy ended, for there was a gap in the logic. There was no proposal. The cooperators were to be asked the vague question of what in general they wanted to see happen. It would be scarcely surprising if the answers were unhelpfully vague too. However, a specific incident was about to occur which would galvanize people into more purposeful debate.

---

[*] A reference to a Liverpool department store's nude statue, which had long been a subject of ribald comment.

9. Responsibility and the stewards: 1976

- Bad luck saps morale
- Gloom everywhere

At the end of August KME dismissed two cooperators for timekeeping offences. The timekeeper went quietly but the other man complained that he'd been framed and produced a doctor's sick note. The timekeeper pleaded that he had innocently signed the clock card without realizing that the worker wasn't at work.

The dismissals created severe vibrations in the cooperative. A spirited meeting of the shop stewards was held. Stewards had talked to their members and were supposed to come to the meeting with proposals to deal with lateness and absence. The shifting moods of the meeting reflected the difficulty that KME's stewards faced in trying to specify their role.

Dick Jenkins	We've been too relaxed. We've been inclined to fight the management over the years. Perhaps the stewards shouldn't be so ready to fight every case.
Anon	The management should be firmer – it's passing the buck by getting people on the floor to do the work for them.
Dick Jenkins	The people *are* the management.
Anon	But they don't accept that. The people won't do their mates.
Anon	Tighten up the disciplinary code. It indicts management.
Joe Hill	Never mind referring to the management. *We're* supposed to be the management.
Jack Spriggs	There's more acceptance by the people of the need to act than months ago. But

	nobody wants the finger pointed at them. The message I'm getting is, don't brand us with responsibility, but we won't kick if you do something.
Harry Miller	If you set very tight targets, you might get a reaction from the floor.
Jack Spriggs	The events of this week have shown us that we need to act. They expect us to act.

The stewards agreed that anyone who was absent for any reason without prior permission could work no overtime that week.

The debate was rekindled by the author's question 'Are you going to stand united if the shop-floor objects?

Anon	We'll split like we did over the manning.
Harry Miller	Are we stewards or managers?
Dick Jenkins	The people themselves will decide before this new proposal is implemented.
Harry Miller	We didn't come here with the harsh proposal we've now agreed.
Anon	The mass may not accept the proposals.
Anon	But we're here to use our judgement.
Jack Spriggs	The stewards are, by the nature of the role they play in this untraditional structure, taking a management role and the people are expecting action, and would be disappointed if we didn't propose something. The soundings will be done. The temperature will be taken.
Harry Miller	The temperature was taken before.
Jack Spriggs	But it *wasn't*. Surely we've learnt that from last time.
Anon	Tony has said time and again at these meetings – if *we* are not formulating policy, who *is* formulating policy?'
Anon	The trouble is we still haven't found our true role.

Anon   We've lost our shop steward role.
Author   You've lost the role of reacting to other
              people's initiatives. You've gained the
              role of taking initiatives. Indeed, you've
              been lumbered with the role of having to
              take initiatives because, if you don't –
              nobody will.

After the meeting Jack was optimistic. 'The new shop steward role is more purposeful.' Dick was less impressed. 'They can't accept it.' Dick was right. There was little change.

Bad luck saps morale

Notwithstanding this disappointment, a few hopeful signs did ensue. The July trading result showed a loss of only £5,000 before taking TES into account and the bank extended the overdraft facility till the end of 1976.

The factory was busy, more was being produced on Sundays, radiator output was reaching thirteen thousand in some weeks, and in September the overall loss was only £26,000, with some weeks showing breakeven – and this before adding in TES.

Sadly, KME's wretched luck was about to knock the cooperative sideways again. British Steel Corporation was experiencing production problems and could not maintain supplies to keep the radiator lines going. KME had to buy expensive steel from stockholders during the period. BSC supplies were later restored along with a price rise which KME could not quickly recoup – given the cooperatives' tardiness in raising radiator prices.

Nevertheless, radiator output remained high – indeed the November 1976 production of nearly fifty-six thousand units was the highest ever achieved. The problem was that the lack of steel prevented KME from making the most popular sizes, and so stocks grew unbalanced and customers became upset. Factory morale dropped as people were messed about to keep the place running. The only consolation was that KME's competitors had the same problem.

Spriggs knew that a worker, Dave Tomlinson, was seeking fifty signatures to call an extraordinary meeting of the cooperative. According to Spriggs he wasn't getting much support. It appeared that Tomlinson was saying that convenors shouldn't be directors and vice versa. It was a very sensible proposal, given that Spriggs and Jenkins were still at the head of the management, the cooperative and the trade union structures.

The first AGM of the cooperative was held on 25 October 1976. (The company's AGM had taken place in June.) It was very quiet. According to Spriggs, Tomlinson and others had been planning a *coup*, but hostility had grown towards them and their dissent had petered out.

Gloom everywhere

Nationally, the International Monetary Fund (IMF) was negotiating with the Labour Government over conditions for financial support for Britain. Locally, the Merseyside employment picture remained appalling. Courtaulds was shedding jobs; Albright and Wilson was closing; there were redundancies at Hygena; Kraft Foods was under pressure – there seemed to be no end to the gloom. A local firm created a silly political stink over KME supplying a few radiators to Liverpool Corporation and so a large corporation contract was kept away from the cooperative and awarded to Carron's in Scotland.

KME asked Government for an extension of TES beyond the twelve months; IPD wanted to raise the rent from £207,000 to £433,000; radiator stocks were still unbalanced and Spriggs was far from happy. 'Bob's just deskbound,' he gloomed, 'and output based on perpetual overtime isn't secure. We've got a factory of post-mortems, not a factory of planning.'

It was easy to see what he meant, but KME *did* have

plans. The trouble was that they were naive and optimistic, and worse, they weren't actioned with any great professionalism. Monitoring and improving performance were tasks which neither the management nor the convenors seemed to relish. Hence they were done badly. A new totting-up absenteeism and lateness scheme was introduced, but it had little effect. People found their way round it and KME's timekeeping controls were too flabby to cope.

By early December, Spriggs' depression was much deeper. 'We've got absenteeism, extensive rest breaks and yet we're working overtime . . . People now believe that they can't be sacked – no matter what they do.' There were distinct signs of stress in his approach. 'The workers are saying that if you can't get rid of a fellow like the one we reinstated then you can't get rid of anyone*. . . Bob's struggling – perhaps it's beyond him. We're physically being influenced by the way others are acting – people are crashing out like at the end of a wedding. The amazing thing is that all these practices happen at Triumph and Ford, and if it's everywhere, having the IMF run Britain won't change it. The young ones are the worst – they're arrogant and seem to think the world owes them a living. It's no good the Labour Government fighting to survive if the people won't.'

A week later, Spriggs had recovered his resilience. Despite the dip caused by the steel problem – even with November's record output of fifty six thousand radiators the loss was still £133,000 – the half-year loss to September was down to £9,000 after crediting £368,000 TES. KME could have broken even with 10 per cent better prices. Their lack of commercial sense was mortifying, but they just wouldn't be persuaded. Every proposed price rise in radiators was reduced. There had been no questions at the mass meeting which had been told that,

---

* The two dismissed cooperators had taken KME to an Industrial Tribunal alleging unfair dismissal. The timekeeper lost, but the worker won and had been reinstated.

with an increase in efficiency, the cooperative could establish itself and that 'departments should use every facility to turn out their full programme'. Spriggs wasn't sure that it would have a great effect but at least it would sow the seeds for further ideas in 1977. Turnover in 1976 had been £6.8 million compared with 1975's £4.8 million and the loss had come down to £954,000 (£1.2 million in 1975) before crediting any TES.

Obviously, a further injection of money would soon be required.

The Government might be more sympathetic this time. Unemployment had topped one and a half million. KME's loss was being reduced again and all the local redundancies would put pressure on the Labour Government to provide further help, though the IMF's crisis conditions included large public spending cuts.

The interruption of steel supply had been a cruel piece of misfortune. Radiator output was averaging over fifty thousand units per month, and yet the last two months of 1976 had lost KME the same as throughout all the previous five months. Just as in 1975, the cooperative had been making significant progress and then morale and performance had both been sapped – in 1975 by the inadequate cash from Government, in 1976 by a combination of ineffective administration and steel shortage. The year again ended on a dispiriting note.

10. Devolution, unemployment and the Labour Government: 1977

- The same old story
- Management on offer
- KME's 1977 budget
- Devolution opens the door
- The unexpected gift
- Filling the gaps
- Another downturn

KME's leaders girded themselves for 1977, the cooperative's third year. Progress would depend on the three p's – publicity, politics and performance.

KME would publicize itself by accentuating growing 'productivity' from the static labour force (conveniently ignoring the growth in overtime) and reduced losses (conveniently ignoring the subsidy of TES). If only a profit could be reached then KME could exert pressure on politicians such that Government funding might become a possibility. The performance gap wasn't due to lack of business. One of KME's biggest customers (Tricentrol) wished to order between 75,000 and 100,000 radiators for 1977. But could KME make them?

There was no cushion of stocks in the warehouse, for the cooperative had temporarily stopped overtime in order to conserve cash and, without it, output had dropped below thirteen thousand radiators a week. A few cooperators had been re-allocated to radiator work as part of the enfeebled demanning and redeployment plan, but it had made little difference to output. The output rate of KME's vital radiator welders was the limiting factor. Absenteeism and the steel shortage had further aggravated the problem of building enough radiators of the right mix for customers, who were desperate for supplies. Indeed, KME's prospective sales were rising as merchants converted from Stelrad to KME's Toprad in the wake of Stelrad's twelve-week delivery delays.

KME was unable to take proper advantage of this opportunity despite the reintroduction of extensive overtime. Costly overtime couldn't offset the effects of absenteeism and the costs of steel, electricity, fuel oil, maintenance and protective clothing were all tending to go out of control. Extra trade was a mixed blessing as KME failed to reflect the excess costs in the selling prices. It would have been an ideal moment to raise prices and change the charging basis to the near universal practice of invoicing at the price ruling at delivery date. KME carried on invoicing at the order date price despite the booming market.

Even with TES, the cooperative was short of cash. British Steel alone was owed £250,000 and the leaders didn't want to send out too many cheques because that would drive KME's overdraft beyond its £320,000 limit. Harvesting cash was going to be difficult. Radiator stocks needed to be rebuilt, not reduced; the humidifier company owed KME cash, but litigation was in the air as each side blamed the other for low sales; IPD was seeking arbitration on its claim to double the factory's annual rent to £433,000; Accadiair, as always, owed the cooperative a huge amount, but KME couldn't prise it out of them.

The internal problems remained. Spriggs complained that he kept telling people inside that KME was losing money 'but they want to believe that we're flourishing. The media are seeing us as doing well – they're beginning to believe my lies.'

Jenkins visited Israel to talk over orange juice supplies. It was always the convenors who made these trips. Their necessity was not always apparent and rarely did Lewis accompany them. It was only a small indulgence perhaps; their version of jet-set wheeling and dealing. Nevertheless, it created gossip and resentment in the administration at Kirkby.

The same old story

Once again the leaders visited Manchester Business School. It was like playing a well worn record. The MBS executives told them that KME's financial reporting was awful. The quantity was excessive and the quality pathetic. Budgets weren't flexed to allow for the level of activity being different from that planned. (This wasn't wholly true, but it might as well have been for all the use which was made of the adjustments.) The information didn't show whether the fault was with volume or price. ('And if you can't tell, how can you act?') The manufacturing variances hadn't been analysed properly; superintendents didn't know the hours budgeted and spent on jobs; there was no monthly narrative for management to act on; there was no clear forum for policy making and performance appraisal; control of buying seemed amateurish and yet was the single most important element of costs since it represented 54 per cent of turnover; the management structure needed strengthening, with a radical improvement in its competence and its powers to act.

The executives provided draft copies of better financial control documents. These were never used, though the volume/price analysis was incorporated into KME's own controls – with no discernible effect. The MBS executives also challenged the way the cooperative was structured and said that there shouldn't be the same representatives controlling both top and bottom of the enterprise because it had emasculated and demoralized the management.

Management on offer

KME didn't change, and its management team fumbled on, preparing the 1977 budget for the leaders. The budget's realism was suspect since, on past evidence, the figures would be made to show a profit almost regardless of any probability of its achievement. The budget would again assume that standard budgeted costs would be achieved, despite mounting evidence that the cooperators could not manufacture to those costs and that gross cost overruns would likely continue. Meanwhile the leaders were talking of a new disciplinary code which the stewards would have to agree with their members prior to its implementation. Unfortunately it was positive, productive, willing performance which was required from the cooperators. A code of punishment would help; but not much. The other desperate need was for competent commercial management. The Meriden cooperative had re-entered the news with the announcement that GEC would lend it £1 million to finance excessive stocks of completed motorcycles. GEC would also help by providing Meriden with temporary management assistance. In the wake of this news, GEC was approached by KME to provide a commercial manager on loan, and although the large company wasn't over-eager to become involved at Kirkby, a suitable man was located. He was briefed about KME and also visited the factory and met Lewis and the leaders.

Hence, the cooperative had the chance to overcome one of its handicaps so far as attracting managers was concerned. It wasn't a matter of salary differentials or cost – GEC would pay him. It wasn't a problem of KME's image in the job market – the offer was there. It wasn't a problem of competence – they were being offered a good manager from one of the most professionally managed and commercially successful companies in Britain. He could call on other GEC managers to help out the cooperative too. The difficulty for the key figures at KME was that the GEC man wouldn't be under their thumb; they couldn't dominate or threaten him – they might themselves have to change and to tackle their managerial dilemmas. Faced with this unpalatable possibility, they dithered, and, in the end, the offer floundered and lapsed.

The cooperative's indifference and indecision put paid to any progress. The leaders patently didn't want to improve the performance of the cooperative if that risked their losing one iota of control. KME never took up the offers of free training for their production superintendents at GEC's Trafford Park factory either. Nor, despite repeated invitations, did they ever accept any of MBS's offers of help. The leaders sheltered behind their wish to hire permanent managers who would be committed to the cooperative. The hollowness of this claim was crystal clear. Throughout its life, KME never recruited one solitary manager.*

Meanwhile, back at more mundane levels, trouble had again brewed over timekeeping. Jenkins had caught one office worker clocking off another. Both were sacked. All the APEX members walked out, including financial controller, John Bandell. In the end, the sackings were commuted to three days' suspension.

Later, there was a mass meeting which confirmed the suspensions. At the meeting, Spriggs mentioned the need to reduce absenteeism. Somebody said that more communication with the shop-floor was an absolute must.

'But they've got it,' complained Spriggs afterwards.

'That's not so,' he was told, 'people don't realize what's wanted.'

'But they do,' he persisted, 'I keep telling them to work better.'

'Ah yes,' came the response, 'but they just hear you sounding like every manager they've ever known.'

The leaders knew that they needed more labour in the press shop 'but that would kill people's Saturday and

* Author's note: It's hard to be precise, but my best guess is that a good commercial manager would have altered and improved the radiator prices and terms; got the costings of contract presswork right; brought in contract business; and would have forced the drinks operation to price up to the market level or else close down. The annual benefit would have been between £200,000 and £600,000 – more if coupled to a productivity deal on radiators. What stood between KME and this improvement was the pride of the handful of key figures at KME.

Sunday . . . we never have the people. The critics out
there think that if only you let the people do as they like,
it will all come right.' But as one steward complained
privately, 'Jack only gets us together to give us a
bollocking.'

KME's 1977 budget

It was a dodgy foundation for the next negotiations with
Government. Still, while there were politics, there was
hope. There was a meeting on 3 February 1977 between
the leaders and senior civil servants, Ken Binning and
Brian Hilton. If the officials could see the context of the
overall cash flow, they could see what needed to be done,
they said. They had to know the up-to-date position in
case politicians or the British Steel Corporation asked.

'We have a legal position as subordinate creditors,' they
continued, 'as well as a *de facto* political interest . . . If
our role became important, the purpose of the grant
would have failed. The cooperative is managed by itself,
not by us. We're not shareholders,' they pointed out.

'That could be arranged,' responded Spriggs archly.

The officials agreed that KME would run out of cash
in two months if losses continued at £100,000 per month.
It might, mused Binning, be imprudent to trade after the
end of March. Spriggs reacted immediately. 'If you are
asking us to cease trading on the thirty-first—' 'No, I'm
not,' came Binning's quick response. The exploding parcel was being passed round again.

Lewis intervened, for, unusually, the convenors had
brought him along. Had it been a meeting with politicians
they would have excluded him.

Lewis went through the budget for 1977. There would
be a new slimline, cool-top storage heater with which
KME would enter the domestic market for the first time,
he said, conveniently ignoring KME's lack of marketing
expertise. Presswork demand was booming; the new Accadiair design was attractive and there would be good

demand. The drinks operation was expanding and there were air curtains, ice-making machines, caravan fridges, acoustic panels, the infra-red grill, a gas fire which might be the first of a range – it sounded excellent. But the new products were mainly speculative and dependent on adequate cash. There was no cash flow forecast to accompany the budget, nor any allowance for inflation. Nor was there a capital expenditure plan, although KME had committed itself to spend £40,000 on a shrink-wrap machine to package radiators – since KME's loose wrapping system was becoming unacceptable to its customers. Despite these deficiencies the delegation insisted that the 1977 budget was based on experience and sound research and they were confident that it could be met.

The civil servants stated that there seemed to be a good commercial case and it would be better to see Varley soon since money would be required. The convenors came away satisfied. We're better than Meriden, they felt, who are only cry babies. 'Yes,' said Spriggs, 'we beg with dignity.'

Binning insisted that KME's state be kept quiet. Publicity would do no good, and yet, if the bank would help in the short term, Government would be willing to look at the medium and long term. The exploding parcel was moving once more. The bank was again being asked to be the first to step forward. The Department was seeking to make any consideration of Government aid a prior commitment by the bank. If the bank wouldn't help, they wouldn't either. It was the second attempt to push the bank into the front line.

The problem was that none of the discussions about money were facing up to the difficulties of running KME. As *The Times* had put it (21 January 1977) 'One can, perhaps, only wonder about the kind of governmental thinking that could be prepared to pump nearly £4 million of public money into a cooperative enterprise and at the same time leave it so exposed and vulnerable in terms of its marketing and future development prospects.'

The various negotiations continued week by week, and then KME's political position was suddenly strengthened by an event which, at first sight, appeared to have no connection with the cooperative.

Devolution opens the door

On the night of 22 February 1977, the Labour Government's combined Scotland and Wales devolution Bill fell in the Commons, principally because of the objections of Labour MPs from the North-East and North-West of England.

The Government's political equation was transformed. It would now be faced with the sustained enmity of the Scottish National Party's eleven MPs. The Government could readily be beaten in the House of Commons if all other parties lined up against it. The rebellious Labour MPs from the English regions had shown that the Government whips couldn't even be sure of a full turn-out on their side. The political implications were clear. The Government would have to offer inducements to its party interests in the regions. Merseyside's Labour MPs might well demand action to reduce unemployment. The devolution upset had handed KME a weapon. The timing was immaculate for a new request from the cooperative for Government funds.

The political community was still in turmoil when, a few days later, the Bullock Report on industrial democracy was published. It was a whimsical document from KME's viewpoint. Its complicated proposals undervalued the problem of the dual roles of policy making and policy execution, i.e. the major difficulty which was shackling KME and preventing any real enhancement of its efficiency. The Bullock committee opted for a single-tier board system which would certainly invite the habit which they were seeking to eradicate, namely the growth of management groups which would pre-empt decisions outside the board of directors. It was not clear that the

Bullock authors understood the job of management or how it was carried out. They had presented some patchy analyses of the problems coupled to a deeply defective proposal. The report was promptly rubbished by every management body, rejected by some unions and ignored by Government. It was a gross disappointment.

Mulling it over, the convenors felt that the cooperative's bargaining position might be stronger yet, since KME could have a value as an experiment in industrial democracy – though devolution was the real arm-twister for Government. Consequently, the meeting at the Industry Department on 3 March was more political, though pleasant. Silk was there as well as the officials and Alan Williams, the recently appointed Minister of State in the Industry Department, who had been assigned KME by Varley.

KME hadn't yet been to the bank. 'We thought we'd better come to Government – which we all support,' said Spriggs, 'since we're concerned about eight hundred people's jobs.' He implied that Government should guarantee the bank's loans.

Williams pointed out that this would be the same as giving money in Parliamentary terms, and IDAB would never agree. 'IDAB was set up as a form of jury over ministers . . . In the last year we haven't turned down an IDAB proposal; we have to carry IDAB with us.'

'Are you saying that the Department is not prepared in any circumstance, to overturn IDAB?' asked Silk.

'It's highly improbable,' said Williams.

'It's a ministerial decision,' insisted Silk.

'Yes,' said Williams, 'but I'm working on instructions.'

Binning came in crisply. The proposal, he pointed out, would need to take account of the sensible amount of money which would be wanted for the expected level of certainty. It should be properly capitalized over three years, not be a temporary expedient, and should include a contingency sum so that KME could be maintained in a robust form if something went awry. This would raise the numbers, but there was no point in massaging them down if the case then became implausible. Loss-making activities should go; the bank's support should be a minimum of £500,000 to make it clear that others than Government were involved. The proposal would have to show the terms on which KME would want the balance of the cash shortfall from Government. Industry Act criteria *did* have regard to social circumstances, he pointed out.

The convenors were suspicious. When officials wanted to increase the money, there was usually trouble. It could be a way of making the proposal so grand that rejection would become inevitable. The leaders tried their original ploy again. 'If the Government discharged the bank's responsibilities . . .' Spriggs couldn't complete his proposal, for there was a sharp reaction from Williams and the officials. 'This would kill you with IDAB.'

Binning tried again. 'My worry,' he said, 'is how the company is to operate, its finances, the shape and motivation of KME, how and who is to run it and the marketing and pricing policy.'

'Our fear,' responded Spriggs, ignoring these issues, 'is that you can't represent verbally to IDAB.'[*]

'Alan,' wheedled Silk, 'you must know what KME is likely to ask for and what the chances are.'

'That depends on how you are going to remedy the deficiencies at KME,' answered Williams. 'Can you emphasize improvements in productivity? Meriden's had notable increases.'

'They've also got managerial help,' reacted KME.

Binning reminded them that the Department had lists of people who could give limited help – mainly retired senior managers – though it would be much better if KME found managers who were committed to the cooperative

---

[*] This was understandable. The worker/trade union tradition is that influence is obtained by oral presentations face to face. The concept of paper analysis is unappealing since it gives no chance for personality to influence decisions. There was a collision of cultures at the meeting as well as an element of escapism on KME's part.

idea. (It was a great suggestion, but apart from Collinson where were these paragons of open-mindedness? Sadly, when managers appeared, as from GEC, KME didn't seem to care for them.) Nothing significant was decided. Nevertheless, it had been a friendly and constructive meeting. The question bothering the KME party as they left the building was 'Why?' The evening papers soon told them. In the wake of the Post Office cuts, Plessey had declared 4,000 workers redundant and 1,000 of them were on Merseyside. Unemployment benefits for the 1,000 could cost the Government £3 million a year. There was a major row in the Commons in which Heffer declared that Merseyside was becoming a disaster area. The Prime Minister announced that the NEB was to see what could be done to offset the effects. On top of the devolution revolt, the precarious basis of the Labour Government's Commons position was under growing threat as by-election losses drove Labour towards a pact with the Liberals. Once again, KME was riding a political flood tide.

The bank was asked to raise its overdraft facility to £600,000 to show its support for KME's prospects. The 1977 budget was withdrawn from the Industry Department by KME – it had been too optimistic and there was no point in giving the IDU the chance to tear it to shreds. Their analysis would be central to the assessment by IDAB.

KME was again advised to speedily improve the industrial situation in the factory, for otherwise the place would be finished, since without improvement, no politician could back further aid. Fifty new workers were recruited as the cooperative tried to increase its output. Yet the stewards' meeting on 8 March 1977 was the usual depressing experience for those who hoped that the cooperative could be galvanized into action by the glitter of funding and the fear of closure.

At the meeting, steward Archie Bredon was frank. 'There isn't an overall understanding of our problems and what the membership can do about them. It's been easy street because of the likes of yourself and Dick and others who've helped you.'

'We were going somewhere,' Spriggs replied. 'Now we're hurtling down a mountain road at a hundred miles an hour and we're going to reach a bend and fly off the road.'

'Overtime is a sign of prosperity,' interposed Joe Hill, 'and it's difficult to convince people that we're going downhill.'

'We're not being honest,' asserted Freda Staples. 'Some of the management work against us and we're accused of wearing two hats.'

Others agreed that attendance and work performance were the problems. 'You can't get them in for thirty-five hours, let alone forty.'

'That's right,' responded Spriggs, 'I lost some of my dignity begging people to work better.'

A new tack was tried at the end of this meeting. An adviser had prepared a short, pithy statement of KME's needs for stewards to take back to their sections. That way they couldn't distort and accidentally misrepresent the main issues. With the statement went a brief questionnaire which each steward and section were jointly to talk over and fill in so that it could be analysed and actioned at the next stewards' meeting. A brief, brutal résumé of KME's present performance and prospects was also given to the stewards to take away so that they would be accurately briefed. Not one questionnaire was ever completed and returned. No further discussion ever ensued with the directors or at the shop stewards' meetings. It sank – though not without trace. The reaction was unhelpful. As a result of the meeting some stewards were in 'a state of turmoil' according to Spriggs. 'It shows that you can't tell people the truth . . . Most people aren't knowledgeable – not even curious . . . They're looking for a villain and think we should be leading the fight against the directors, not be the directors. The stewards aren't interested in responsibility.' Lewis's view was that the stewards panicked at being finally faced with KME's grim state in writing and got so frightened that Jack had to calm them by saying that, in effect, what they'd been told wasn't true.

Some cooperators were trying to improve output, but for every sign of hope there was a signal of deterioration. A superintendent had told the spot welders that he wasn't satisfied with the output and quality of their work. He hadn't been too willing to listen to their explanations and the welders had promptly downed tools, saying, 'We're not even discussing it with you. Get the message? We've decided that we've done enough.'

A couple of days later tempers had cooled, although people were still putting pointed questions to the stewards as some workers tried to find out the truth of KME's prospects.

The leaders were adamant that there was to be no further attempt to involve people before the negotiations were concluded with Government. They could not take the risk of more disruption. This was the stated reason for never acting upon the deadline for the questionnaire. They were advised that it would be a good idea to present any further political support as being conditional upon certain changes in the way KME ran. The leaders were interested. 'We've got to face it some time, and this could be shown as a *fait accompli*. There couldn't be any argument then.'

Silk had met Varley, Employment Minister Albert Booth and Junior Industry Minister Bob Cryer, and it was clear that KME couldn't be allowed to go under at this time. One of the closing Plessey factories was right across the road from KME and the directors temporarily entertained the idea of offering Plessey space so that it could move its operations across into KME's factory. The plan came to nothing. GEC were also making several hundred people redundant at their nearby cooker factory. It all helped KME's case.

There was a long meeting with National Westminster

on 15 March. Spriggs was at his best, knowing that he had done all he could to influence the bank's auditing team to report favourably on KME's future.

'The loss in the half-year is about £300,000,'* said Spriggs, 'and after TES its only £9,000. Turnover in 1976 is 40 per cent up on 1975. We are forecasting a loss of about £400,000 in 1977/8 before any TES and about £250,000 profit the following year with £750,000 profit in 1978/9. Carey said we'd been underfunded, and since we are talking about capital expenditure too, we are probably going to Government for £2 million. We need your facility to go up to £600,000 to help Government put in their longer term support.'

Burgess, the Regional Director, was firm. If the bank stood by KME it would have to be for working capital and not as replacement for previous losses. 'The long-term money has got to come from another source to take out these hiccups.'

'Government has indicated that money is available,' responded Spriggs. 'An indication of support in principle from the bank would be helpful.'

'We're interested in commercial ventures,' said Burgess, 'but we can't be insensitive to social needs and we'll help Merseyside . . . Our problem is that our board hasn't a track record of KME profitability on which to judge – our support would probably be conditional on medium- and long-term support from Government.'

'It is a lot of money – £600,000 – but to us it's cosmetic,' said Spriggs. 'We agree that the main goal is Government help.'

Back at KME, Lewis, Bandell and the directors then finalized the 1977 budget. Lewis had previously said that £750,000 was needed for capital expenditure over the three years. He had agreed with Spriggs that some of the product targets could be met without it, but others could not. In the end, a four-page application letter accom-

---

* These were the best six months (May–October); for the nine months April–December 1976 the loss was £690,000.

panied the budget which was sent to Varley on 16 March.
It was a strange document. It did not ask for £2 million.
The application was for £860,000. This was half the figure
which KME had been advised to seek. Capital expenditure had been cut to £511,000 and the trading predictions
were highly optimistic. Once again KME had believed its
own naive, optimistic forecasts and had asked for an inadequate sum.

In its new 1977 budget KME planned to expand sales
by 34 per cent and turn over £9.8 million at a loss of
£280,000. (It was more realistic than the withdrawn
budget which had forecast a turnover of over £12 million.)
It wasn't an implausible target if only financial and production efficiencies could be raised. There was no reason
why £4.5 million worth of radiators couldn't be sold to
yield a profit. The 1978 forecast was now for a profit of
£454,000 on a turnover of £12.3 million, and for 1979 a
profit of £785,000 on a turnover of £13.7 million.

The alarming feature was that KME believed its own
optimistic assertions, which suggested that the quartet of
Lewis, Bandell, Spriggs and Jenkins weren't learning anything significant from their experiences. The cooperative
had already lost more than its forecast £280,000 for the
whole of 1977, and it was only late March now.

There was no obvious way that the current loss of
£115,000 per month would be slashed so quickly that the
rest of the year would break even. KME was leaving itself
short of cash. It had preferred to disregard the warnings
from Binning, Burgess and its advisers and had once again
asked for too little in the hope of raising its chance of
getting more Government money. Basically different assumptions seemed to be at the heart of the disagreement.
The advisers were trying to build a viable business. KME
was seeking relief from immediate crisis to keep jobs
going for a few months longer.

Then, on 1 April, KME made a decision of the kind
which was the despair of its friends. The leaders and
stewards awarded everyone an unconditional wage rise of

the incomes policy limit – £2.50 a week for the bulk of the workforce and 4.5 per cent for the more skilled workers. No effort was made to amend the target scores or working practices. Just as a year earlier the leaders had taken the view that anything extra would have to be paid for in addition, the incomes policy limit was a right. They had no plan to raise productivity and wages through any self-financing scheme which would reduce the trading losses.

Fortunately, the politics of KME's case were still promising. Nobody else on Merseyside was displaying any tenacity in the face of the mounting employment crisis. The EETPU stewards at Plessey were accepting the firm's voluntary redundancy terms and as Spriggs observed contemptuously 'the white flags are flying everywhere'.

The bank told Varley that it would increase KME's overdraft if Government would take its share of the load. National Westminster had handed the exploding parcel back to Government.

The unexpected gift

On 25 April 1977, Spriggs and Jenkins were sent for by the Industry Department. It was a short evening meeting with Williams. Government had agreed to give £860,000 as a grant – not the loan which had been requested. The Government evidently felt that one might as well be hung for a sheep as a lamb. The convenors were told that the grant was nothing to do with KME, but the unemployment figures had shot up that week and the pressure was on. An official advised the convenors to go quickly before anyone changed his mind.

The new grant was announced in the House by Varley in response to a carefully placed question by Silk. It was thought that this would minimize any row. IDAB had advised against the grant, said Varley, but 'in view of the present severe and increasing unemployment in Kirkby, the Government would give this limited commitment.

KME's representatives have assured me that they will not apply for any further Government assistance in the future.' It was the first time Varley had gone against an IDAB recommendation.*

Bob Cryer batted a series of Commons questions straight back at the Opposition and revealed that IDAB had considered 367 cases since its inception in 1972. In only seven cases had the Government concluded differently from the Board. The political row fizzled out.

Spriggs told the *Financial Times* that the money had been asked for 'more as a precaution than anything. We won't need any further help because we are already breaking even and will be making a profit† by the end of the year.' He didn't mention TES. The cooperative's political difficulty was only too clear. They couldn't again claim that they'd been shortchanged. They had been given everything they had asked for.

As soon as the £860,000 grant was announced to a mass meeting at KME, some cooperators started to walk out of the hall. They didn't intend to listen to any more, reported Spriggs. They'd got another nine months.

KME lost an average of £32,000 per week throughout April, May and June 1977, though, since the whole of the domestic heating industry was suffering from the slump in house building, KME's radiator sales were holding up well in the circumstances. Dimplex Industries and the state-supported radiator firm of Penrad were both to call in the receiver during May.

KME's leaders were anxious to capitalize on 'the new enthusiasm' which they had detected following the

* As later evidence to the PAC showed, the Department of Industry believed at the time that the new grant would not achieve its objective. The money was granted despite their belief that KME just wasn't viable.

† The *Financial Times* had received a scrappy letter alleging that KME's previous 'profit' had ignored the £80,000 per month of TES. The letters editor tried to check it out, but the address didn't exist. The letter was thrown away and the revelation about TES not used, until it could be substantiated.

announcement of the grant. There was a meeting at KME to discuss management changes and fresh ways of coaxing effort out of people. Some of the lads were keen on reorganization, said the leaders, and the press shop was flat out on two shifts, but yet there was no special effort from the welders even for the most worried appeal. The leaders were depressed about this and claimed that people got away with what they could. 'One of them told the superintendent that they'd have tea breaks all day if they could do it.' This wasn't a strictly accurate picture, as the convenors would assert in less stressful times. The welders had a difficult job. It was repetitious, sometimes heavy and fume-laden, and the welders felt that they were carrying the rest of the factory and were put out by the sight of the blow men (relief workers) on other jobs and the 'tea party' on the overmanned paint plant. They were proud of using heavy welding rods, which actually made up for the relative crudity of the radiator seams. Metal had to be poured into some radiator ends to fill the gaps. They were proud of a crude, rotten solution to an easily solved technical problem.

Spriggs had told the stewards that the grant had to be accepted by 31 May or it might be withdrawn and that Varley had said that satisfactory changes would have to be made at the cooperative if the money were to be paid. Spriggs was embroidering the situation. It was not a condition of the grant, but it was useful to shelter behind such a claim and use it to push forward with new plans.

Filling the gaps

The leaders wanted, they said, to look at organization structure. But they didn't. Even less did they want to discuss management style. They wanted to talk about promotions and appointments in the existing system. The problem was that KME needed an enhancement of its management skills, and internal promotions would achieve little in this direction. Matters could have been improved if the appointments could have released people to obtain training elsewhere. That never occurred. Nor would they bring in assistance. Lewis privately alleged that the convenors wouldn't let anyone in who might threaten their power. The convenors always claimed that Lewis didn't want someone who might show him up. They were both right. They all agreed that they only wanted permanent managers who were committed to KME, although they knew that the jobs were unattractive and so nobody of quality would come. However, it gave Lewis and the convenors a cast-iron excuse. 'A temporary manager has nothing to lose,' they claimed. The fact that such freedom might produce less self-interested decisions was conveniently overlooked. KME's leading figures wanted to repel any threats to their positions or their self-esteem.

A long discussion ensued about who should be promoted from inside KME. Various characters were assessed and the risks of their appointment considered. To their credit, the convenors proposed to promote one of their fiercest critics, Jack Eccles (no relation to the author).

Once agreed by the convenors, the proposals were put to the stewards as ideas at a lengthy stewards' meeting on 10 May. The people concerned had not been approached to see if they would accept. This was the lesser of two evils. If people had been asked already by the directors, the stewards would have reacted to that pre-emptive action. As it was, the stewards were being put on the spot. They had to agree or else put forward their own alternative ideas. Either way they would be seen to be taking responsibility by the shop-floor. Several of the proposed supervisory appointments were of stewards.

Spriggs went through the situation. 'We can't just take the grant; we've got to indicate what we've done to straighten ourselves up. We've tried a number of things and they've failed. Communications and management organization aren't good. We need to tell people what has to be done and we have to reorganize at the real pinnacle.

In over two years, there's been no meeting of management, supervisors and stewards to discuss what is needed for progress.'

Spriggs and Jenkins then tabled the new employment agreement. None of the other stewards had seen it and they were required to react on the spot.

'Section four,' said Freda Staples, 'refers to monitoring our own performance. You're leaving it to the shop stewards and local supervisors to sort things out. You're leaving out the most important people – the people on the floor.' (Before the meeting she had confided that 'we need stronger management. Jack thinks like a steward and acts like a manager. My husband Tommy suggested self-controlling work groups two years ago. It was laughed at.')

Jack fudged his response and seemed relieved to receive another intervention. The atmosphere became a trifle querulous. 'There isn't enough communication between the radiator producers and the sales force . . . There've been no meetings, no liaison, and the lack of a works manager has been a grave difficulty. Who's been doing the liaison?'

'The meetings were all stopped,' said Harry Miller, accusingly.

'Only the daily ones,' replied Spriggs, though he had just said that the lack of meetings had been a grave difficulty. 'We've got to force the general issue,' he continued, 'and yet it's been said that nothing will change because no one's prepared to take a grip on it.'

Joe Hill made an important point about the role of the shop steward. 'Why weren't we brought in more often? Look at the nonsense of the shrink-wrap.' (The radiator wrapping machine had been installed in the wrong place with a lot of disruption. Everyone could see it needed to be moved as soon as it was put in.)

'We're on our own,' said one steward. 'Yes,' responded Archie. 'This area's docile now. My union [EETPU] could throttle Plessey if it wanted to.'

One thing was readily agreed. Lunchtime clocking on and off could be removed provided people didn't abuse it. (The defunct cooperative advisory council had been in favour of this change. 'All it meant,' said Spriggs later, 'was that people spent more time off site at lunch hour.')

Norman Kelly brought up a new aspect which raised the question of how the various groupings at KME were accountable. 'When the recent APEX problem came up, the members said that if there were changes in conditions, they'd want a meeting before the shop stewards accepted it.' It was a critical point about the shop stewards' mandate. Here they were, under pressure to make progress, being given some new proposals on the spot without any chance to consult their members before the decision.

Spriggs reacted. 'If we have several unions doing different things we'll get nowhere. It could destroy this committee. It'll go against your policy over the last two years of having collective responsibility.'

Jack was concerned. He'd spent years under previous managements welding together the disconnected groups and unions into a united body. He saw dangers in sectional accountability. Some sections might go out of the convenors' control and set up their own ideas of what should occur.

Kelly persisted. 'It's not to overrule or be overruled by a mass meeting, but before there's a mass meeting we should let our members know exactly what they are considering.'

'We must go via a mass meeting,' said Jack.

Harry Miller objected. 'Surely that cuts across membership of the union and gives all decision-making to the mass meeting.'

Dick Jenkins intervened. 'It's been long agreed and operated that, unless a policy cuts across trade union procedure and policy, this joint committee will decide and recommend to a mass meeting.'

Kelly withdrew his objection, and the new employment

agreement was carried unanimously. Nearly all the twenty-four stewards present had spoken, most of them several times.

The leaders then tabled the list of fifteen vacant managerial and supervisory positions, together with the list of proposed apointees. Apart from a proposal to recruit a commercial manager, all the promotions were internal.

People skirted round the personality implications of the promotions. It was difficult to discuss the suitability of individuals when they were in the room. There was muted aggravation about people being promoted to control virtually nobody – which was later to develop into complaints that the convenors' friends, their critics and ex-council members had been bought or silenced by promotion. In the end, all the proposed promotions were passed without variation.

Late in May, Lewis talked over the management issue from his perspective. He had a problem keeping an organized team. 'I've told my managers that the directors will do as they want and if the managers don't like it, they can go elsewhere. The leaders spent £7,500 on racking without consulting me. I never considered Colin Lewis as works manager. [Colin Lewis (no relation to Bob) had been promoted to works manager from his job as toolroom foreman.] If the managers come up with paperwork people like it, but it gets eroded. There's a complete lack of systems discipline, though sales is the basic discipline. Our application for Ministry of Defence listing will force us into putting in proper systems. Dick and Jack haven't read my proposals in the three weeks they've had them.'

'We don't need a commercial manager. Sales is our biggest problem at the moment. We signed up Transglobe and I never even got a hydraulics engineer. It ended up with an estimating engineer. I've been pressing for a contract presswork agent, but Dick says its paying money for nothing.' Bob then went on to describe how bad were the commercial controls in foods and radiator marketing and how poor were the managers.

'Bob,' he was asked, 'how can you tell me all this and then say you don't need a commercial manager? Are you going to do it all yourself?'

Lacking an answer, the conversation switched to other topics. 'The best thing that Jack and Dick could have done,' said Lewis, 'would have been to go off and get some grooming in business. The stewards' committee has now, in effect, become the council. It's a smart political move by the directors.'

Another downturn

In mid-June there was a nasty article about KME in the *Sunday Times* which insinuated that Lord Peddie of the Agrément Board had unfairly licensed the KME-built Accadiair product because of his cooperative leanings. The paper apologized the following week. KME were not charmed at the campaign which they suspected was being waged against them, though they had been pleasantly surprised at the lack of reaction to the £860,000 grant.

The trouble, confided Spriggs, is that the press could uncover a lot. 'The stopping of work in the afternoon is getting worse. We're going to act while we've got money, not when we haven't. I've been too soft.' He was told that his political flair had meant that he'd absorbed pressure from groups in KME, but at the overall expense of the business. KME should change its style, because there were six conditions of corporate collapse.*

– one man rule
– non-participating board
– unbalanced top team
– lack of management depth
– weak finance function
– combined chairman and chief executive

* See John Argenti, *Corporate Collapse: the causes and symptoms* (McGraw Hill, 1976).

KME had all six.*

There was a mass meeting on 14 June because, although the new employment conditions had been based on excellent intentions, nothing at all had changed. Spriggs opened briskly. 'We've called this meeting because we've come to an impasse on the question of attitudes and the future of this establishment.' He reminded people that their cry in 1974 had been for the right to work, but where was that enthusiastic support now? 'We can fight with governments and industrialists, but we are not able to control ourselves. There are fanciful rumours about the sums of money people could get if the place closed, but it is nonsense. We could have nine directors, but it doesn't matter how many people make the decisions because you are the ones who will make the major policy for this company . . . I was naive to believe that in 1974/5 the workers alone would create the self-discipline, the productivity, to move forward without the need of supervisors being necessary to discipline people. Yet we find sunbathing and card schools, a little intimidation where people have done extra work. These are not mythical situations – they are fact. People tell me, "It's about time you did something about it Jack." Jack is only one man, you know.

'If we get it right we could keep rewards moving forward . . . We cannot go back all the time asking the Government to fund your losses . . . £3.9 million was a once-and-for-all grant. We have also heard that the directors would not go back after this last application. Providing we were progressing I would not be red-faced if we

* None of these strictures had any effect. The author's notes are spattered with lists of proposals put incessantly to KME. In the end they became a ritual. The author would spell out the inexorable needs as he saw them. Spriggs would agree, but either ignore the points or point out the difficulties of action or produce some contra-evidence, no matter how tangential. Jenkins tended to look amiably but pityingly at their deluded adviser.

went back to Varley . . . it's about time we got away from scores . . . we should each do a good day's work.'

Spriggs then hinted at a special deal for the welders in view of the 'horrible job' they have to do. He wanted people to work to the breaks. 'It is a heartfelt plea and a demand that unless you give us, I cannot represent you any further. You must go forward together. It is not a threat. I am sick at times of worrying about the next step. I want you to help me to help you. This platform is ready, providing you are ready. We are in a wonderful position to take advantage of our cash situation and I would hope that you would grasp it with both hands.'

It was difficult to see that Jack's speech did more than exhibit his worries, but then any proposals were yet to come. The author reminded the cooperators of their economic position:

'Last year we hoped that TES would help us to new ways of working that would raise efficiency, but the year was frittered away. Last autumn we could have had the market by the throat. People were begging for radiators and we were short-ordering them. People were begging for Accadiair. We couldn't supply them. We were actually sending tools back for presswork contracts because we couldn't get them through the place even though all the budgets said it was possible.

'We don't need stop-watches in here. We barely need a sun dial. It is very obvious what could be done if people had a mind to do it. We got £860,000. There was nobody else to give it to but us. Courtaulds were closed, Thorn were closed, Tate & Lyle weren't organized, Plessey was falling to pieces. The only people who looked as though they knew what they were doing were KME. And we walked in through the door at exactly the right moment. The timing was immaculate and we were dead lucky . . . at the moment we are drifting along losing about £30 per head per week, and we can't have money haemorrhaging out of the place at that rate for ever . . . It's like running out of coal in the house, and instead of earning more to buy more, we start burning the doors and the cupboards and the floorboards. We'll keep warm for a while but in the end we won't have much of a house. The chance of our getting money a fourth time is about as big as Southport's chance of winning the FA Cup . . . I don't want KME to come to an end and be buried and have a gravestone put up which says "Well, we could have made it if we had tried, but we couldn't quite be bothered."

'We could look back, proud of what we helped to create here, something new that would be remembered just as much as Liverpool is remembered for winning the European Cup. Either we work through the day doing the maximum we practically can and trying to solve problems rather than waiting for others to do it, or we will continue to drift on until a bitter and painful end. The remedy is very clearly in your hands.'

Spriggs took the microphone and asked people to outlaw sunbathing. 'People see groups on the back road and are writing to MPs saying there appears to be a holiday camp. Are there any observations from the floor?' There was silence.

The meeting then accepted the revised codes of conduct and employment, the principle of a check-off system for union subscriptions, and the new administrative appointments. Jack half promised that overtime would increase and benefits would be available provided progress was being made. The meeting ended. Bob Lewis hadn't been there. 'No,' said Jack, 'he doesn't come to these kind of things. Pity.' Lewis was never invited on to the platform. His role was in a strange half-world. In fact he did come to some mass meetings and stood on the floor amongst the cooperators, listening to Jack.

After the meeting, there was a revealing exchange over costs and prices. 'There would be a chance of selling more,' stated Spriggs, 'if we were more competitive. We could send our men into the market with better prices.*

* KME's radiators were still slightly underpriced, notably from that strange habit of letting people order at old prices after the announce-

Creda approached us to manufacture storage heaters for them. The contract's gone to Germany. Bob should have gone in lower.'

During this, Bob arrived and reacted to Jack's assertion. 'If we'd gone down to match the price we would have been twenty-five per cent below manufacturing cost!'

They were asked if they priced on actual or budget costs.

'Actual,' said Jack.

'Mainly on budget,' said Lewis.

'We're costed on past costs,' persisted Jack, 'and if we beat them . . .'

'No,' interrupted Lewis and Bandell. 'We're pricing on budgeted costs which we never get down to.'

After all this time there was no agreement on the cost bases. No wonder cost variances were never properly investigated. It was infuriatingly incompetent.

Bob arranged to meet the supervisors to try to improve operating efficiencies. It was suggested that the supervisors should be asked to consult with their stewards so that the foremen could come to the meeting with ideas which they would 'own' and to which they would be committed, rather than have them wait for Lewis to tell them what to do. The suggestion was ignored. The convenors insisted that the stewards should remain the sole controlling body since the advisory council had 'failed to take some load off the stewards'. In fact they well knew that the council *had* tried to fill the decision-making vacuum and had been smashed for its pains.

The working mood in the factory was mixed. There had been a ten-minute saving on the lunchtime break as people cut back their extra time. 'It's the first time we've seen a positive mood after a mass meeting.' Against that, the leading figures were sniping at each other privately.

---

ment of a price rise. On the other hand, KME believed that Carron was down to a three-day week and that the main makers were giving customers a further, hidden sales rebate.

'Bob wouldn't know the names of some foremen. He's in the office all the time.'

'That was a big piece of learning for Jack over budget costs,' said Lewis. 'They complain about me not holding meetings – but they told me not to have meetings with my managers.' It was hard to know where the truth lay. The only obvious fact was that KME was the worst administered factory the author had ever encountered.

Still, the convenors felt that matters were improving. The loss came down in some weeks; stewards were now asking for actual costs; the plight of the welders was being recognized by the rest of the factory – though nothing was done. KME remained a low trust factory – exactly the opposite of the predictions which self-management experts would have expected.

11. An independent survey: 1977

- **Scuppering the survey**
- **Main findings, observations and recommendations**

The author was now trying a different route to improve communication and performance at KME. Two MBA students were brought in from Manchester Business School during their summer vacation; Paul Chaplin to analyse people's attitudes/decision making and Roger Cowe to investigate the financial information needed for effective supervision within KME.

The directors agreed, with reservations. Spriggs was worried that the study of organizational power would be seen as an excuse by the directors to avoid action at the forthcoming AGM. He wouldn't agree to the use of questionnaires by the team or to small group meetings during working hours. However, the convenors accepted the condition that everyone surveyed would receive some feedback via a summary of the findings. It was the author's test of a management's sincerity. Acceptance indicated a genuine desire to face problems, even if they were embarrassing; rejection meant that the sponsors were trying to use an independent analyst to provide information for their own use.

Chaplin and Cowe were well received by the cooperators. Just about everybody was eager to talk. A handful were guarded. The pair felt that KME's top people were sceptical about the project's worth, and many cooperators doubted that there was a way out of KME's present mess or that the report would be used.

The research team's first impressions were depressingly predictable. There was, they found, a great deal of commitment coupled with concern and fairly widespread disillusionment. Jack was highly respected and had tre-

mendous personal authority; Dick was a much less liked
and more shadowy figure. Both convenors were felt to
interpret opposition to their actions as hostility to KME
and so were caught between being held solely responsible
for the cooperative whilst finding it difficult to relinquish
any power.

The leaders were running the place fairly autocratically,
though with semblances of democracy, which they justified by KME's commercial plight. It was difficult to see
how they would be willing to give away their power,
however, even if KME became profitable.

The central dilemmas, declared the team, were those
arising from the dual role of convenor directors. People
had no way of protesting at management decisions which
had been initiated or agreed by the directors; management felt threatened and uneasy at being responsible to
on-site directors who were ostensibly non-management
yet who actively managed the enterprise; it was never
clear whether Jack and Dick were acting as directors or
as convenors. Positive leadership rather than traditional
reaction was required from stewards and this was placing
much greater responsibility and strain on them.

There was no 'management team' the researchers
found, but managers worked as individuals under Lewis
'who likes to give the impression of being hard and go-
ahead, and may welcome the chance to hide behind Jack
and Dick at times, although bemoaning his lack of room
to manage as he sees fit'. However, the researchers did
accept that Lewis had plenty of ammunition to show how
the directors sat on him.

There was little information on performance going to
anyone but Lewis, Spriggs and Jenkins. Many people
resented this as 'a general policy of keeping people in the
dark'. The team described the monthly accounts as 'quite
comprehensive, but not easily comprehensible'.

The researchers could understand the frustrations of
those who had been on the council and the many cooperators who found that things had not changed much; that

Jack and Dick had too much power, but that the leaders' inexperience in business had contributed to KME's problems. Many of the company's organizational methods remained through inertia – hardly changed or challenged since 1973. The directors' style of leadership reflected their skills and experiences through their pre-KME union work. They were known in KME as 'The Big Two' and also as 'The Brothers', or, when things were going very badly, as 'The Brothers Grimm'.

The researchers' findings were reinforced by a party of German managers who visited the plant. According to KME, the visitors had been impressed; but this is what the Germans actually wrote after their visit:

The impressions during the factory tour were overwhelmingly negative . . . The factory struck us as neglected, underfinanced, with no 'go'. People seem (or appear?) to work slowly and in a disinterested way (although the company belongs to them). Technical possibilities (e.g. for rationalization) are obviously not used at all. The workers do not seem to identify with the company, although that is needed because of its character as a model. A higher stake in the company is needed to bring it into profitability. The model, which is in itself very praiseworthy, suffers somewhat from lack of interest and possibly from the ability of the management . . . We are convinced that this company will go on working at a loss. A pity, the idea is good. Without it the factory would already be closed. But even this firm must live in a competitive environment and make a profit.

In late August there was a mournful meeting between the author and the research team as they reviewed their findings.

'Where on earth can we find the impetus for change?'

'Hardly anyone is prepared to walk forward.'

'Some stewards are being appointed as militants to give workers their undivided loyalty. Otherwise they've no channel to complain – the people are trying to retrieve the stewards back into their fold.'

'Can we educate the stewards and managers through seminars?'

'Tony's tried that route and failed.'

'Jack's not prepared to take any risks – even the ones that are necessary.'

'The trouble is that Jack falsifies the question by saying that if he and Dick are in the way they're prepared to step aside. That isn't the issue and they know they'll never be voted out. It's an easy suggestion to make which simply stifles discussion of roles.'

'There's no strong character in that top management team. Their problem is of marketing and pricing.'

'The drinks manager claims that it's profitable. He never gets any profit figures, so how can he *know* it's profitable?'

'People are talking of an autumn money crisis.'

'Archie Bredon thinks Jack has given up.'

'There's still lots of trust in Jack from the shop-floor – perhaps too much.'

'The trouble is the workers can't formulate the questions let alone understand the answers.'

'Lots of people feel that the cooperative structure should be separate from the union structure.'

'But then who would they represent themselves to ?'

'We'd need a clear management channel. It could work if union issues went through a collective bargaining route.'

Chaplin and Cowe became disillusioned about the prospects for change. Jack, they reported, was the obstacle. He was resistant to just about everything – in the nicest possible way. He was dismissing their ideas: 'It'll make a good book.' Spriggs had said that he wished that stewards would discuss more, hold group meetings and have more autonomy, but yet was against committees or giving the stewards an advance agenda for the stewards meetings.*

The team felt that the leaders had the wrong picture. At mass meetings, claimed Spriggs, the shouters are no

---

* Nobody made regular reports of those meetings. The only time that minutes were ever taken was during a brief period in 1976. The man responsible was promoted, left the committee, and minutes ceased. The tradition was informal and oral rather than formal and written.

longer shouting. He deduced that they'd been won over. Paul thought they'd given up.

The transport manager was extremely unpopular and known to be a close confidant of Jack's. Every Friday they and their wives went to the Wooky Hollow night-club together. He was known throughout KME as 'the third director'. He told Paul that no more than three people wanted the council back. In fact, many wanted its reinstatement – including a number of stewards.

The research continued and people became franker with the two researchers as they built up a reputation for discretion. A widespread dislike of Dick Jenkins was beginning to surface. Critics felt that he threw his weight about. Yet without Jack nobody really threw any weight about. A meeting had been arranged between production and sales managers for 26 August. Jack was off-site. Dick's response was to postpone the meeting since Jack wasn't there, despite the fact that the marketing manager had interrupted his holiday and travelled 150 miles to be present. Virtually nothing happened without Jack involving himself or being required to involve himself. This gave him an excruciating load and it wasn't surprising that he was away having a minor operation.

On Jack's return, the author tackled Spriggs and Jenkins yet again. They denied the duality of their role though admitting that 'we will probably end up in the lunatic asylum'. They resisted the idea that people could want to take responsibility saying, 'It is no use debating issues if there is no choice.' It was pointed out to them that people didn't know the choices, and weren't doing what the leaders felt to be the 'only choice'. The people wouldn't be talked into action. They would have to talk themselves into it. Discussion was useful if it led to commitment.

'Should we scrap the new document on principles and make it tougher?' mused the leaders. Performance depends on commitment and implementation, not on the formality of documents, they were told by Chaplin and

Cowe, who insisted that people *didn't* know the facts; *didn't* know what to ask for; received little encouragement if they did; and hence were little better off after the effort. In contrast, the leaders believed that people went away dissatisfied because they heard things they didn't want to hear.

The team's work was thorough, despite their being barred from stewards' meetings and from the AGM. Paul held 161 meetings with a total of 177 people – 34 of whom were seen between two and five times. They included 31 past and present stewards, 17 supervisors and 14 in management grades.

Chaplin and Cowe produced analyses and specific recommendations together with the promised summary (see pp. 205–7).

The analyses and conclusions were well argued and were essentially the same as those of every other outside expert who had looked at KME – which was important. The convenors were unable to complain that contradictory advice justified inaction. Every analyst saw KME as being organized ineffectively for the tasks which it faced and there was little divergence in their remedies.

Scuppering the survey

The convenors met the team on 6 September to discuss the implications, the actions which should ensue and to finalize the summary before it was distributed to the many people who had contributed.

The meeting was appalling. A near verbatim summary of the key exchange would read as follows:

Team   We've interviewed a number of people.
Convenors It's just a few mouths.
Team   No. We've interviewed two hundred people.
Convenors But they all say the same.
Team   No. They say different things.
Convenors That shows how confused they are.

It was the nearest the author ever came to losing his temper and walking out and leaving the leaders to their own devices. The convenor directors just didn't want to know.

(Furthermore, they didn't want anyone else to know. The summary was never distributed to the cooperators. The leaders reneged on their promise. Even in 1978 the leaders didn't consider it wise to distribute the summary or even confirm that it was available. Right to the last, cooperators (some of whom had been in management positions) expressed regret that no summary had been sent to the cooperative. They were later surprised when the author told them that it had been delivered as promised. They were not startled at the leaders' behaviour in suppressing it, even though it had been watered down by Paul and Roger to make it more palatable and to minimize friction within the cooperative, as well as to deflect criticism from outside – in the event of a leak.)

Meanwhile, the meeting between the researchers and the leaders proceeded on its metaphysical way.

Convenors The people don't want to change themselves.

Team Maybe, but change must come from the leadership, who are in the responsible positions.

Convenors People won't do more unless they get paid. On our shrink-wrap we've got eighteen men standing there, yet the electrician says he needs an electrician's mate there in case he collapses switching it on! People won't come to meetings or say anything.

Team It's disappointing that people won't stay behind and learn but some companies do it in working hours because it's worth it.

Convenors People don't want to hear the bad news. We've tried to delegate responsibility.

Team But not authority. Or accountability.

Convenors Do they want us to be convenors or
            directors? If after our struggles it was taken
            over by someone else, we'd feel cheated.

Team   What you're saying is not that people won't
            behave better than in a capitalist enterprise,
            you're saying you can't even get the same
            collaboration. [Silence from convenors]
            You're creating a self-fulfilling prophecy.
            There's not a contradiction between
            demands for strong management and for a
            say in things. If you hold responsibility
            tightly, they've no choice, and when they
            want information, you regard any interest as
            self-seeking. So why should people feel
            responsible or show any signs of wanting to?

Convenors They're interested only in pay day and
            maximum overtime.

Team   There's lots who were interested and found
            that they couldn't get involved or were
            slapped down.

Convenors It's nice for them to say they did try to be
            involved. I don't think they tried very hard.

Team   Perhaps they did try but not in ways you
            recognized.

Convenors Only fifty out of four hundred turned out to
            elect the AUEW council man. What Paul's
            been told is lies.

Team   By two hundred people?

Convenors Yes.

The author had just written a chapter on KME* and in
October 1977 it was given to the convenors, marked to
draw their attention to the key features and to the specific
actions which were vitally necessary at the cooperative.
They took not a scrap of notice. At the end the author
had scribbled on their copy: 'The problem is that you two

---

* 'Control in the democratized enterprise' in *The Control of Work*, eds.
Purcell and Smith (Macmillan, 1979).

are KME's biggest asset, whilst simultaneously being its biggest liability.' Not surprisingly, the convenors found this provocative. The author was trying desperately to goad, cajole and kick them into reconstructing their own hopelessly inappropriate roles and so eliminate the vacuum which was crippling KME's competence. It had no effect.

Main findings, observations and recommendations of the Chaplin/Cowe survey

Findings
- a general lack of financial information throughout the factory
- little adequate budgetary control for most functions
- widespread concern about the dual roles of director convenor – most want their power shared and roles separated, despite admiration for their leadership
- widespread dissatisfaction with the level and quality of information
- many, including stewards, want a council of some sort
- there is a widespread lack of confidence in top management, especially with respect to commercial expertise
- shop stewards are becoming increasingly unpopular
- discipline is isolated as the main problem – shop-floor blames foremen, who blame lack of support from management; everyone complains of inconsistencies
- most people are still committed to the survival of the factory
- little change is seen in the way the factory is run, and many see a reversion to traditional management and union attitudes
- there is a lack of meetings of all sorts, and a general lack of open discussion

Observations
The specific proposals we have made are open to debate and negotiation, but they are based on the following fundamental observations. We believe these should be accepted by all, if any changes are to be of benefit. Running through all of these is the contrast between the superficial, or formal, and the 'real' situation. By 'real',

throughout this section, we mean that which is perceived by people to be the case.

- KME is not an ordinary company – despite the conventional legal position of the company, the fact that the workers are the shareholders leads them to expect a 'real' share in control, without which the share in ownership is meaningless
- the role of the unions is confused – for director convenors, stewards and officials
- There is a vast difference between procedures and the way people see things as happening
- there is much criticism, but little disrespect or disloyalty – dissent often indicates a greater commitment to KME and should be encouraged; in KME there is not the same need as in conventional companies for the platform always to have the full backing of the members
- motivation will only come from 'real' involvement – especially in the absence of conventional incentives, and the lack of faith in management
- communication must be two-way – people must understand, and have a 'real' chance to disagree
- a change of approach at the top could begin change – it does not have to await a massive change of attitude on behalf of many others; improvements in delegation, clarification of accountability, coordination and communication could help attitudes to alter

Recommendations (summarized)
- extension of the board – to include two external directors, two directly elected from the shop-floor and one steward from outside the two major unions, in addition to the chairman and secretary of the shop stewards' committee
- formalized procedures for the stewards' committee – more notice of meetings, a published summary of discussions, a clearer role for stewards
- training – for managers, foremen and stewards; also better induction for new workers
- a training and communications officer – to be responsible for the above training and for all communications within the factory, including a regular newsletter
- incentive payment scheme – no specific scheme is proposed,

and any scheme must be the result of extensive factory-wide debate and general agreement.

- discipline – closer adherence to present procedures, and the introduction of a final step involving a disciplinary committee
- shop-floor autonomy – to set targets and monitor performance, and to agree methods of working; foremen to act as leaders
- management – greater communication and coordination
- absenteeism – the personnel department to be increased to allow more home visits; factory-wide uniform treatment of absentees in relation to overtime
- the constitution – to be clarified, with full discussion throughout the factory; also to be made clear to new workers
- financial information to be more widely distributed, including weekly performance reports to foremen, stewards and the shop-floor
- wider involvement in budgeting

Paul Chaplin
Roger Cowe

October 1977

12. Depression and struggle: 1977

- Autumn manoeuvres
- Merger thoughts
- The conference season
- Pressure from everywhere
- The application that never was . . .
- The internal problems come round again
- Passing the parcel
- Another rebuff
- Enter the consultants
- A Christmas present

Parallel with the research study, life at KME went on. The losses were not abating and if there was a new mood of determination, it wasn't reflected in the results. KME lost £750,000 in each half of 1977.

Radiator production had been well up in the first six months – some 20 per cent above 1976 – but orders were down as builders merchants reduced their stocks in the face of economic stringency and high interest rates.

KME's overtime was cut to avoid having production outstrip sales, but production costs remained high and Constor and drinks continued their loss-making way. Spriggs was disgusted at the lack of progress with contract presswork. 'Bob's been telling us how well he's in with British Leyland, but when we went to Longbridge with him, we found his contacts were at a very low level.'

Absenteeism was approaching 15 per cent and the convenors told the Industry Department that KME might need to bring in a receiver and then the whole thing could be dumped back onto Government. Binning said privately that the cooperative was finished. Spriggs was again asked what he was doing to involve cooperators and the answer was – very little. 'I've been unable to change the way I work,' he concluded.

Autumn manoeuvres

A fresh reconstruction plan was sent to Government. It involved vacating the administration block and part of the factory, thus concentrating operations, with Government buying the whole freehold and developing the spare space and land for other industrialists. Vacating the whole site and moving the three good products to a new factory was also mentioned. KME was limbering up for its fourth assault on politicians' sensitivities.

Spriggs also wrote to Prime Minister Callaghan inviting him to put KME into the NEB or into the projected Cooperative Development Agency. The letter upset Silk who claimed that, in going over his head, KME would lose its political allies since Callaghan and Varley had both played blue murder with him, complaining that they'd been persuaded to support KME again in April – even if it had been for unemployment reasons – and four months later the begging bowls were back. It was decided to pacify Silk by inviting him to address the AGM – it wouldn't be easy to ignore seven hundred pairs of eyes. Wilson and Heffer should be invited too. Many of the cooperators were their constituents.

Alan Williams was being criticized by other ministers for not sorting out the KME problem once and for all. It wasn't his fault that KME had put forward a half-baked proposal in the spring, but he was culpable in having failed to ensure that the scheme was workable and would be carried out.

Spriggs wrote to Williams in August 1977 virtually proposing that the Government should insist on conditions being met by KME as the price of any further assistance. '. . . the main reason we have not got into profit is because we have not put into operation the right sort of criteria.

Your officials and ourselves all recognized the need for some tough but realistic plan that would be made to stick for KME . . . We all say it but nobody seemed to do it. We must all share some guilt for this, and we at KME recognize our failure to grasp the nettle . . . It needs a clear, precise role and no-nonsense conditions to make it work. The workforce have indicated their willingness for such a line to be taken and my colleagues and myself are ready . . . but it needs precise conditions clearly defined . . . it has been stated by the officials that there are limitations to the [Department's] involvement – but the closer cooperation lent to Leyland and Chrysler shows more involvement than just financial assistance.'

The letter, coupled to the verbal requests to Williams to intervene, could scarcely have been a clearer cry for help. The leaders could see exactly what had to be done, but their shop-steward commitments were preventing them from taking the responsibility and blame for shutting down the drinks operation and sacking their mates. If only the necessary actions could be imposed from outside, then Government would have sacked the people and the convenors could escape from their terrible bind. But would Williams have been able to take the responsibility on his shoulders? It appears not, for there was never any response from Williams to such pleas. Apart from Binnings' attempt in February 1977, neither the officials nor Williams showed any desire to assist KME out of its cruel state. Their tactic was to leave the cooperative hanging, twisting slowly in the wind until it expired.

However, the Department did at least seem worried about the convenors still being guarantors for the factory's rent. Jack and Dick were deeply worried, too, though to their eternal credit they never let it feature in arguments nor allowed themselves to be bought by promises to remove the burden. Rather the reverse; they were always watching for the accusation that their interest was personal rather than collective. The Department could look foolish and callous if the guarantee was invoked and would have to bear the load of any repercussions over the convenors' martyrdom.* 'Well,' said Jack, cheering up at the thought of officials having these problems, 'at least we're keeping them guessing.'

Jack was still fretful about the cooperative's lack of manoeuvring room. 'We'd have got the moon if we'd asked for more than £860,000 last February.' For the first time, he looked defeated. Following a stewards' meeting to discuss the state of KME, stewards reported back ineptly to the cooperators. Some had even said that KME had only a fortnight to live, and this had created despondency, but their confusion was understandable for they hadn't been told of the plan to concentrate operations at one end of the factory. 'It wouldn't be helpful,' stated Spriggs privately.

The leaders knew that KME's application – if one could say that a variety of tentative ideas was an 'application' – would go to IDAB where they could expect a rebuff. They scratched around for a new weapon. 'What about a gesture to Government and to our liquidity if we laid everyone off for two weeks?' asked Jack. 'The workers would accept a *fait accompli*. We can ram it down their throats like we did over worksharing in 1974'. But KME was boxed in, for a layoff would have broadcast its plight to its creditors.

Spriggs began to pull out of his depression as the search for political leverage created more activity. The external climate was improving. The *Liverpool Daily Post* was being critical of Government aid to the North-West. Scotland was receiving £46 per head in selective industrial assistance with an unemployment rate of 6.7 per cent. Merseyside, with higher unemployment, was getting £7. The ghost of devolution's resentments lived on. Pressure on ministers would soon be accentuated. The next un-

---

* In fact, officials were deeply anxious to help Spriggs and Jenkins over this matter, but daren't give them advice for fear of conniving at some conceivably dubious act.

employment figures were imminent and the Labour Party conference wasn't far off.

The Industry Department's Mrs Cohen seemed keen on KME's new reconstruction plan to hive off part of the factory to other tenants, though it was a puzzle to the leaders that the Department was trying to help. 'When an official is keen, I'm suspicious,' murmured Spriggs. Silk seemed 'far too happy' according to the leaders, but perhaps he'd been pledged to secrecy and knew more than he would say. There seemed to be tremendous activity at the London end.

Cynical hindsight might suggest that officials were using the opportunity of a KME plan so expensively grand that its rejection would kill the cooperative once and for all. After all, KME was already on its knees.

Merger thoughts

KME's creditors were becoming restless and the Department had to dissuade the Inland Revenue from embarrassing ministers by taking action over its overdue tax, whilst Government was processing a proposal for aid. Government wouldn't want KME to collapse at this moment for, near by, Otis Elevators was shaking and the GEC cooker factory was under threat of closure. Indeed this was one source of hope to KME. A plan was being floated to amalgamate the two operations. After all, KME had made cookers once. Such an amalgamation would help the local political climate for the leaders knew that some local labour MPs were jealous of the money and attention being spent on KME. If GEC's plant could be given assistance, it would help to bring them over to the cooperative's side. Furthermore, if the AUEW could back the proposed coalition, then the Government might feel that the trade union movement was behind KME. Up to now it had been conspicuously disinterested.

The prospect later broke down. GEC might have been

interested a few months earlier but now felt that it wouldn't be appropriate.

The convenors weren't surprised. The GEC workers were about to be told 'cooperate or perish' and were apparently in no mood to be more productive just to get from a three-day week up to a five-day week. If the redundancy money was reasonable then the Christmas period was a good time to give up. People seemed quite ready to accept unemployment – except at KME.

The conference season

The Public Accounts Committee produced some new strictures on Government behaviour over KME. '. . . temporary support for an enterprise which appears most unlikely to achieve viability on ordinary commercial terms only postpones difficult decisions', asserted the committee. If criticism created any effect, industry ministers ought to have been distancing themselves from KME as fast as they could; but they weren't. The Labour Party conference at Brighton was imminent.

Williams made it clear that KME shouldn't carry on trading on the presumption that Government was going to help. Nevertheless, ministers had apparently pencilled in 5 October so that an announcement could be made at the Brighton conference. KME was a symbol, a card to be played, a trick to be performed. Yet no announcement came. On that day the Cooperative Party chairman gave his fraternal greetings to the conference. He said that workers' cooperatives were the most exciting development in the cooperative movement in recent years; much of the credit must go to Tony Benn, and he wanted to explode the myth that workers' cooperatives were a failure. They had grown up out of the bankruptcy of capitalism. It was capitalism which had failed, not cooperation. He wanted to see more state money going into research, finance and expertise for such cooperatives, rather than to propping up ailing private enterprises.

During the unemployment debate at the conference, Birkenhead's delegate said that unemployment would be worse on Merseyside if it weren't for KME, which deserved all the support it could get. KME hoped that Varley and Williams had noted these sentiments.

During the conference, Spriggs had endeavoured to keep up the pressure by sending an appraisal to Williams which showed that if drinks and Constor had been cut out, the weekly loss in September would have been only £2,000, excluding any saving of overheads. (KME had no intention of following this logic by actually closing these operations – not unless Government gave funds and took the responsibility by making it a condition of aid.)

Nevertheless, the urgency in Whitehall had abated. There had been no emergency resolution for ministers to face at Brighton and postponing any announcement from the 5th might defer the embarrassment of a refusal of further aid. Once the conference was out of the way, perhaps KME could be allowed to sink without a political brawl.

Pressure from everywhere

The stress level at KME was rising again. The leaders had heard that Thorn was installing a new radiator production line at Gateshead and was telling the trade that it would take over KME's business when the cooperative folded. Tricentrol – KME's biggest customer – was becoming concerned at the prospects of KME's demise, for the gap in their supplies couldn't be filled domestically and so imports would inevitably grow. KME's radiator sales were now booming as merchants re-stocked for the winter trade. Yet KME was having to run down its steel stocks to conserve cash and would soon run out of radiator material. As if that wasn't enough, another British Oxygen strike was about to bring the radiator lines to a halt through lack of welding gas.

Everyone was putting pressure on everyone else.

Spriggs told Silk that if the trade went to Gateshead it would be one more example of another region taking over the North-West's business. Silk told Varley that Government would be seen as a bad manager if it just gave up after putting £5 million into KME. Callaghan was leaning on truculent Labour MPs by treating the new devolution proposals as an issue of confidence, and so he might not need to buy back support on Merseyside.

Varley had put a Cabinet paper to his colleagues based on the grand plan to buy and develop the whole Kirkby site. His paper was negative. It was considered by the post-conference Cabinet on Tuesday 11 October and was referred back to the EI Cabinet committee. EI had recommended rejection of the grand plan. Benn and Booth had resisted in Cabinet and so Callaghan had sent the problem back for EI to seek a less expensive solution. Cabinet had baulked at the idea of choosing on the basis of the £5–7 million cost of buying the factory and refinancing KME.

The application that never was . . .

The subsequent meeting with Williams must have been a corker. The convenors pulled one of their most elegant stunts. Williams began to tell them that with the high cost of the application, the Government could not see its way clear to . . . 'Just a minute,' said Spriggs. 'We didn't present these proposals. They were just ideas. Your Mrs Cohen has blown them up into full scale applications. On the basis of these figures we *concur* with the Government rejection.'

According to Spriggs, Cohen was furious and so was Binning. Officials' hours had been wasted; but KME had, in effect, scrubbed it all off the record. The cooperative had not really been refused its application; in a weird sense, it could claim that there had been none. The officials' tempers were not improved by Spriggs' insinuation that ministers had not been in receipt of all his letters and so had been misled.

Williams took it well considering the mess it created for him. 'Full marks for ingenuity.' It seemed that the Department hadn't considered reducing the existing operation by ditching the foods and Constor operations and carrying on without Government buying the factory or hiving off any factory space. The leaders promptly suggested this and returned to Kirkby to work out the next survival strategy.

KME had to put a new proposal in quickly to Government. The leaders felt that if the Inland Revenue found that no proposal was before Government, there would be no reason for it to hold off any longer and it might lose its inhibitions and demand that KME pay up. It could be a cunning way for officials to invite the Revenue to smash the cooperative. (There is no suggestion that there was any such plan. It just indicates the suspicion of the leaders. It also explains why, at various stages in KME's life, the cooperative felt it necessary to have an application before Government at all times. *Any* application would do; its sense scarcely mattered. Its very existence was its own justification.)

Four days later, Williams had the convenors' new outline plan for Government support to the tune of £1.02 million. One-third of it would be for capital investment to reduce costs and increase throughput. The drinks and Constor lines would be closed and 150 cooperators made redundant. They proposed that Government should safeguard the investment money through a condition that the Department could only release funds for capital works so that KME couldn't again divert investment money to cover trading losses. The balance of the grant would come from extending the bank overdraft to £1 million but with repayment guaranteed by Government. The plan was ingenious, though Government could find it tricky to fund redundancies.

The leaders were also asking for support on the basis

of KME's work as an experiment in industrial democracy. Following the furore over the Bullock Report, the convenors felt that the Government might be in need of solid evidence about participation.

The internal problems come round again

Having indicated to Government that the cooperative was planning to cut its activities, the question was how to proceed internally. 'We boobed over the £860,000. When we got it, Bob and John abused the position. The losses went up to £40,000 a week.' Reduced labour loading would only be implemented after a full discussion section by section and would have to be endorsed by a mass meeting. 'If we agreed a layoff number with the stewards, it would be halved by the shop-floor inside an hour,' gloomed Dick. In the old days, he continued, people didn't believe the management because they didn't know what was true. It wasn't the right moment to point out to the convenors that this was perilously close to the cooperators' current feelings about them.

The grim cash situation had been reported to the stewards who wanted Jack and Dick to tell the cooperators rather than report back themselves. The leaders were contemptuous of this feeble lack of guts, but it wasn't wholly the stewards' fault. There had been no prior discussion, no agenda, and no agreed statement and, since the leaders had always been the oracles, why should stewards stick their own necks out to be exposed to abuse from both convenors and workers? The damage which resulted from the stewards' incomprehension was terribly costly for KME. Vast orders were flowing in for radiators which couldn't be produced due to the British Oxygen strike. By the time the strike ended some cooperators had been laid off for three weeks on basic pay. The production manager asked the returning teams to each do five more radiators a day until the order backlog was down. Their reply, according to Spriggs, was 'What will we get for it?'

By this time Spriggs and Jenkins were well distanced from the shop-floor. Listening to them complain about people's ignorance, disinterest, selfishness, sabotage and laziness, they sounded like every cynical, thwarted production manager you could meet. 'They won't do it,' was their claim, as the two convenors defined the cooperators so as to exclude themselves. It was even possible that they were knowingly distancing themselves from the shop-floor in order to reduce the feeling of being rebuffed by their colleagues.

Passing the parcel

The leaders were trying to juggle all the factors inside and outside simultaneously. King had produced an American company which might want to buy Kirkby, and the Department seemed very interested, for if KME left their hands, their relief would be enormous. Yet KME had to find a way of preventing the Department from inducing the Americans to wait and then pick the bits up cheaply from the receiver. (The IDU had already suggested this.) The convenors didn't want to become trapped in a business plan which tied them up politically as the two grants had done, with Government again saying that they'd got all they asked for.

The bank had to be kept sweet for it had behaved impeccably, and whilst it was fair to play a rough game with politicians and officials, KME couldn't afford to alienate National Westminster. Their meeting with the bank went well, but whilst the bank wouldn't want to be seen to put the knife in, it was clear that it could only go so far. However, Spriggs was able to tell Williams that National Westminster 'could find nothing in the application that it could not support'. This wasn't surprising since the application left Government taking all the new risk. Spriggs also reported that the bank had stressed that it would not be the one to pull the rug from under KME, mindful as it was of the social implications of the loss of eight hundred jobs. The bank had again neatly handed all the prospective odium back to Government.

Government also had its hands full. Another 1,500 local jobs were at risk at Courtaulds, opposition to the new devolution Bills remained strong and unemployment was still high. In an effort to win back support from its rebellious English regions, Government ordered two regional NEBs to be set up. It was a strengthening of the offices already in Newcastle and Liverpool. They would have money and the powers to invest, though anything major would have to be referred to London. It wasn't impressive – particularly to those who felt that the two regions should have autonomous development agencies on the lines of the envied Scottish Development Agency. Government announced yet another job-boosting consultants' study in an effort to cope with Merseyside's 12 per cent unemployment rate. The new work by P.A. Management Consultants was seen as a last ditch attempt to solve an insoluble problem. Simultaneously, the Environment Ministry launched an inner-city partnership scheme to try to solve the urban decay of central Liverpool. All the razzamatazz couldn't disguise the severe limitations of these political sops.

Another rebuff

The convenors were called to a meeting with Williams on 7 November where he told them that both IDAB and ministers had concluded that the £1 million proposal offered no more scope for viability than the withdrawn plan. Government could not recommend any further injections of cash or guarantees to the bank. A lively debate ensued.

KME   Our lack of surprise doesn't mean we haven't got a case – we have. We didn't fight to let a Labour Government kick sand in our faces. We've been left exposed and the Department could have helped us with more than money.

Williams　We don't have the ability to give you
　　　　　managerial back-up.* Part of viability is
　　　　　getting the managers you need.'

[There was a debate about the difficulty of changing
affairs in a democratized enterprise.]

Williams　What conditions are needed and why can't
　　　　　they be put in spontaneously?

[Williams was playing the daft laddie trick. He wasn't
lacking in insight or intelligence. He just didn't want to
know.]

KME　　　The conditions should include stronger
　　　　　management with a mandate to operate and
　　　　　having wider control in the cooperative plus
　　　　　the ditching of some products and people. We
　　　　　know we've been in cloud-cuckoo-land and
　　　　　that we need to take the organization by the
　　　　　scruff of the neck.

The leaders then suggested that the NEB take over the
cooperative – the Secretary of State had the power to
order this.

Williams replied warily. 'I've no objection to telling the
NEB that we've turned it down on the basis of the proposals put to us. If the NEB is set up to take a more
imaginative line . . .'

It was put to Williams that the main barrier between
KME and the Industry Department was one of trust. It

---

* This was the Department's usual nonsense. KME wasn't asking for
management – just the imposition of certain conditions. Government
couldn't pretend ignorance either, for these were the conditions which
the Department felt were needed too. There was the perpetual contradiction that the Department claimed the management skills to
appraise projects, but disclaimed such skills when asked to advise or
help. Its worry was that advice could leave Government directly
responsible for what ensued if KME took it. But there were ways
round that and, indeed, it was to meet this and other circumstances
that the NEB had been created.

seemed that KME didn't trust the officials' impartiality, whilst the Department didn't trust KME's budgets or promises. Why didn't the Department commission an independent consultancy study so that a jointly reliable document could be available? Williams looked apprehensive. There could be legal objections. There was Section 332 to be watched. The Department had looked at KME's accounts, and it might not be proper to encourage KME to continue. Government might be liable for the consequences.

Williams recapped. 'I can't reverse a ministerial committee decision. We can't tell you how to run the business – we are not businessmen. I don't think the new plan is a viable operation as it's proposed. You've expressed a wish to have KME looked at by the NEB; we'll ask them, and you may initiate an independent study. We cannot do that, but we won't announce anything because that would force you into a 332 situation with your creditors. In the absence of a firm proposal, I cannot take it any further at this stage.'

Spriggs had one final go. The Department had a responsibility to the eight hundred jobs. 'I've got a lot of strength in Kirkby. Our people will do various things to secure their jobs. We need to keep it at a calm level.'

Williams reacted quietly to the threat. 'I'm not going to move it from a calm level.'

'Kirkby is in a very difficult, rotten state,' added Spriggs.

'That's why you got the £860,000,' replied Williams.

Enter the consultants

The choice of consultants was no problem. The deciding factor was simple. The leaders felt that the Department would do its best to discredit a positive consultants' report, so it had to be done by the firm of P.A., the management consultants who were doing the Merseyside study for the Industry Department. The officials could

222 Under New Management

hardly rubbish a report on KME from the same consultants they were employing. It was a grim game which was being played and KME was well able to anticipate problems and act adroitly.

P.A. accepted the commission to 'appraise the facilities, organization, products and product markets of KME and their potential for development into a fully self-sustaining business enterprise', knowing that their report would form the basis of a plan to be put to the NEB and Varley. Ward of the NEB was promptly on the phone to P.A. criticizing KME's management, mentioning Section 332 and making his resolute opposition clear.

The convenors were fascinated by a news item the following day. Williams had been in Liverpool that morning as part of the Government's propaganda push, driving a bulldozer on an advance factory site. 'That was crafty,' said Jenkins. 'He never said a word to us yesterday. Perhaps he thought eight hundred of our lads would lie down in front of his bulldozer.'

Spriggs was urged to brief Silk who had arranged to see Varley, but Jack was reluctant to spell out Williams' concerns to Silk because 'it will show that we haven't delivered our promises'. 'But it may convince him that you're serious this time,' Spriggs was told. 'Don't you realize how annoying it is when you continually claim that you'll be competent in the future when there's mounting evidence of failure? It shows that you won't learn. You've just got to level with Silk and do what you say you'll do.'

Silk inquired about the likelihood of KME having a sit-in or would it go quietly? Robert was being placed in the unenviable position of a go-between. 'The Government should really advise us to end it,' mused Spriggs, 'but they won't do the dirty deed. They'll just try to keep safely out of the way. The appointment of consultants was a tremendous card to play.' He was advised to prepare a specific plan of action to reduce the workforce and cut out the poor products. It would be no use if P.A. said that a good market existed, but there was no indication that KME could organize to meet it. The cooperative had to be able to retort, 'We have a plan.'

Ward visited KME on 18 November and was as wary as before. KME's record didn't warrant support, he indicated. Ignoring this opinion, KME wrote a formal application to become 'fully integrated' into the NEB. Ward wrote back that the NEB was 'obliged to observe certain criteria . . . difficult to make direct investment . . . not prejudicing your proposals . . . or wanting to build up false hopes . . . we'll need a detailed look . . . let me know when you want another meeting'. It was a well constructed reply, cool but not rejecting. KME was advised to confirm the application and ask whether its track record precluded NEB help, regardless of a favourable P.A. report. If the NEB said 'yes', it showed enmity regardless of prospects; with a favourable P.A. report, a 'no' could lock in the NEB.

Williams pointed out that KME's new 'application' hadn't contained any specific proposal, so that they couldn't take it as one. Spriggs wrote back by return, pointing out that it was an application in principle, because substantive detail could only emerge after the P.A. exercise, 'since you, as Minister, proposed we get in consultants'. The application, he insisted, should be duly recorded at the Department. Williams repeated that there was no application and expressed puzzlement at the suggestion that it was the Department's idea for KME to bring in consultants.

Both Williams and Spriggs were right. The idea of consultants had come from KME – for the Department to hire. The notion that KME should hire its own had come from Williams. It was just another aspect of the tortuous game which was being played.

P.A. would not be able to prepare a detailed operating plan for KME for some weeks, but hoped to have its analysis of the cooperative's 1978 budget available by Christmas Eve. The leaders soon asked P.A. to undertake a longer, detailed survey of the enterprise as well, in the hope that the prospect of further business would encourage the consultants to report favourably on KME's prospects. The convenors had guessed that P.A. would otherwise hedge its bet in its Christmas interim report, worried that the Department and the NEB would both try to pick holes in P.A.'s analysis. The consultants wouldn't want to risk looking naive or foolish. P.A. had to go on making a living in the North West.

The leaders also considered offering unconditional acceptance of the P.A. report so that nobody could say that the cooperative was in the way of progress. The trouble was that even if Government accepted P.A.'s interim report in principle, there would be more holes in their agreement than a sieve. By hiring P.A. to do the full study, Government couldn't ignore it so easily and KME could also claim that the NEB was being given the time it wanted to do its own analysis of KME.

In the meantime, the cooperative made another stab at obtaining more TES – reminding Booth of closures and redundancies at GEC, Otis, Plessey, Birds Eye, Hygena, Meccano and Courtaulds – but it was no use. There was no provision for KME to receive more. The bank offered to help if KME got into real trouble. Cash was getting tight and the leaders felt that Whitehall was just waiting for KME to blow up. Jenkins went into hospital after a mild heart attack. Everyone showed signs of stress. The directors had a knock at Accadiair which still owed KME an extraordinary £460,000 and they pressed it to produce some money from its bank, under the threat of halting production of its product. It was vital for KME to keep going over Christmas, otherwise it could disappear unnoticed amidst the festivities.

Spriggs was hoping that P.A. would come up with a positive report because it would raise the question as to what ministers and IDAB had been told by the officials. Both IDAB and the IDU could look silly if P.A. said that KME could be profitable. KME wrote to Varley with calculations which purported to show that supporting

KME had saved Government money over the three years when compared with the cost of unemployment and lost taxes and rates – even before any balance of payment considerations over imports.

A Christmas present

At Christmas, P. A. submitted their report. They expressed doubt about KME's ability to reach its optimistic targets in 1978 but said that, if Constor and drinks were closed and redundancy of the 20 per cent surplus workers was accepted without reservation, there was a chance of reaching breakeven, and that if some of the factory costs could be shed by concentrating operations, then KME 'should begin to show some profits consistently for the first time in the history of the company'. It was a lifeline for KME to grab.

13. Hanging in the balance: 1978

- The internal problems remain
- Yet more advice
- Pressure on the bank
- The big push
- A new resolve
- P.A.'s rescue plan
- P.A. tries again
- The application for £2.9 million
- End of the big push
- The political climate
- Officials undermine P.A.'s plan
- The plan sinks

The year 1978 dawned with a depressing list of redundancy threats on Merseyside. Otis, Plessey, Courtaulds, Triumph/Leyland, Tate & Lyle, Birds Eye – all had some major employment problem.

KME was teetering on the brink of trading collapse, but the political climate was favourable, for Varley was believed to be sympathetic and might need some political credit on the Left. The TUC was working out its proposals for the forthcoming April budget and the reduction of unemployment through employment subsidies was high on its list.

Despite P.A.'s lifeline, Spriggs spent a bad Christmas. He'd just about had enough and nearly told the bank that it wasn't worth going on, but this, he felt, would be defeatist. Part of Spriggs' unhappiness was the knowledge that implementing the P.A. recommendations could be painful. He realized that KME needed to demonstrate to Government that it knew what it was doing and had the skills to do it. Bluntly, KME had never shown either quality in its business affairs.

The tactic with Government would be to show that an independent report had demonstrated that KME could quickly reach breakeven and insinuate that Government was holding back the cooperative.

The interim P.A. report was sent to Williams on 9 January and KME emphasized its conclusion that a future could be assured, provided that the cooperative was put on a proper footing, which, stated the directors, all at Kirkby were prepared to do. Short-term aid of £250,000 was requested for the seven weeks which P.A. needed for a more detailed analysis of KME's prospects.

KME wanted P.A. to proceed, partly because the consultants were a protection for the cooperative; it would have to be a totally insensitive Government which let the place shut down just as the cooperative was taking the professional advice which critics had so often urged.

The leaders visited Williams on 16 January to discuss the P.A. report. The discussion was amiable but inconclusive. The problem with short-term aid was publicity. There seemed to be no way that public money could be given without a Government statement. Its statement would inevitably include a reference to Section 332, in view of KME's questionable solvency. The press and the creditors could pile in and the whole enterprise could collapse.

Williams wondered whether the bank would extend the overdraft whilst P.A. carried on its investigation. KME was wary. There would be no point in contorting both KME and the bank if the prospect of Government aid was non-existent. Aid would depend on the P.A. report and viability, responded Williams. 'All projects have to be considered on their merits, notwithstanding that you have had projects turned down before.' (KME knew this and was already exploiting Government's inability to decline to inspect even the daftest proposal.)

A full appraisal via IDAB and ministers would take three weeks, continued Williams, so the earliest decision date would be Easter. Since Government had no detailed proposals from KME, the bank was the best source of immediate funds. It was agreed that KME would receive a minute of the meeting which it could show to the bank.

The Department had been more helpful than it needed – after all, their open-door policy had covered them against accusations of unhelpfulness. Behind their friendliness lay the knowledge that Plessey was again ditching people on Merseyside. You couldn't afford two company failures in one town in a week.

The internal problems remain

The directors returned to Liverpool and were urged to ask the workers not just for a 10 per cent increase on radiators, but for 20 per cent, which would take the weekly target to 14,400. The main need was a Stakhanovite burst of radiator output to convince P.A., NEB and the Government that KME could do it.

Back at KME, Spriggs asked for only 10 per cent more output. He appeared to have no other plan. However, the stewards were told that any further state aid would be conditional on extra performance. Although absenteeism was getting better, the leaders didn't feel that working bell to bell would improve output. 'They'd just spin it out.'

The leaders were urged to connive with Lewis and Bandell and get them to hit KME with a Schedule 11 wage claim so that salaries would have to rise and managers could be hired at sensible rates without causing ructions in either workforce or management. The workforce would probably back a strong manager. The convenors agreed. 'They'd kick us in the teeth if it saved their jobs,' said Jenkins.

Spriggs was depressed and feeling helpless. 'The stewards say it's up to the top but they won't do anything – they wouldn't even move a resolution . . . There's no way people on Merseyside will do anything. Some people will only wake up from their deep sleep when they get their cards in their hands . . . it's all very well talking about self-government, but when you ask them to take some responsibility they say "You're not on" . . . people are leaving before lunch on a Saturday and Sunday . . . we need a bloke to run this place who looks the part.'

'But what about you, Jack, they know you're not bluffing?'

'I don't know how Dick and I could change, given our history. What elixir could I take to become a Mr Hyde and not a Dr Jekyll?'

Had Jack thought of leaving himself? 'I did walk out during the BOC strike. We had two hundred bottles of gas available from Holland. They rejected it. I stayed away for a few days I was so annoyed. They were confused. They didn't know what to do.'

Couldn't he level with the stewards? 'I'd sooner level with the fellow in the toilet. I don't trust the stewards much. We aren't helping ourselves. If I tell them the bank's refused, there'll be a reaction and they'll worry about this week's wages. The radiator men are asking what we're going to pay for productivity and they think I'm just putting the pressure on to get more output.'

Meanwhile there were other distractions. Three of the warehouse men had put a cat through the shrink-wrap. It was dead when it came out, but opinions differed as to whether it was alive when put in. It was a grisly incident. The men were suspended for three days and the local press and the RSPCA arrived. Spriggs was scornful and used the incident to point a comparison. KME had a dead cat and the press came in. Yet people were being killed in industry and there was no story.

Yet more advice

The convenors went yet again to Manchester Business School. The deduction and proposals were just as before – just as sane, just as necessary, just as practical. They took away yet another set of management control documents, another suggestion for technical contacts to improve their welding technology. No action ensued.

The author tried to force the issue and wrote to Spriggs and Jenkins. 'KME's vital tasks scream out loud and clear. There has to be a sign of effective action at the cooperative. No one can help while the problems remain in 1978 just as they were in 1977, 1976 and 1975. Twelve were listed.

1 Shortage of money
2 Negligible capital investment
3 Old-fashioned equipment
4 Little product development
5 Insufficient management
6 Poor management control systems
7 Little communication of operating information
8 Inefficient organization structure
9 Disorganized shop stewards' committee
10 Indifferent labour practices and productivity
11 Unwillingness to change
12 Unwillingness to tackle problems

'So long as the last remains – so will all the others.' The letter had no effect.

Pressure on the bank

Sadly, the external pressures were taking all KME's attention, even had it been willing to face the internal implications. The bank refused to extend the overdraft – put off, it seemed, by the part of the Industry Department's minute which had mentioned Section 332. It was going to be difficult to induce National Westminster to change its mind, and P.A. might also be reluctant to proceed. The consultants could look silly if they failed to spot KME's bankruptcy. They might not even be paid themselves.

It was vital to shift National Westminster. The cooperative's lawyers were clear that KME was solvent. Fortunately, the bank was malleable because it appeared to believe that the Section 332 reference had been deliberately inserted into the Department's minutes, though Spriggs explained that this wasn't so – KME was not being singled out. Government always did the same, and one could see why from the case of Upper Clyde Shipbuilders.*

National Westminster relented. The convenors told a meeting at the bank's Lothbury office that they wouldn't shirk their duty to shut the Kirkby factory down. 'The Government officials may be manoeuvring us into a position where you, the bank, will appear to be the problem, not them,' said the leaders, pressing on the bankers' sensitive spot.

The bank was uneasy. 'The way you and your colleagues took this on commands great respect, but we cannot start on the slippery slope of forgetting our depositors.' The convenors were able to satisfy the bank that they had a coherent plan for consolidating at one end of the factory and ditching the poor products and the relevant workers. If the bank wouldn't help, the leaders wouldn't go back on their agreement – they would put KME into receivership. Fortunately, their resolve wasn't tested. 'We'll give the £250,000 by raising the overdraft limit to £850,000,' said the bank. 'Nothing's changed, but we've been impressed by the way you've put the case.' After three months, they said, either Government had to help or the leaders had to liquidate the company rather than appoint a receiver. The convenors agreed. A lot could happen in three months.

The onus would now rest on Government as well as on P.A. The Cabinet wouldn't be too happy if the private sector would help KME but Varley wouldn't. The industry ministers needed a solution which took KME out of the way properly, perhaps via the NEB. The money was there, and the sympathy – if only there was a glimmer of hope. Ministers, it was said from Westminster, recognized

---

* The *Sunday Times* that week had carried a story about the UCS creditors' attempt to force Government to pay up on the grounds that they had only supplied goods in the belief that UCS was Government guaranteed. The attempt had failed and the creditors were left without redress.

that the previous solutions weren't properly designed to make KME self-sustaining.

The big push

Internally the problems remained as tricky as ever. P.A. had already expressed doubt that KME could produce fourteen thousand radiators per week. They had to be convinced by performance. P.A. wasn't going to believe promises alone. 'Our luck has been political,' said Spriggs. 'We've never been really successful commercially.' They'd never really tried hard enough to make their own luck, and that, agreed Spriggs, was the only way to succeed – just like his beloved Liverpool Football Club. He was urged to reverse the power play in the factory. 'The radiator men are saying that if you, the leaders, do this, we'll do that. You're in a powerful position to say to them – *you* do this or there's nothing further.'

Spriggs was distressed throughout this period with only the scent of occasional verbal battle to rouse him from near despair. He had precious few allies outside KME and effectively none inside. This wasn't totally fair to Jenkins (whose wife was seriously ill, thus distracting him from KME and adding to the onerous load of responsibility) or Bandell, but everything rested on his shoulders. It needn't have been so, but it was. No wonder he was waking up in the early hours, worrying.

A new resolve

It was agreed to hold a mass meeting so that Silk could spell out the grim choice and back up the convenors. 'It's no use going on as we are,' said Spriggs. 'We've been pussyfooting about and going nowhere fast – using taxpayers' and bank money and carrying on in the same old way. We've got to tell them the whole truth, including the drinks and Constor closure, take the risk with the press, and if we can't get our action plan we might as well stop now. The stewards have been saying the membership won't do things, but the stewards are a blockage in themselves. I feel like a tongue being pressed.' He resolved to thank Silk publicly. 'He's spent a disproportionate time on KME and any praise would be well deserved – and it's election year.'

It all sounded like good stuff. The question was – what *was* the action plan? The central theme would have to be – *performance now* or there's no tomorrow. But Spriggs still wanted to tell them to 'work the programmes' so that the drinks people couldn't gallop on making yet more unprofitable products. 'No,' he was advised. 'Shut the drinks – performance *is* the word. We want maximum performance out of that factory – even if people have to clamp radiators together with their teeth. Don't talk programmes – everyone equates that with scores. We need far more than those numbers.'

Spirits were lifting. Silk, Lewis, the author – everyone was pleased that Spriggs was grasping the nettle. He was committed. 'We can't live in fairyland any more.' It was even possible to find the odd laugh – as when IPD's company secretary said that if only they made King their managing director, the problems would be solved. 'He's another at-a-stroke merchant,' chortled Spriggs.

Before the mass meeting, the stewards met. Spriggs put forward the stark choice. It wasn't just output which was required – the radiator quality was bad too; in fact, 'the defect rates are fantastic'. People would have to go. 'General Custer would have been proud of the number of last stands we've had. He only had one. The bank can't pull the rug from under us politically. Only Government or ourselves can do that. The stigma will be with you. The chance will go and it will give the capitalists a magnificent platform. We won't be put in a gas chamber and martyred – we'll just be given a P45.'*

The stewards argued and squirmed. Why didn't man-

* Employment form to pass to the next employer – if there was one.

agement take responsibility and why weren't they changed
if they were failing? 'Management stopped the council
and took the responsibility, so they can't blame the
workers now.' Others took a different line. 'We're not in
the popularity stakes as stewards – we've got to look at
our members' long-term interests.'

The mass meeting was crisp. Spriggs spelt it out as did
Silk, whose speech was reported in the press as a 'stern
warning to expect no more Government help and to stand
or fall on their own profitability'. The leaders told the
meeting: 'We aren't going to carry on deceiving the Government and the bank that KME is on the verge of success
when we know it is not going to be true. We can't go on
using our magic calculators. Nobody now believes KME.'
Spriggs continued, 'Constor and drinks will shut down
immediately. You must back the platform or we'll all sack
ourselves. The workers can't give management the responsibility and then go on vetoing what's needed by not
doing it. The power is in your hands.'

One steward (who should have known better having
been at the earlier stewards' meeting) protested that the
problem wasn't output. 'You can't blame the men. It's
due to having insufficient workers.' The platform didn't
have to reply – a worker dealt with the fatuous point. 'If
you put the scores up twenty per cent we could still be in
the house Thursday afternoon [i.e. having already finished the whole week's work] or we'd be asking for overtime; that's how much scope there is for improvement.'
He was applauded.

Another production worker was also clapped. 'I can
end at one p.m. and sit there till four p.m. having done
my stint, but we're being asked to produce extra to carry
more superintendents and indirects.' (There was a lot of
feeling about the burden of non-productive workers, even
though the ratio was low. Nevertheless, it was rare to see
any briskness in the general office. The tempo was usually
languid.)

Archie Bredon tried an ingenious way of forcing the

cooperators to commit themselves. He proposed that the company be put into liquidation because 'that's the bottom and if we're not prepared to move off it, we might as well pack up now'. It was rejected with only two votes in favour. Spriggs made it clear that the platform was virtually begging for a six-week period of maximum output. KME needed a big push.

The effect was slightly spoiled afterwards when Spriggs re-affirmed the commitment to close the two product lines but was vague when asked about the surplus workers. Spriggs told the press that nobody would be sacked or made compulsorily redundant.

He wasn't going to announce redundancies publicly. It wasn't clear to anyone what the workers would think when they read the press reports.

Nevertheless, there was a head of steam for action. The next stewards' meeting started buoyantly – 'good to know the truth', 'should have done it two years ago', 'let's start with the plan we're going to draw up today'. Then it began to fall apart again.

'Why don't we let the management manage? We're paying them to manage with you at the head.'

'Dick and I don't see ourselves as managing the situation,' responded Spriggs.

'What happens if the management propose and we don't let them?'

'They manage how we allow them to manage,' contradicted Dick.

Archie wanted progress. 'We've got to talk about restrictive practices and about overmanning.'

There was the usual inconclusive argument between those who claimed that the stewards had to give a lead and back it, and those who wanted someone else to do it – management, Government, convenors – they didn't mind as long as it wasn't them.

'Where's the lead?' Archie asked. 'I thought the lead was going to come out of here, but it appears I've got it wrong.'

As one steward put it, 'If we're not going to get rid of the surplus people then overmanning doesn't matter. The problem of leaky radiators is that people are in a hurry each day to get to the card schools. 'We've got to face the fact we've only got a four- to five-hour shift.'

The meeting had gone on all morning. After lunch they were joined by Lewis and Bandell ('this is the first time we've both met the stewards'). Lewis then went through a long calculation about the numbers of radiators, output rates, manning levels. It was full of puzzling numbers. Archie broke in. 'We've talked enough about what we need. We need to move and we haven't made a single commitment to action.'

'You have to go back to your members,' reacted Jeff Hurst. 'We have to provide leadership,' he was told bluntly.

A blackboard was wheeled forward and proposals listed on it:

– 40-hour week   rejected
– increased productivity   agreed
– women to weld radiator bosses (not nights) agreed
– reduce blow men (covering for breaks)   agreed
– cut out tea breaks (not welders)   agreed
– forget scores   agreed
– let managers manage   ?
– directors to stand back   ?
– tighten discipline   rejected
– reduce absenteeism   rejected
– provide more information   agreed
– create disciplinary committee   agreed
– departments to govern themselves   agreed
– expand the board/have workers' executive   ?

Observers could see that there were three interesting points about the list:

1 There was no backing for harsher discipline or an extended week, nor mention of redundancy.
2 The list was of desired policies. There was no list of actions to make them work.

3 The three unresolved items all related to the key problem of
   leadership, power and control.

   The meeting went on all day.
   'What are we going to say if the welders say *they'll* do
it, but what are *we* going to do [in return]?'
   'One welder told me they could do it if they were paid
and could then go home. That shows they *can* do it.'
   'We know that. That's not in dispute.'
   'The two convenors should come round the floor every
day. One hour a day would be a real investment.'
   Outside the meeting Jack was far from complimentary
about his senior managers. 'Bob's not really interested –
he thinks going round the factory is a distraction from
work. He'll sit in an office drawing up complicated charts.
Then you ask him for information and he takes three days
to get it. After the £860,000 we got no accounts. We were
losing £40,000 a week and Bob and John kept it from us.
He didn't know the facts. Bandell told me about the high
overtime yet Lewis had been signing the sheets. We were
making Constor on overtime and doing nothing in the
week. Much of Lewis's work is clerical. He shouldn't be
doing it. Bob also wants a twelve-week effort, not six.
The people will see that as another management con.'
   Meetings were held with the radiator department day
and night crews. Some people wanted to know what other
sections would do. Others were wary of committing themselves to promises they might not be able to keep. Everyone bitched about supervision, inefficiency and others
having an easy time.
   Welders said that they had a rotten job. 'But you won't
come off welding will you?' 'No' was the reply. Then they
recovered to say, 'You won't let us come off welding,'
but their 'no' had been true. There were requests for
more money. Their steward got annoyed. 'But there's no
poke [money] there. Can't you get that into yourselves?'
   The exact effect of the meeting was unclear but the
next week's radiator output was 13,500. There was an

enthusiastic mood in the factory. Production meetings were at last being held. P.A. was suggesting the recruitment of a commercial manager through their recruitment consultancy. The Ministry of Defence gave KME a registration as a defence contracter. Knowsley Council offered £75,000 a year rate reduction if KME would vacate half the factory and the administration block.

The local Birds Eye factory announced 450 redundancies and the threat of complete closure with the loss of 1,500 jobs unless behaviour and output improved. The workers struck, but soon returned, agreeing the redundancies and accepting all management proposals. The Triumph car factory at Speke was under threat, racked by a sixteen-week stoppage, and Leyland soon announced its end, with the loss of 3,000 jobs.

Two hundred were to go at F.D. Garments, Ocean Steam was losing 300; Courtaulds announced closures at Aintree and Wrexham; and Booth Concrete was closing, making 100 people jobless. Cammell-Laird gave notice to 160 outfitters and 400 jobs were in the balance at Tate & Lyle. In mid-March, Lucas announced the closure of their Victor works in Liverpool, where 1,200 people were employed. In less than three months, 8,000 jobs were on the slide, at a time when Merseyside unemployment was at 11.5 per cent.

Varley went north to launch a publicity campaign to emphasize that the industrial strategy was finally on the road to success. Pitting publicity against the closures was a sick joke to many North–Westerners. It was scarcely surprising that officials found 'a widespread lack of knowledge among industry of the aims and progress of the national industrial strategy'.

It was reported that P.A. had drawn a total blank in its search for a new formula for Merseyside. The well-trodden ground was yielding nothing new. KME tottered on, the only place where shop stewards were even putting up a fight. As Spriggs observed, 'Every cloud has a silver lining, and we're the silver.'

P.A.'s rescue plan

P.A.'s draft full report was very encouraging. The seventy-five-page document concluded that, provided that KME's workers would accept 'their normal responsibilities', the company could earn a trading profit in the coming year based on conservative, nay pessimistic, assumptions. Radiator sales could exceed 13,000 units per week, even with KME raising prices. Radiator production would exceed 12,000 per week (it had been averaging 12,900 during the big push). Accadiair would go up in volume and price. Contract sales would expand. Activities would be concentrated at one end of the factory after the sale of the Constor and drinks businesses, and the workforce would come down to 645. A profit of £50,000 should be reached in 1978/9 and results would then improve further. It would need £2.9 million of new funds of which £1.5 million would finance capital expenditure to increase efficiency and capacity. P.A. concluded that there was an improved climate and tempo at KME. Confidence, drive and enthusiasm had all increased. The six-week big push had paid off.

The weak point in P.A.'s draft was the proposal for management. What KME needed, it claimed, was a top class chief executive. P.A. had not fully grasped the problems of control and accountability in a cooperative, nor the unique, sapping effect of the convenor directors' interventions in day-to-day management. The consultants wanted this new wonder-man to be joined on the board by Lewis and Bandell, plus an outside non-executive chairman. The two worker directors were to stay to help develop company policy 'whilst continuing with their normal jobs with the cooperative'. They should keep out of day-to-day management and Spriggs should head up Industrial Relations and Jenkins run Personnel. It wasn't clear on whose behalf the chief executive would be working and with what mandate. The blunt fact was that it wouldn't work. Spriggs and Jenkins could not give up power, and cooperators would urge them to intervene day to day. P.A.'s proposal could have been agreed sincerely but it would have broken down quickly. The chief executive – if one could be found to take such a post – would have either blown up or buckled under. There needed to be a constitutional mechanism for ensuring effectiveness. The structure had to be right.[*]

Spriggs woke up worrying in the middle of the night. He recalled the many discussions about separating policy-making from policy-execution and the need for a two-tier board. The next day he told P.A. that some cooperative features must remain and that too much of a swing back to traditional management must be avoided.

There needed to be room for management to manage, but the stewards had to be involved so that they couldn't just go off and oppose. Shop-floor representation should be sustained through a modified form of advisory council – though that would be the last thing it would be titled. Spriggs wanted to get the shop-floor involved, but without risking the loss of his control. Nor did he want to disappear out of the picture – and what would happen if he and Jenkins were outvoted on the expanded board? What would the new management do if its instructions were disobeyed? Spriggs' and Jenkins' power would have to remain as a backstop, or they would never accept the changes.

---

[*] This criticism is not intended to belittle P.A.'s analysis. They had done a thorough job under some difficulty. Their report did illustrate, however, just how difficult it was for managerially-oriented analysts to get to grips with the political structure of the cooperative and the pressure upon the convenors to take charge of everything. P.A. was not alone in proposing a plan which had industrial sense but naiveté about a cooperative led by such a powerful duo. The rational-logical management model which P.A. was suggesting would have been adequate where the various pressure groups accepted and abided by a common perception of management. At KME, this common view did not exist, as the stewards' meetings kept demonstrating.

P.A. tries again

P.A. came back with a new plan, which was also rejected. It showed a policy executive board (PEB)* of Spriggs and Jenkins – with Jack Jones as chairman – making policy for the management group to execute. Unless Jones would become involved – and no one had even asked him yet – it looked like the same old discredited structure with the convenors as *de facto* managing directors, controlling a powerless management team led by the unknown newcomer.

Another suggestion was made. The Policy Executive Board should be expanded by adding shop stewards and employee representatives and Spriggs and Jenkins would remain the sole directors of KME Limited as a backstop against the PEB causing problems. This avoided having to pay anyone else directors' fees, though it admittedly gave the convenors the chance to get up to their old trick of controlling the place whilst denying control. The solution might have been elegant but it wasn't ideal.

There was another feature which was added after discussions. All policy executive board meetings would be joint meetings with the shop stewards' committee. The majority of stewards would not have votes, not being on the PEB, but they would be there, involved in the discussion with the stewards. The stewards *couldn't* then claim that they weren't informed or involved, yet, apart from the two to four stewards on the PEB, they *could* say that they weren't actually the responsible policy makers. This complicated idea steered a path between being the least which had to be done to improve KME's control structure, but not being so much that the convenors would baulk at their loss of control, though Spriggs was concerned that the two groups might war together with the 'stewards being concerned with ideology and the PEB

---

* It would be 'non-executive' in management terms. The word 'executive' was being used as in a trade union, where the executive generates policy for members to agree and officials to carry out.

representatives becoming crusaders of business efficiency'. It is hard to know whether this scheme would have worked, but it was certainly ingenious.

The second appealing feature of the new scheme was its value as an experiment in industrial democracy. It could be put to Government as of inestimable value as the Labour administration floundered round trying to work out how to proceed from the discredited Bullock proposals. If KME could play this new card whilst putting the cooperative's management system on its feet, Jack's early morning insomnia could be the best night's sleep he'd never had.

The application for £2.9 million

On 28 March the revised P.A. report went to Williams with KME making a formal application for the £2.9 million to install P.A.'s plan. Spriggs told Lewis and Bandell that if Government gave the money he'd not go back again., 'What we do now is final.' The IDU said that it was the best report they'd ever seen on KME but that it still wouldn't be accepted by IDAB because the action plan hadn't been carried out – the workers hadn't been sacked and no managers had been recruited. It was pointed out to Spriggs that he must satisfy the IDU and IDAB and carry out as much as possible. He argued that there was no money to do so. (The workers from the abandoned Constor and drinks operation were still sitting around KME doing little and drawing a wage, though they could have been seen off with three months' wages.)

The problem for KME's analysts, whether friendly or hostile, was to gauge whether the new proposals showed that the leaders had seen the light or were grasping at the PEB in order to retain power. The inaction over redundancies inevitably raised suspicions in Whitehall about the directors' real intentions.

KME's friends were just as wary. The directors had, they said, to get out of day-to-day management. 'We must be involved,' retorted Spriggs. 'Yes,' he was advised, 'but not so involved that you dominate. It gives the management a let-out and they give up.' The convenors were told that neither must chair the PEB, nor call meetings at short notice so that the chairman couldn't get there, so it would become natural for Spriggs to take the chair. 'You'd be back to a one-man band.'

End of the big push

The six-week spurt in output was also at risk. When making the appeal, Spriggs had implied that an incentive scheme would be introduced so that people would be rewarded for continued performance. There was no coherent discussion about an incentive scheme during the six weeks. Indeed the debate between the leaders and Lewis was primitive.

Their basic equation was the number of people, the hours worked, radiators produced and the bonus money. Yet the key figures at KME all knew that people were turning out overtime radiators in normal hours. 'There's two hours' leisure time in each working day. They're flogging it for five hours then relaxing for the rest of the day, having already 'worked' their two hours' overtime.' (In other words, the work standards were loose. A reasonable work effort cannot normally be doubled.)

The result was a direct labour cost of £1.51 per radiator instead of the budgeted £1.10, and the loss of output greatly increased the overhead which had to be allocated to each radiator. It wasn't clear how the projected bonus would relate to output or value added; nor had it been decided how to cope with absenteeism, indirect workers, associated departments or defective radiators. In the end, it was agreed that the bonus should be based on thirty-five hours and sound radiators; it would be paid to all, with the direct workers involved getting more and the welders a special extra. Yet people's wages could still go up if they took more time to produce a given number of radiators because the overtime effect would outweigh the incentive.

The scheme was never finalized and the six weeks effort petered out. The drop in output after the six weeks was seen by Spriggs and Jenkins as 'showing that they won't work except for money'. It showed nothing of the kind. What it did show was cynicism and low trust by workers who had been half-promised a scheme and then found that there was no plan of action, or even a proposal to put to them. Evidently the cooperative's leaders were viewed no differently than a traditional management. Nor did Spriggs' and Jenkins' views of their people differ from that of a poor traditional management.

By this stage, they had a very low opinion of their fellow cooperators. The terms in which they spoke of the workers and the stewards were those of distaste, cynicism, frustration and bewilderment. The cooperative's internal behaviour had moved to a vicious circle of mutual suspicion and distrust. The convenors would not be convinced that there could be a virtuous circle. No productivity scheme was ever introduced. The 150 surplus workers continued to sit around, demoralized as well as demoralizing those whose work was carrying them.

As from 1 April, everyone at KME was given a 10 per cent wage rise – the maximum allowed under Government guidelines. For the third year running it was not connected to productivity in any way. People had been expecting a rise. Losses were averaging over £100,000 per month.

Spriggs told the stewards the outline of the P.A. plan. (He didn't offer them copies. They didn't ask to see them.) He said that the directors were charged with interfering too much and that P.A. proposed that they 'should be put out to grass'.

The leaders intended to ask P.A. to develop a productivity scheme. This could take eight weeks for a full study.

Later, there was another fruitless interchange between the convenors and KME's advisers.

'These people haven't educated themselves over the years.'

'But what have you done to educate them?'

'We give them the information they ask for.'

'But how can they ask if they don't know what to ask for? Are you saying the people are beyond redemption? It's difficult for you to share power with people who you feel are ignorant. That's preventing you doing what's organizationally necessary. You won't suffer the nonsense that goes with the sense and so you don't get the sense anyway. The fact is that KME is very badly run. You've been advised over the three years that you've got to run it better and that there are ways to do it. You've continually rejected that advice and you've continually failed.'

'This family has been protected for far too long – since 1971.'

'Then why do you continue to protect them by taking it all on your own shoulders?'

'I'd love to get out of the day-to-day operations.'

'Then start discussing the PEB *now*. Our worry is that £2.9 million will cause a relaxation again.'

'We can't afford to relax.'

'But *they* will and if you don't set up a proper structure you'll find acute difficulty in getting a chief executive.'

The political climate

The external tide was ebbing and flowing daily. The Government was about to back down from the Bullock proposals and publish a White Paper which would have a proposition for two-tier boards instead of Bullock's single tier. KME's leaders and the author viewed this as a sensible abandonment of Bullock's unworkable proposals. Even so, the CBI was still determined to object, claiming that legal compulsion and uniformity were undesirable ways of making progress on participation.

The tide flowing in KME's direction was the growing

assault on the failure of Labour's regional policy. Callaghan had declared that 'industrial peace might remove the aura that surrounds Liverpool'. But, as the *New Statesman* pointed out, the area was becoming the Bermuda Triangle of British industry. Unemployment dropped everywhere except Merseyside. What made it galling was that the reputation was not connected with actual militance since, in Liverpool, radicals were proving hopelessly incompetent at organizing resistance to factory closures and their rhetoric was little more than empty blustering. The Liverpool Trades Council called on the Labour Government to nationalize the country's two hundred largest companies. The *New Statesman* reported one delegate's cutting reaction: 'How do you expect this Government to nationalize two hundred companies when it can't even keep a penny off a loaf?'

The fact was that KME needed a new start. The PEB needed to be started as soon as possible to involve the stewards in the forthcoming redundancies. Left to itself, the stewards' committee would fall to pieces over this problem and leave it all to the directors, who would then duck the action themselves.

The leaders cheered themselves up with two snippets of information. The Triumph workers were only going to get about £1,500 redundancy each, which would make it easier to pay people off cheaply at KME. The leaders had mixed feelings about Triumph's closure at Speke; fearful that once it was safely out of the way, interest in Merseyside would again wane; hopeful that Triumph's lack of fight would leave the field clear for a gesture to KME. Secondly, KME at last introduced a radiator price rise without a period of ordering grace. There wasn't a squeak from the trade.

Officials undermine P.A.'s plan

The meeting with Williams prior to the £2.9 million application going before IDAB, was a microcosm of the problem which KME had to face with the IDU. Briefed by them, Williams began to put pressure on the P.A. plan.

Williams The report indicates considerable growth.
Spriggs Yes. On our main product lines we cannot meet demand.
Williams If your competitors expand, will KME be able to meet its targets?
Spriggs Yes. KME's been competitive.
Williams But won't other makers invest if the market expands?
Spriggs Yes they will. But with capital investment at KME, there's no reason to feel that KME won't remain competitive. We have expanded volume and market share in a flat market.

They were fair answers. Jenkins chipped in to point out that the case wasn't KME's but came from P.A. 'We've done what we were urged. We've invited international consultants with wide terms of reference and they've come up with the answers. Perhaps you should carry on talking with P.A.'

Then the IDU's John Andrewes intervened, and the tactic became clearer. (Williams had revealed their basic propositions. KME's expansion plans would be branded as implausible. If the market remained flat, KME couldn't prosper because it couldn't raise prices and steal more market. Alternatively, if the market did grow, competitors would prevent KME prospering because of the low prices they would offer with their new, low-cost plants. Either way KME would lose. Spriggs' answers had countered that basic denigration.) Now Andrewes tried the historical and short-term arguments simultaneously.

'Your trading record makes it difficult to have confidence though you're one of the few companies who've made a bank think politically.' (The past was being used to bury P.A.'s plan for the future.)

'We accept, Minister,' he continued silkily, turning to

Williams, 'that there is a short-term boom in radiators arising out of the BOC strike.' (The IDU was also trying to discredit P.A.'s projections with the flash-in-the-pan argument and yet again demonstrating its poor judgement. The boom was to continue right through the remainder of KME's life.)

The leaders were trying to counter the Department's mistrust of their future intentions, for the past was littered with KME's broken promises and missed forecasts. 'We've demonstrated that we've prepared by closing the two lines – the publicity killed the businesses – but we did it.' (The weakness of this argument was that they hadn't sacked the surplus employees.) Williams was again reminded that the £2.9 million plan was P.A.'s independent view, not just something thought up out of thin air, though Spriggs was insinuating that P.A. had *recommended* that £2.9 million be put into KME, when the consultants had actually said that this was the sum needed to make it work. It was, recalled P.A. ruefully, a slight but significant twist of their report. Williams said it all had to be sorted out this time. 'Eric Varley is determined to grasp the nettle.'

'Yes, Alan, but he's using your hand to do it.'

KME asked to see the new IDU report so that they could be best advised by having a commentary on the P.A. report. It was refused, just as Varley had refused in 1976. The team returned to Liverpool convinced that IDAB would turn the application down. It would become a political decision. Varley and Williams told Silk that they were on KME's side. The leaders didn't believe a word of it.

P.A. had turned out to be a good ally and its report had been so positive that Spriggs was feeling optimistic about the political battle. 'It will really expose the officials if they knock this one back and the place closes.'

Heating and Ventilating News highlighted Stelrad's expansion plans. Its new radiator plant at Mexborough would add 30 per cent to the market leaders' capacity and help its customers 'who are becoming increasingly dissatisfied with growing delivery dates'. It appeared that Lewis had known about the investment for months, but hadn't told Jack, and it had nearly dropped P.A. and KME in it.

Spriggs promptly wrote to Williams pointing out that Stelrad's plans at Mexborough were welcome because it would make the market more orderly and stave off import penetration which was difficult to reverse once established. He repeated KME's desire to liaise with the NEB and mentioned that P.A.'s report was cautious because the NEB would be running a critical slide-rule over the analysis.

Through the Welsh Development Agency, Government was about to pump £600,000 into the revived Penrad radiator factory. Williams could scarcely claim that there wasn't a demand for more radiators.

National Westminster agreed to give KME another month's grace. The bank wasn't going to pull the plug on KME, and besides, the ending of Constor and juice purchases had improved KME's overdraft position.

It was clear from the Westminster delay that a political struggle was occurring over KME. On 10 May three of the four P.A. consultants met Williams and his officials, together with Junior Industry Minister Bob Cryer and Harold Walker, the Junior Minister from Employment. The officials were hostile but were quite unable to discredit P.A.'s analysis; nor was Williams, as he asked questions from his officials' brief. Cryer later said that P.A. 'rang rings round the officials'. However, P.A. was unable – quite reasonably – to put its hand on its heart and promise that KME *would* make a profit, but, since P.A. was staking its reputation by agreeing to provide managers for KME, it was evident that P.A. believed its own analysis and was fully committed to KME's success. P.A.'s senior consultant Marsden was unable to find out where the analysis was defective, and nor would the officials specify what they thought would occur at KME or why viability was suspect. 'Viability,' murmured an official, 'is a matter of judgement.' He wouldn't explain what was the basis of official judgement, though the Department was later to make it clear that viability was achieved when an enterprise became self-supporting without further Government help. The P.A. proposals and the Government's £2.9 million could well have achieved just that. Evidently the IDU thought differently. It didn't accept P.A.'s view of the length of the market boom, though it did agree that imports would flood in if the cooperative went down quickly.

One of the unpersuaded civil servants was a market research statistician who had analysed the market and disagreed with P.A.'s allegedly optimistic forecasts for radiator sales. Marsden was at a disadvantage because the P.A. team hadn't brought their own market analyst, not expecting this to be a problem, since the IDU team had seemed to accept the P.A. report when they had visited Kirkby. The argument continued, with the statistician casting doubt on P.A.'s figures. 'How can two of you disagree?' asked Williams innocently. This undermining of P.A.'s case by the Department was to have an embarrassing sequel some months later.

Once P.A. had left, Cryer became infuriated when a junior civil servant said that P.A.'s commitment was worth little because 'they would lie their way out of it'. The other officials also took up this point. (Marsden was later to become angry over these sly aspersions about P.A.'s integrity. 'We were confident enough in our findings to back KME up with managers and we had good managers available too. The offer lay on the table. We had done this role in many other similar situations. It's part of our normal business.')

The plan sinks

The Cabinet committee which considered P.A.'s application was chaired by Varley. He had put in a neutral paper, so other ministers took a lead from his lack of support. The IDU's advice was strongly negative. Benn and Booth reserved their positions and so it went to full Cabinet on 11 May, where Benn and Booth were joined by Foot and Orme. Most of the Cabinet were against the proposal, on the basis of the information supplied to it.

That evening a courier delivered a letter from Williams to Spriggs' home. The Cabinet had concluded that the application could not be justified under the Industry Act criteria. It had been rejected.

14. The cooperative fights back: 1978

- Enter a mystery company
- The past catches up
- Takeover attempts – one down and one to go
- Jim's election gambit rocks the boat
- The storm breaks
- An unexpected development
- But who was in the trap?

Not a word of the rejection spilled out, even though Benn had leaked it to the *Guardian* as he emerged from Varley's Cabinet committee meeting. Secrecy was vital for KME, for once rejection was out in the open, Government might choose to brazen out the row. In fact, reasoned Spriggs, the Labour Government might welcome a row, for wasn't it now trying to save itself by showing that it was as Tory as the Opposition?

On the day of the rejection Callaghan spoke in Manchester on industrial democracy. He hoped to promote cooperative development, a more powerful NEB and workers on company boards. The leaders found it sickening. Callaghan declared that the North-West wasn't a particular problem area, for unemployment was a world-wide issue which would best be solved by an improvement in the world economic situation. For a Prime Minister seeking re-election, it was strangely complacent. Jim wasn't making any friends in the North-West. *Engineering Today* wrote that the Government's indifference to Merseyside's plight 'has created the impression in the area that the Government . . . is now totally cynical about unemployment in Liverpool and its surrounding areas'.

The Lib-Lab pact was due to finish at the end of the session of Parliament and a truculent fatalism seemed to have settled over the Labour administration.

Despite this, the political mood was not wholly against cooperatives. Labour MP David Watkins had published a Fabian pamphlet* commending cooperatives, having piloted the Industrial Common Ownership Bill through Parliament. Left-wing MP Norman Atkinson and right-wing ex-Industry Minister, Nicholas Ridley, united in calling for the creation of worker cooperatives. Atkinson's interest was in finding an alternative to state monopolies, whilst Ridley thought that denationalizing mines and ports into cooperatives would inject some commercial discipline into workers' minds.

The *Guardian* suggested that the forthcoming Cooperative Development Agency could promote a cooperative where the workers wanted it to work and where there was a genuine demand for goods and services at commercial prices. There was a need to avoid money gurgling down some self-indulgent drain. 'To succeed, worker cooperatives must be about finding ways of efficient self-responsibility – not avoiding them.' KME's analysts could not have put it better.

The leaders had reacted to the rejection by searching for support. The bank appeared to be resolved to absorb whatever pressure came its way without precipitating a crisis at KME. KME had been worried that P.A. would distance themselves from trouble and back-pedal out of the minefield as delicately and speedily as they could. In fact P.A. took the rejection as an affront to their reputation and seemed quite determined to stand by their analysis and to press Williams to say why their report had been found wanting.

Nevertheless, Spriggs was dispirited. 'We were on a definite promise that we would get Government support if we could prove viability, which P.A. demonstrated.' He was worried that if the political vacuum persisted until Parliament rose for the summer, the cooperative would die unnoticed. Neither management nor stewards at KME

* *Industrial Common Ownership*, (Fabian Society, 1978).

yet knew of the rejection for fear that output would drop
as workers became demoralized. It was assumed by the
leaders that it was better to keep them in the dark because
people would not be galvanized by the challenge.

Enter a mystery company

Silk asked Varley for a meeting over KME and was told
that it was Williams' job. 'Why don't you do your own
dirty work, Eric?' Silk persisted. Varley said that it
wouldn't change anything. His attitude seemed to have
hardened.

Silk told Spriggs that Williams was negotiating with
another concern which would employ about three
hundred people on the KME site. It can't be warehousing,
mused Spriggs, perhaps the mystery men want to retrench
on to radiators alone and build up that business. He was
absolutely right. A principal in the Industry Department
had visited the Heating and Ventilating Exhibition at Birmingham where the Stelrad central heating people from
Metal Box had confided their worries about the unhelpful
effects on the market and on import growth if KME
folded. Could they help? Unknown to KME, talks started
between Williams and Stelrad – Europe's biggest central
heating firm.

The radiator market was booming and both Sankey and
Tricentrol had offered to buy enough radiators to take up
the whole of KME's output for the next year. 'Varley will
say that's just part of the flash in the pan,' grumbled
Spriggs. Tricentrol was even prepared to put up £200,000
cash for forward deliveries of radiators – if it got priority.
Knowing that this would alienate other customers, KME
declined. Matters were not that desperate – yet.

A different possibility now came to the fore. Through
the trade, the leaders knew a firm called Hill Foster, a
marketing company which imported Feroli boilers and
radiators from Italy. As KME's troubles mounted, the
possibility had grown of a takeover by Hill Foster and an

association with Feroli. Hill Foster employed only twenty
people though it turned over £3.5 million a year, but it was
KME's only known lifeline since ministers no longer believed in KME, its management, its marketing, its leaders'
promises or in the cooperators' motivation. Yet the mistrust could have been reduced if only the leaders had taken
one resolute act towards commercial sense and shown a
sustained commitment to organizational competence.
But they wouldn't do it. The idle drinks and Constor
workers were still sitting there. Even sympathetic ministers couldn't support leaders who ran away from every
nasty problem. KME was steadily digging its own grave.

Williams met the leaders on 6 June. On the way to the
meeting, Silk spelt out the key issues. 'A public campaign
would kill the business and you'll be dead once the House
rises on the third of August. Ask the Department if it's
got something up its sleeve.' None of the KME party
picked up the significance of this last point.

Williams opened strongly. 'The Cabinet view is that
massive sums of Government help have been put into the
enterprise and I've managed to create one thousand jobs
for far less cash on Merseyside.' (Williams was referring
to Schreiber at Runcorn and Vauxhall's second shift at
Ellesmere Port.)

'P.A. said it's not fully commercially viable . . . money
not merited . . . everything's highly marginal . . . We
won't get viable jobs with the present unit . . . We're
looking for a partner too and we will negotiate with a
principal and they could involve you . . . You have only
one possible partner, because we've all kept confidence,
even though we're very worried about the bank, and so
other prospective buyers haven't been alerted.'

P.A.	They'd probably want to sack everyone and make them redundant.
Official	That could be better for the jobs.
Spriggs	They won't necessarily remain docile at Kirkby if they're sacked.

Williams   Buyers won't come if there's militancy.
Making a hue and cry won't get money out of Government.
Spriggs   Some industrialists welcome people who want to work. Perhaps publicity would bring home what sacking means to those in Cabinet who are against us.
Williams   Nobody is against you. The rug would have been pulled out a year ago if that was the case.

[This wasn't true. The £860,000 had been given to counter unemployment because there was no other obvious recipient on Merseyside. It had little to do with Government being attracted to KME.]

Williams repeated that KME was clearly not viable. Spriggs was disgusted. 'I never thought to hear this Tory talk. It's not you Alan – I think you've been wound up to say it.'

However, the officials made it plain that KME alone could not be deemed viable. Hill Foster would have to put in some money since viability meant no more injections of public funds for several years. KME would have to fit into the aid system; only that day the Permanent Secretary had asked for a confidential briefing note so that he could face the Public Accounts Committee over KME's recent history.

Spriggs tried fishing. 'Is there anything that Government can throw on the table to help us in our search?'

'We'll be looking for another company too,' responded Williams.

After the meeting, Silk said that Government wanted to help, but needed a scheme which would succeed. 'They believe you'll get nothing from the bank, the NEB, or Hill Foster and you'll go into liquidation and someone will pick you up.' Williams, he claimed, was very committed to saving the jobs, but worried about KME.

(Silk then told me privately that the Department had

a prospective buyer for KME – as firmly as they could have in the circumstances – but they couldn't presently discuss it with Jack. More than that he felt unable to reveal.)

Back at KME the leaders were fearful. 'Benn's the albatross round our necks even though he's been our helper.' Their central worry was the officials' sanguine acceptance of liquidation.* Did officials realize that although a receiver would have the use of the lease, a liquidator wouldn't, so that King could take back the factory and let it out as warehousing? The bank had declined to change the terms so that a receiver could be appointed instead, though it was willing to extend the overdraft agreement to August so that negotiations could continue with prospective partners.

It seemed unlikely that the NEB would be amongst them, for talking to them 'was like talking to the wall' reported Spriggs. Ward had visited the factory but made it clear that the NEB was interested only in commercial deals. There was no hint of any social, regional or industrial democracy perspectives, despite the NEB's brief to promote such matters and its ability to 'recommend on matters of particular importance within its region'.

This was disappointing but not in the least unexpected, for the convenors regarded the regional NEB as a pathetic joke and recognized that nationally the NEB would not want to jeopardize its shaky future further, by becoming more identified with lame ducks. At least Hill Foster offered a slight chance of salvation. Its managing director had visited the Industry Department and revealed that

---

* Back in January 1976, Varley had been given an Industry Department memorandum which pointed out the positive role of receivers in reconstructing industry. 'In the assisted areas a new employer, if he purchases assets from the receiver, is eligible for help under Section 7 of the Industry Act. This, rather than the propping-up of failed enterprises is and should remain the principal contribution the Industry Act can make towards dealing with redundancies.' It was a fascinating example of advice on industrial intervention given to Labour ministers.

the plan would be for Hill Foster to take on KME's radiators with their 10 per cent market share, use Kirkby as the distribution base for its French and Italian imports and perhaps later plough in funds to the enterprise. 'Later' was the worrying word.

All kinds of figures were flying round about aid, purchase of the site, new radiator lines and the like. Hill Foster wanted the convenors to be executives in the new set-up — probably as industrial relations and personnel directors as in the P.A. proposal. It certainly wouldn't have them continue both as directors and convenors and the implication was that it wouldn't have them on site at all as worker representatives. The convenors recognized that they would almost inevitably be drawn into mischief if they continued to behave as an uneasy amalgam of steward/manager under a new management, for the workers would look to them for leadership and the shop-floor remained the source of their strength.

Yet they didn't fancy reverting solely to a shop-floor role, since they hadn't worked on the factory floor for years and life there wouldn't be exciting enough after their recent experiences. 'The shop-floor has had good leadership for years', said Jack, 'and although there'll be some sniping, that's all there is throughout the union movement on Merseyside anyway. We'll go back to being a traditional organization at KME and let other people worry about industrial democracy.'

The past catches up

The poignancy of this problem was being heightened by their current battle inside the cooperative. In an effort to improve the trading position they had worked out a temporary incentive scheme for radiators. This wouldn't be a repeat of February's big push, for they didn't fancy being rebuffed. This time there would be money for effort. They would set a target of 13,200 radiators per week and if this was achieved on average for five weeks, welders would get £100, the other radiator workers £70, and other workers £40. This would be coupled to a layoff plan because it would be daft to pay a bonus and keep two hundred people idle.

The danger was that the simple scheme would pre-empt alternatives if new methods raised the factory's capacity. Nor did the leaders have a fall-back plan in the event of output not quite reaching 13,200 a week. What would happen if there were plant breakdowns? It was only too easy to halt the paint plant.

None of it mattered. The workers turned the plan down. Some tool-men felt that they wouldn't be rewarded properly; some workers wanted the same money as the welders, and the layoffs 'just seemed to be a few women and absentees'. The stewards reported that the current incentive was the early finish. This didn't produce a single extra radiator but the hidden warning was that a financial incentive might not work. A bell to bell scheme might result in little extra output – it could just be spread over more hours.

The leaders were scathing. The stewards had fallen down again in not sorting out and commending the scheme properly, they claimed, and everyone had defended their own area. The scheme was abandoned due to dissension. Nobody even came back with any alternative suggestion. The directors were beginning to wonder if the unreality on the shop-floor could only be dissolved by liquidation and a fresh start.

In fact, the plan had not been properly debated with the various groups. The leaders had simply pressed their pre-arranged plan on to the stewards, who had no intention of getting into the firing line after the experience of the big push in the spring. Stewards just didn't have the nerve to try to force the new scheme on to the cynical and mistrustful workers. The leaders were now reaping the full reaction to the way they had chosen to run the factory over the previous three years.

Takeover attempts – one down and one to go

Silk provided more news on the Department's mystery company. Apparently it would take the plant to a purpose-built factory near Liverpool and employ two hundred people in total. This would scarcely satisfy KME's workers. But who was it?

If it's TI, or Thorn or Stelrad, mused KME, they're not buying jobs and plant. It would cost a lot to move the plant and some of it is clapped out. They'd be buying 10 per cent market share complete with a way into KME's stockists and getting up to £4 million of tax losses. It was difficult to know whether to take this mystifying possibility seriously. The only helpful piece of news was a trade whisper that Thorn and Stelrad had agreed not to attack KME's position before 1981. Whilst KME had raised its prices by 6 per cent, Thorn had lifted its prices by 8 per cent. Catching up with the competition was proving hard. What KME didn't realize was that since the cooperative's price levels had depressed the whole market, as soon as KME raised its prices, all its major competitors seized the chance to raise their too. If KME had only had competent commercial management it would have realized that it could have driven up its prices substantially in the buoyant market.

The Hill Foster negotiations continued and Department officials seemed enthusiastic, though Bob Cryer was arguing with Varley that the cooperative should be maintained in some form. Signor Feroli visited the plant, which created a factory rumour that the takeover would be coupled to big discounts off Italian holidays! Hill Foster was pressing KME for speedy agreement and the convenors had already reluctantly agreed to the reintroduction of a forty-hour week as part of the deal, recognizing that Hill Foster would have to sort out everything before they took over. There wouldn't be a snowball's chance of changing conditions without resistance once the firm had taken control.

Hill Foster would be taking on a mammoth task, but it

might succeed if the prior conditions were negotiated properly. The leaders were wary because Hill Foster appeared to be making no commitment and would only come in if Government funded the required two hundred redundancies. There was no mention of Hill Foster's own promises.

IDAB turned down Hill Foster's proposal, which surprised the convenors, since Government had wanted a new management at KME and now it was being rejected. They swiftly induced Hill Foster to withdraw the application before ministers could reject it too and leave another refusal on record.

The puzzle was why Hill Foster's application hadn't found favour – for KME assumed that it had been for roughly P.A.'s £2.9 million – though figures of up to £3.8 million had been mentioned. Hill Foster continued to press the convenors to sack two hundred people and introduce an incentive bonus scheme immediately. The convenors were told that a new Hill Foster application was before Government, this time for £250,000, and Hill Foster also revealed that its rejected application had been for £4.7 million. So that was what IDAB had turned down! KME had never seen the application and everyone was now embarrassed. 'We should have been sensitive to it. We've been like birds in the nest waiting for worms to come – but they haven't. We've never been to Government with Hill Foster. It's been divide and rule. We've got to get back to Government fast.' With Hill Foster having talked of £2.9 million, then asked for £4.7 million and now £250,000, what confidence could Government have in the firm?

Mutual trust was dwindling rapidly. The firm wouldn't act before KME's workforce reduced itself, and the convenors wouldn't back Hill Foster's plan without commitment from Hill Foster as to what would ensue. The officials were finding the firm's tactics frustrating, as was the bank, which couldn't get Hill Foster to commit itself to anything concrete.

The leaders' will to fight was being sapped. Forced liquidation was on the cards as desperate measures were taken at KME to keep within the overdraft limit of £850,000. Stocks of raw materials had been run down to liberate cash and BSC was becoming very reluctant to supply while so much money was owed already.

The idea that KME could use its cash flow to pay off the two hundred surplus workers was fanciful,* claimed the leaders. There wasn't any spare cash flow – creditors were being fought off all the time. John Bandell's ingenuity in juggling cheques was already enough to win him any talent contest. There just wasn't any more.

And what could they say to the remaining 530 whose jobs would still be insecure? (There was a considerable element of self-deception in this argument because two hundred redundancies would have obliterated half the weekly losses and exhibited KME's commercial resolve to Government and Hill Foster. It was the whole KME story in a nutshell. Action was vital but the leaders couldn't bring themselves to take it. The pain was too great). Yet the convenors had thought about sacking people, knowing that it could not occur on the hallowed 'last in, first out' basis because 80 of KME's precious 120 welders would have gone. Even so, the welders might leave anyway, for Hill Foster's proposed forty-hour week could be judged to be a major change of conditions so that welders might refuse the new contract and claim redundancy, confident that they could get other welding jobs. Some workers were looking for a cash handout and so might want the cooperative to close. (Even in 1978 with 20 per cent local male unemployment, jobs could still be bought out for as little as three months' wages. Many workers had a time-scale which appalled not just middle-class analysts but their own union officers and

---

* It was, by then, becoming almost impossible, but KME had already paid wages to the idle drinks and Constor workers through the summer which, as a lump sum, would have readily funded the redundancy payments at the time of shutting down those lines.

stewards too. As one Triumph steward had said, 'Our members will walk all over us for the redundancy money.') If a few of KME's young welders opted for redundancy, radiator output would be temporarily crippled.

The leaders were also deeply suspicious of Hill Foster. The firm was an enigma. It kept changing its deadlines. Why couldn't it see the need for commitment – not as a gesture to KME but as a reassurance to the bank and to Government?

Spriggs and Jenkins were bitter with Government. 'They told us that if a new firm came in their attitude would change, but it hasn't. It's our Labour Government playing games. That Saatchi & Saatchi advertisement – 'Labour isn't working' – it's true isn't it?'

Bob Cryer had told the leaders that the hostility of the officials had to be seen to be believed, though one senior official reacted to the insinuation that anti-Benn feeling lay behind the rejection. 'That's claptrap. It's simply not a viable commercial proposition and it's been judged by the same criteria applied to any other request for Government aid. To put more money in would be a waste of resources.' The implication was that adding to Britain's import bill and paying out yet more in dole money was a more effective use of resources.

The leaders knew their own bargaining position was weak. 'We've lost a lot of friends saying we'd do things and then going from bad to worse. Three thousand Triumph workers wouldn't shed any tears over us.' Hill Foster was probably being warned by officials not to be talked into taking on KME and finding itself lumbered with a disorganized venture and with the convenors still in control. 'Given the history, that's reasonable,' said Spriggs. 'Perhaps Hill Foster and the IDU believe that we're too close to the shop-floor and will never change. Silk says that and he's a friend of ours. Even you say that Tony.'

The leaders were boxed in. If they agreed Hill Foster's

present conditions, there could be new ones the next day
– already the firm was suggesting that, once it had taken
over, the convenors should stay away from the factory in
their spare time. 'After a few months, they'll boot us,'
they decided. And how could they stand on a platform
and deliver a message full of 'ifs' and 'buts'. They ignored
a telex from Hill Foster requesting their unequivocal commitment within an hour.

On 16 August the leaders visited Silk in London. (Some
workers believed that they were going to bring back the
Government's new allocation of money.) Hill Foster had
yet again shifted its deadline, this time to 7 p.m. that
evening. Silk reported that ministers wanted to give the
£250,000, even if IDAB rejected it. The convenors stifled
their worries and agreed that they would hold a mass
meeting the following day to announce the action plan –
sackings, forty-hour week, the lot – on one condition. Hill
Foster had to obtain the backing of National Westminster;
the leaders would take these drastic steps if the bank
backed Hill Foster. Silk telephoned Hill Foster from his
corridor office in the House of Commons and all but
promised the Government's £250,000 if Hill Foster proceeded. The firm accepted. Things were looking up. KME
had made a move, and it had been reciprocated.

The next day the bank again told Hill Foster that it
must put in some financial commitment, but no commitment came. The firm once more insisted that the redundancy notices be issued and the action plan introduced at
KME. At 5 p.m. Hill Foster pulled out, blaming Spriggs
and Jenkins for the breakdown.

The following week Hill Foster reactivated its interest,
with Hill Foster now urging KME *not* to hold the action
plan meeting or let out any information. But leaks were
already occurring. The *Kirkby Reporter* wrote of an imminent takeover. The *Financial Times* claimed that KME
was urgently seeking more funds to meet recommendations by P.A. which had mapped out a prosperous
future for the cooperative. Some recommendations, it

reported, had not been carried out and there were reports of low productivity. Because of the Benn rescues, KME and Meriden were regarded with disfavour both in Whitehall and in the cooperative movement, continued the *Financial Times*, apparently being briefed information from the Industry Department.

KME suspected that these were leaks by officials attempting to sink KME at its most vulnerable time. Some cooperators were shocked by the article, others didn't know whether it was good news or bad and so it agitated people without activating them.

KME's radiator output was dropping despite the backlog of orders. Absenteeism rose again and only two of the four multiweld machines could be operated. In retaliation, the tack welders dropped their targets and reduced output further. 'They're living in cloud-cuckoo-land. We'll have to tell them the brutal truth,' said Spriggs. 'Some of the things we've kept inside are giving me nervous pains. I'll shock them with the Government rejection letter. We can't mess about like this much longer. We were naive to believe that people would respond when we got the £860,000. They didn't. They went worse. If only we'd used our ruthlessness as a union movement to run the business, perhaps we'd be strong as an organization now.' As if KME didn't have enough trouble, the paint plant broke down and three days' output was lost.

There were two compensating incidents. KME had now managed to sell the drinks business to an Irish firm* for a creditable £135,000. It was probably the best commercial deal the cooperative ever concluded, though the bank wouldn't let KME use the money and, instead, placed it into a special deposit because it had come from selling off assets which secured the overdraft. (National Westminster didn't fancy applying it to a reduction in KME's overdraft limit, fearing that KME would try to wheedle the limit up again later.)

* The firm later went bust.

The other occurrence was that a new company was now interested in KME via a local merchant bank. This time the leaders intended to insist on a joint approach to Government in case the Hill Foster fiasco repeated itself. They also intended to ensure that the takeover and any Government assistance would be conditional on a clear action plan. That way there could be no nonsense with the co-operators, whose stewards would be faced with a *fait accompli*, which would have the helpful effect of keeping the convenors out of the firing line.

The next week had barely started before the leaders felt that they were going round in circles. The merchant bank and Hill Foster had formed an association under the aegis of P.A.'s Derek Hartland who, KME suspected, was seeing himself as the chief executive of the reconstructed KME. The new group proposed to take over on virtually identical lines to Hill Foster. Again there was no commitment of funds. The only difference was that the two buyers were going to Government as a team.

KME felt that it would make no difference if they added three men in a boat, but since the directors didn't want to be seen to be blocking anything, they agreed to approach Williams. The merchant bank team soon disappeared. In the wake of its departure, Jack and Dick recalled something. They hadn't initially named the new company in talking to the officials, whose first question had been, 'Is it another radiator manufacturer?' Only a firm making UK profits in the same business could take advantage of KME's tax losses. The Industry Department's mystery buyer just *had* to be Thorn, Myson or Stelrad.

The trouble was that there was no other option open to them, though they half hoped that the new Government-funded Cooperative Development Agency might be of help. Lord Oram, the ex-Cooperative Party research officer and Labour Cooperative MP was appointed chairman of the CDA. It would advise, but not fund, cooperatives, though the Cooperative Bank might

provide up to half the start-up funds of new cooperatives
provided the workers showed commitment by putting in
their own money, as in the Spanish Mondragon cooperatives and the defunct SDN. According to *Labour Weekly*
its task would be to 'galvanize cooperative activity'. Government was to appoint the other members of the agency.
At their first meeting Williams told them the KME saga.
They heard him tell them to steer clear of KME.

Jim's election gambit rocks the boat

September 1978 was an irritating month. If only Government would make a last gesture to KME before it was
stymied by the general election. Once called, election
protocol would leave the cooperative out in the cold –
and what if the Tories won? The bank was due to end the
suspense on the 8th. Spriggs and Jenkins resolved to stay
at home that day so that their expressions wouldn't tell
the story to everyone in the factory. Then everything
changed. Just as the TUC Conference at Brighton was
pumping itself up to back the Labour Government, Callaghan announced that there would be no autumn election. Union leaders were furious at the offhand treatment.
They'd been made to look fools.

At the time of Callaghan's statement KME's leaders
were closeted with Alan Williams who, like virtually
everyone in Government, had no knowledge of Callaghan's intentions. Williams told the leaders that an anonymous company was interested and intended to provide
250 to 300 jobs on a site near Kirkby – probably
purpose-built for radiator manufacture. There were
copper-bottomed guarantees, and the mystery enterprise
knew KME, the characters, the history and the products.
Would KME go into receivership the following Monday
(11 September) so that Government could announce that
the new people were coming in? he asked. He believed
that the convenors agreed.

Williams offered to speak to Employment Secretary

Albert Booth so that wages and redundancy money could be processed quickly. It seemed that Williams was arranging for the bank to have a receiver standing by to manage the business via a cosmetic receivership. He had evidently squared the bank to vary its conditions to incorporate a receivership rather than a liquidation. Williams wouldn't name or discuss the company which would be taking over. He'd gone far beyond the reasonable ministerial function, reflected Spriggs afterwards, as he read the headlines of the cancelled election.

The convenors returned to Merseyside with Williams convinced that they had categorically agreed to the receivership plan and would agree it with National Westminster the following day (Friday 8th) – the only day left to them. Government was trying to tie them up without information time or manoeuvring room. 'They don't want you to have an inch; they know you'll only expand it because you're slippery customers. But you shouldn't be shoved into giving up control on a promise by Williams about an unknown third party which he cannot bind.'

The directors' only weapon was that the receivership needed their permission. Their worry was that their refusal risked three hundred jobs, because the promise was of continuity of employment for those kept on, and since the Industry Department team knew the leaders desperately wanted to save jobs, the officials believed that the convenors had agreed to receivership and would deliver the vote of KME's workers.

The convenors went to the bank the following day. It appeared that the Industry Department officials had persuaded the bank to vary the debenture agreement and allow a receivership. But KME wouldn't agree. The mystery company must come clean and talk.

It refused. It would only come in once the receiver was appointed. Williams was sympathetic to KME's view but wouldn't put pressure on the firm. In that case, said Spriggs, we'll go into liquidation. Officials urged him not to do this but were told by Spriggs that the business could fold up at any time and that KME's second largest customer was already importing £7 million worth of Danish radiators. Hill Foster had a full list of KME's customers and could offer them Feroli radiators immediately.

There was, felt Spriggs, a terrible state of flux in Whitehall. They'd set up a takeover by capitalists and now it wasn't fireproof. The officials had bounced the ministers into it. On Friday evening an official rang again. The minister wanted to meet the convenors on Monday morning and the other company was prepared to be there too. The leaders stated firmly that they would only attend the meeting if the other company identified itself to them when they arrived. 'We won't negotiate with masked men.'

They were risking the loss of the mystery enterprise and of the jobs, but felt that negotiations were worthless if the other company was going to play games. In the political turmoil of the cancelled election, KME was taking the crisis to the brink. The mystery men cancelled the meeting. They intended to remain anonymous.

On Monday (11 September 1978) Spriggs asked Williams for a clear summary of the Government-backed proposal. It was quickly prepared and telexed to KME five minutes before the mass meeting.

Spriggs read it to the cooperators. It confirmed that the secret company would run the factory as the receiver's agent, and employ 250 to 300 people who would continue to make radiators while the secret firm sorted out its acquisition and then moved to its new factory near by. It would only negotiate once the receiver was appointed.

The leaders put their pre-arranged resolution to the mass meeting which pledged one hundred per cent support for the platform's rejection of voluntary receivership or liquidation and called for Government to support the cooperative in an open and constructive way. The convenors had delivered the vote, but not the way the Department believed had been promised.

Williams was reported as being shocked and unable to see the sense of rejecting the mystery company's lifeline.

Silk gave the impression that he too wanted the three hundred jobs to be accepted. The other company was reported as having gone away. KME didn't know whether to believe that, but their trade contacts had confirmed that the firm was Stelrad. The officials seemed to be accusing the leaders of changing their minds from Thursday to Sunday. On Thursday the plan had been agreed, they asserted, because everyone believed there'd be a general election. 'Now they say we've gone back on our word because we're still dealing with a Labour Government. Williams thinks we've kicked him down,' reported Spriggs, 'but his officials had set him up.'

The argument would become complex. Williams would be certain to blame the convenors for pushing three hundred jobs down the river. But the cards weren't all in Williams' hands, for the Department could face a major embarrassment. The previous Permanent Secretary, Sir Anthony Part, had retired from the Industry Department in 1976 and was now a director of Metal Box, Stelrad's parent company. What was the Department doing in trying to nudge KME into its arms?

Rob Rohrer of the *Sunday Times* was on the scent, having heard of the liquidation threat from a boilermakers' union official at Cammell Laird. Despite Rob being a friend, Spriggs was furious over the leak. 'There's a conspiracy of trade unionists and socialists on Merseyside who want us to go down.' He was very agitated. The strain was telling.

Neither Spriggs nor Silk wanted publicity. Yet Rohrer was picking up information from Westminster and the radiator industry. KME told the Department that Metal Box's interest had been known in the trade for at least a week. The local press believed that the Merseyside Industrial Development Office had been looking for a factory site for them for months.

The leaders were now recovering as the flux intensified. They were back in the rough and tumble they exploited so well. Spriggs was talked round over the question of publicity. Rohrer pointed out that it was no use KME going quietly under. Government seemed to be trying to jostle the cooperative into submission and it would be no good if, after the event, people said they could have helped but it had all happened so quickly and quietly. The leaders were worried that the story would be traced back to them. But Rohrer already knew it.

The storm breaks

'Secret takeover bid angers workers' coop' headlined the *Sunday Times*. Stelrad was named as part of 'an extraordinary manoeuvre' by the Industry Department to force the cooperative to close despite the consultants' report that the firm had a profitable future. The newspaper disclosed that there would be no negotiations with the worker directors and stated that, for the Kirkby workers, the consultants' report gave a key test of senior civil servants' sympathies since they appeared to have been unable to fault it. Opposition to Benn lingered on. 'Anti-Bennery is a favourite sport in Whitehall these days, and there is uniform hostility to KME,' said a minister. The newspaper continued: 'Throughout the firm's history the influence of civil servants' hostility to the concept of workers' control has been blamed for the poor guidance given to the cooperative, which has always been short of management expertise.'

A sympathetic civil servant explained the opposition over KME. 'Officials have collective memories. They remember the broken promises and the missed targets and they don't really forget – or forgive.'

The effect of the article was vivid. The Industry Department was put into a thoroughly embarrassing position and an official rang the *Sunday Times* to explain how it had misunderstood everything. The paper's journalists were confronted by Department solicitors and learned that a leak inquiry was under way with statements being requested from ministers that they hadn't released infor-

mation. The Tribune Group became active; an emergency
resolution was drawn up for the forthcoming Labour Party
conference; the Institute for Workers Control put forward
a plan for miners to lobby Varley in his Chesterfield
constituency; and Spriggs was invited to speak at the IWC
fringe meeting at the conference. Heffer would approach
the Prime Minister, whilst Metal Box denied that any
negotiations were taking place. (It was right; it had refused to negotiate.)

KME did its best to stir the cauldron, revealing that its
radiator order book was close to £2 million with its seven
biggest customers prepared to order £8 million worth of
radiators for 1979. Sankey alone would double its order
if KME could supply them, and Salvesen Heating was
worried about having to sack men if KME collapsed. P.A.
was reported as intending to send its men to Williams to
defend its report, which Williams had said was first class.
(Only Ward said otherwise, commenting privately that
P.A. were naive.)

The cooperative's stewards were told that the market
demand for radiators made KME's market share and production attractive to Stelrad, whose own factory building
programme was behind schedule. Right now the market
needed KME and its radiators and they should capitalize
on it. Sadly, the author and Spriggs were not in harmony.
Asked what they could do to help, the author told the
stewards 'turn out more radiators to bring in money and
show we can do it'. Spriggs instantly killed the point.
'They fall on stony ground these appeals. The radiator
people don't like carrying people who are doing nothing.'
He legitimized, yet again, the workers carrying on as
before.

The debate between the author and Spriggs continued
after the meeting.

'Are you going to get rid of the two hundred who are
doing nothing?'

'No. It's no use sacking two hundred with full rights
and then we go into liquidation and the rest get nothing.'

'But you improve your chance of survival if you cut the losses and show Government you can act.'

'No, we won't.'

'You've switched. Last week you were prepared to do anything. Now you're prepared to do nothing.'

'But you saw the mood of the mass meeting.'

'You created that. My information is that a number would be keen to go.'

The author's view was that the slimmed-down operation couldn't easily be refused backing, even by Varley. But Spriggs had his mind on political rather than business options. The publicity had made Varley and Williams look deviously anti-Labour and pro-capitalist. The Labour Government was being routed over its attempt to introduce a fourth stage of incomes policy. The Left was lining up to help KME, and the party conference in Blackpool was just two weeks away.

KME's leaders visited the Department once more with a growing weight of support behind them. Customers had again offered to advance money; on Government figures it was cheaper to keep KME going with subsidies than close it; left-wing MPs promised support; fears of rising imports were expressed and the Conservative leader of Merseyside County Council backed KME's survival plans.

An unexpected development

Spriggs, overestimating his political muscle, was in a belligerent mood on the way to the meeting with Williams. 'We can't sack people on the chance that something might save the rest. We aren't going in with a begging bowl. We go on the offensive. We're offering them jobs. Government can't be seen to be encouraging imports. The nice ways have failed. We've got to hit Government between the eyes.'

The meeting itself was wearing. Everyone was fractious; worried as to who was wheeling and dealing. If anyone left the room it caused concern. If two left it was deemed a conspiracy. (It was the only time that people became touchy about this book. One by one everyone joked about it nervously.) The problem for the KME party was that, despite the pre-meeting bluster, they had no plan to put forward. Going up in the lift they were still searching for a card to play.

The faces round Williams' table were familiar by now. So were the arguments. KME still hadn't got rid of the spare workers in spite of its financial plight, pointed out Williams. Jenkins replied that there was no point if the rest were going to follow them anyway, and why aid Metal Box and not KME? The other company's plan was unchallengeably viable, responded Williams, who was careful not to name Metal Box. He was clearly still resentful about the Stelrad fiasco, having had to sell the scheme hard to his colleagues only to see it collapse about his ears. It wasn't much reward for his misdirected effort. As he complained, of all the many cases he had handled he had spent more time on KME than on any other firm. (As one official recalled sadly later, 'KME tried to flush Metal Box out, but it simply flushed them away.)

'After three separate infusions of cash you keep coming back and you've still got much the same problems,' continued Williams, 'and I want it to be a credit to cooperatives. I repeatedly get criticism from the cooperative movement that they have to overcome the reputation which KME brings.'

Money should come to KME conditionally, Williams was told. Nasty decisions would have to be made by a strengthened management. No action – no cash.

'But the other company's proposition is cheaper – probably less than £2 million. We'd need to be very sure that KME would never come back for a grant again. We don't have confidence in your management or marketing ability to carry the action plan through. P.A.'s plan needs everything to go right and even then isn't very secure.'

'We've been drawing up a list of those who have to go, even though it's distasteful,' said Jenkins.

'The Government will take the blame,' pointed out Silk. 'It's taken the credit.'

'We haven't had any credit,' reacted Williams. 'No matter how much we give, it's never enough.'

'KME's not going to give up the business to anyone,' threatened Spriggs. 'There'll be no bits to pick up.'

The KME group asked for temporary assistance so that the interest created by the publicity could be explored. 'That's what TES was given for,' countered Williams. 'What could I say to the textile industry – that TES has run out for them but I've found a magic formula for KME?' The meeting was going nowhere.

Then Spriggs played an unexpected ace. (He had been contemptuous of the Triumph car workers who had taken the redundancy money and then made the empty gesture of asking for a retrospective inquiry into the closure. But if an inquiry had been held in time . . .?)

'Let's set up a working party, Alan, to look into the ways of saving KME. Dick and I will step aside if necessary.' The meeting went round a few more circles whilst people absorbed this idea. KME declined to accept a solution which left only radiator manufacture at Kirkby. 'You agreed that last Thursday and thought you could sell it [to the people]' accused Williams. It was clear that he believed that Spriggs had reneged on an agreement. Spriggs demurred, quoting the cooperators as being against it.

'We could have gone out and raised the roof at Blackpool and gone for Government through the trade unions. That's not the way,' said Jack. 'We're looking for a sensible solution – any plan thrust on KME will be rejected.' (In fact he was telling Williams that he *would* raise the roof it it came to it.) The discussion shifted to the money KME would need to struggle on during the working party's inquiry. The merits of a working party were that it breathed life into the expiring enterprise and met Marsden's need to agree on KME's viability, which mainly revolved round the likely length of the boom in radiator demand. The four months which had elapsed since May supported Marsden's judgement, rather than that of the IDU. There might now be a revitalizing plan which both sides could accept.

Williams suggested an adjournment to see if there was any money available. (He had to extend his terms of reference from Varley during the break, because he had no mandate to agree the new proposal.)

Over lunch the KME group struggled to agree. Spriggs, Marsden and the author were for the working party; Hartland and Jenkins were against. After lunch, Silk reported that the working party was on – if KME wanted it.

'The officials are against the working party,' reported Silk. 'Then it must be a good idea,' chorused the KME group.

On reconvening, Spriggs said that, if there wasn't money, there could be industrial action. 'What – sit-in you mean?' Williams seemed startled. 'If you want to commit suicide that's sad, it's not in your members' interests.'

'The whole of Merseyside is waiting on us,' said Spriggs. 'With varying sympathy,' retorted Williams.

Guided by Binning, the meeting then worked out the conditions. The working party could make more progress if all options were open, including liquidation. Government would need a quid pro quo if it were to commit itself to the findings, and any proposal would have to be viable. There would have to be an announcement of the working party's formation and the cooperators would have to agree that it would be deciding their future. Williams felt unable to be bound by an independent group. Jack and Dick moved in. 'We'll be bound if Government will.' Their offer seemed to be accepted. Both parties would be bound to accept and act on the working party's recommendations. It looked to be an amazing *coup*.

Williams asked the author what organization was needed to make KME work. The author responded reluctantly. 'There has to be a way of not putting intolerable pressure on Jack and Dick. The conditions for money must be watertight so that it's paid on action, stage by stage, and for agreed purposes; there'll have to be external control to make it stick.'

Spriggs turned to Jenkins. 'Tony's just sacked us.'

There was another adjournment. The KME party was still split, but the dissenters were talked round. 'The Government is riding out the storm. If we don't accept what's on the table, there's nothing else, so we might as well get the train home. If we refuse, they can now say they even offered an independent assessment with Government commitment and we kicked it back.'

On reassembling, the proposal to set up a working party was agreed, subject to the limits of Government guidelines. There would be three members – one from KME and one from the Department under an independent chairman. There was another adjournment to agree its membership. 'We won't serve on it,' said the convenors. 'We're not going to be party to assassination.' KME's obvious choice was Marsden. He could argue with the IDU, was committed to the P.A. plan and could be guaranteed to represent KME excellently. He was also seen as totally honest and sincere. The civil servants wouldn't easily deflect him.

Silk was buoyant. 'It's an incredible precedent if they commit themselves in advance. They obviously want a solution. It would have been so easy to show you the door at lunchtime.'

The two sides reconvened again and the Department tabled draft terms of reference, which showed the efficient speed with which the Civil Service can – and usually does – work.* The terms were readily agreed. Williams had spoken to Varley, who chaired the EI committee which would consider KME's plea for interim relief money. A letter from Williams would be in ministers' boxes for the

---

* When it wants to make progress. When it doesn't, it's a different matter.

weekend, and a decision should be made by Tuesday 26 September. The six-hour meeting was over.

But who was in the trap?

Outside, Silk told them that only Binning had been in favour and, indeed, had initially been against it. 'Everyone else was opposed because it was such a dangerous precedent – that's why they were seeking to show that it wasn't a precedent, in order to protect their flank. They think Alan's mad. Varley thinks it's very risky.'

It had been agreed that publicity would be harmful whilst ministers were consulted. Back at KME Spriggs flannelled through another mass meeting which applauded the platform's intention to kick up a fuss at Blackpool. Spriggs told them that more Government money would mean complete restructuring at KME from top to bottom. Nothing crept out about the working party. The only press revelation was that KME had been getting TES. The *Daily Telegraph* warned Government off further aid, though much of its leader article was sympathetic to the workers' plight.

It had been a great week for KME. From the leaders being at the end of their tether, Government was now almost locked into an independent assessment which it would have to back whilst supporting the cooperative meanwhile. Truly there was life after death. The publicity had worked – thanks to Rob Rohrer's tenacity and skill.

KME waited for the clause which would bind both Government and the cooperative. Minister's reactions to the working party were favourable, said Silk, though the Department's lawyers had been worried about the problem of appearing to hand over any of the Secretary of State's powers to the working party. All was proceeding quietly and smoothly it seemed.

The following Thursday, 28 September, John Elliott had the whole story in the *Financial Times*. He had information which KME didn't even know. Williams' office felt that someone in the Department had been talking and Williams was far from pleased. The story hadn't come from KME. Elliott wrote of 'expectations in Whitehall' that KME was on the agenda for that day's Cabinet, because Varley's EI committee hadn't agreed.

As the Labour Party conference delegates were beginning to assemble at Blackpool on Friday the dispirited Williams was waiting for a decision from other ministers over the working party, knowing that the emergency resolution on KME was wending its way towards the conference arrangements committee. If accepted, it would certainly be passed. Benn was fuming over the determination to let KME go, and there was the threat of an unwholesome row at Blackpool.

Spriggs wasn't too perky either, because the uncertainty was worrying and he was in some pain. Another vehicle had run into the back of his car on the way to work, which had done his spine no good. At KME he said little and the workers didn't know what to make of it all. As one steward said, 'They're so despondent, we've run out of rumours.'

The conference was going to be difficult for Callaghan. Silk had been working hard behind the scenes and finally rang 10 Downing Street at 1 a.m. on the Saturday morning to say that if Callaghan didn't agree the working party by 9 a.m., the emergency resolution would be called at conference. The 5 per cent pay limit, oil sanctions, re-selection of MPs and the election manifesto were quite enough. Government wouldn't fight on all fronts. So it gave KME a truce. Before breakfast on Saturday, orders came from 10 Downing Street that KME could have its working party and its interim relief money, provided it called off the hostilities. Binning would spend his Saturday with the Attorney-General's department assembling the press statement announcing the working party. He was still there at 8 p.m. Williams was wondering about his own job, having been dressed down severely, and even Varley had his knuckles rapped. It was unfair to Alan. As the

KME team agreed, 'He's given us a lifeboat – but he's in it with us now.'

Though they didn't realize it, Williams wasn't in the lifeboat at all; he was safely on shore. It was true that Callaghan had objected strongly to the working party idea, since it overturned the previous May's Cabinet decision over the P.A. plan. Williams retorted to Callaghan that it would be *ultra vires* to refuse an application for aid. 'KME,' recalled Williams, 'was the sort of thing which makes for political sackings and resignations.' Although Williams felt that Jack had made a mistake in asking for the working party, in fact Spriggs had by then run out of manoeuvring room. As Hilton recollected, 'He'd kept the thing afloat on a shoestring for a long time, the market had improved and so there was the opportunity to seek a solution to what could be seen either as a heroic fight and tremendous achievement, or as a mess that couldn't go on for ever.'

Williams knew he had them trapped over the working party, since the convenors were committed to accepting the results and any plan could be backed easily by Government because it would be viable; if nothing viable came out of it the cooperators were committed to accepting the end of KME, and if the cooperators sank the solution, Williams would get public sympathy. His senior ministerial colleagues were doubtful – some because the working party device wouldn't assist KME, others because it would. But Williams knew that, no matter what went wrong after the working party, Spriggs and Jenkins would be the villains of the piece.

The convenors hadn't withdrawn the emergency resolution from the party conference but the pressure on them was mounting. If KME played hard, Government could smother KME's political allies by saying that it had been ready to help the cooperative for the fourth time and all it wanted was a bit of credit – and the directors wouldn't even give that. Spriggs played for time. He should have got hold of party chairman Joan Lestor at Blackpool and withdrawn the KME resolution, but nothing would come between him and the fortnightly ritual. He went to the match at Anfield.

Spriggs received the draft press statement via the local police just before midnight. It was soon agreed, including the Department's suggestion of the working party chairman – Professor Douglas Hague of Manchester Business School. As ex-colleague of the author, Spriggs was told of his background on the Price Commission; that he knew Margaret Thatcher well, but was highly regarded by Labour politicians such as Shirley Williams. He would be conscientious and good at the job, and would give KME a fair shake. 'He can start right away,' agreed Spriggs.

The key feature in the press statement was the binding clause. 'The Secretary of State has undertaken that he will exercise his powers to the full extent that they are available to him under the Industry Act so as to give effect to the recommendation of the working party.' KME was exultant. The cooperative was bound by the working party's recommendation, but so was Government. Varley's powers included the ability to require the NEB to take on KME.*

Sunday's IWC fringe meeting at the Blackpool conference was subdued. Gone were the optimistic days of 1975, but the same committed people were present. Stuart Holland chaired the meeting. Spriggs, Benn and Norman Atkinson all spoke. Jack told the story of the cooperative and its uphill struggle with Government. He was depressed by the Labour Government's behaviour. 'It's no good having industrial democracy if we're all on the dole.'

While the KME group was at Blackpool, the Industry Department had announced the setting up of the working party. The journey back down the motorway to Liverpool was quiet, for the group was tired. It had been an excessively exciting fortnight, even by KME's palpitating stan-

---

* Assuming the 'Industry Act' meant the 1975 Act and not the 1972 Act. There was a faint whiff of an official's attempt to backtrack to 1972 – when there was no NEB and so no powers to direct it.

dards. But they'd come a long way in two weeks. From being no-hopers, with everything stacked against them, they now had the Government locked into an analysis which would be more public and independent than anything the civil servants had previously operated.

15. A doomed solution: 1978

- Ignoring the obvious
- Another new structure
- The report emerges
- The press conference
- Worcester's bumpy ride
- A minister resigns
- Suspicion and embarrassment
- The plan disintegrates
- A night to remember
- Exit Worcester
- Worcester looks back

The following day the stewards were told that the working party would investigate everything and that Marsden would fight for the implementation of the P.A. report. The Department had nominated Hilton as its representative. 'If we'd had a choice we'd have picked him, not the hostile ones from the IDU,' said Spriggs approvingly.

'Are we giving away our opportunity to challenge the working party recommendations?' the leaders were asked. 'We're pinned down,' they answered, 'but so are Government. This is the first time, to our knowledge, that Government is bound by the findings before the investigation. It's unique. Everyone else will want the same off them. We don't know how they're going to get out of the implications, but that's their problem.' The leaders said that they would probably be the first two to go in any new scheme and so might 'be committing personal euthanasia'. The twenty three stewards backed the working-party plan – unanimously. The subsequent mass meeting was overwhelmingly in favour too, despite being warned that the working party might recommend Stelrad's much reduced employment level. About ten people voted against the platform.

The working party held its first meeting that day in London and Hague quickly indicated that he intended to write the bulk of its report. The trio had a list of potentially interested parties which included the NEB, Myson (which was interested in the customers, machinery and goodwill, but which wouldn't take it on as a going concern) and Stelrad (which was anxious not to let Myson have KME's 10 per cent share of the market). Stelrad was keen that KME didn't go to an importer like Hill Foster/Feroli and was prepared to develop manufacture at Kirkby. There were a number of other small companies ranging down to the odd one-man band. Apart from one Scottish company which was already fully stretched, the only other likely prospect was a private firm called Worcester Engineering.

Worcester had been built up from scratch by an engaging and highly capable entrepreneur named Cyril Duckworth. The firm had been manufacturing oil-fired heating boilers and, after the trauma of the 1973/4 oil crisis, had rebuilt its operations to include gas-fired boilers. It had since traded very successfully. The profits for 1977 had risen to £104,000 compared to £44,000 in 1976 and, in 1977, it had taken over Danesmoor, a loss-making subsidiary of Delta Metal, and had already turned it into profit, even though it was bigger than Worcester itself. The method was simple. Worcester cut the Danesmoor boiler range from eighteen models to five and produced some add-on packs to give the necessary variety. This immediately made the Danesmoor range more attractive to merchants who didn't have to stock so many different models, and hence could keep down their stock costs. At the end of 1976, Worcester had net assets of £228,000 and equity share capital of £40,000. Worcester was a very efficient, rapidly growing, small firm.

Duckworth had heard through the trade that KME was in trouble and, since radiator manufacture would be a logical extension of Worcester's activities, felt that it would be worth an entrepreneurial trip to Merseyside to have a look. Once there, he met Hartland, whom he thought over-enthusiastic, and Spriggs and Jenkins. He stayed late in the evening and left them saying that it needed a lot of Government money and some hard decisions, including a selective reduction in the workforce. Nothing further had ensued, but now, through Hartland, Worcester's name had been included on the working party's list.

The working party's options soon narrowed, given that it was trying to ensure continuity of production on or near the Kirkby site. This ruled out Myson, though Stelrad was still prepared to proceed with the plan which had created such a furore a few weeks earlier. Worcester also put in a proposal, and although Hague had initially felt that the Stelrad plan was more practical, it was evident that Duckworth, already a millionaire in his thirties, wanted the challenge of expanding his business. He had an excellent track record and was enthusiastic.

This was more than could be said for the NEB, which made it clear from the start that it didn't want KME in any circumstances. Ward was resolutely opposed and tried to impress the working party by telling them of his business record. Each member of the working party took a hearty dislike to him. He stated that the NEB didn't have people to manage its investments and that it would be impracticable to recruit them.

The NEB would have impressed the working party more if it had said that, yes, of course it was competent to handle the public money needed for KME; was perfectly capable of finding a good manager or two and knew perfectly well how to set up conditions which were watertight and could produce a scheme of arrangement which would be agreeable to KME's creditors and to the bank. Then, having demonstrated its competence and confidence, it could have pointed out that its board had no intention of being saddled with a political millstone and then gone on to indicate, as they did to the working party, that if the Secretary of State did instruct them to take the company, the board members would resign *en bloc*. As it was, the NEB was confusing KME's very real problems with its own motivation and managerial competence, which it was understating in an effort to repel the appalling prospect of being lumbered with KME just when it was becoming clear that the Tories would win a general election. The NEB was already being criticized for inaction on Merseyside and a fiasco at KME would have been almost the last straw. All the members of the working party felt that the NEB would have messed up KME anyway.

If the NEB was blocking off choices, so was Government. Despite his ability to order the NEB to take on KME, Varley made it plain to the working party that he was most unlikely to use his powers in that direction.* Consequently, the working party did not intend to recommend an NEB takeover. The result was an elegant reduction in the options facing KME. The NEB wouldn't take it; Varley wouldn't force them; hence the working party didn't commend that route and so Varley didn't have to break his commitment to use all his powers to put the working party's recommendations into effect, because an NEB takeover had not been recommended. You had to admire the style.

Moreover, a new condition had appeared which was somewhat less refined. Despite the fact that the Secretary of State could override the advice of IDAB, Callaghan had apparently let it be known that IDAB had to agree the recommendations or else Government would not support the working party's findings. Spriggs believed that this new retrospective condition was a piece of chicanery

---

* Hague had checked with Whitehall, feeling that it wasn't the working party's job to pre-empt ministers' choices and tell them what to do, which was somewhat at odds with the working party's original task, namely to make just such a recommendation.

and that Hague would not have taken the job if these restrictions had been there in the first place.

The working party plugged on, talking with any interested parties. It found that the bank, conscious of its image, wasn't going to rock the boat, no matter what it cost. King gave the working party the impression that he had a love–hate relationship with the place and kept insisting that he could easily let the factory once it was empty, but was then delighted when any prospective tenant or buyer appeared. Hague visited the factory at 7.45 one morning and was impressed by the prompt, indeed early, start as people worked on their daily stint to give themselves an early finish. He later visited the night shift. Arthur Andersen & Partners were brought in by the working party to check KME's financial condition. They found everything above-board and uncovered one encouraging item. Despite the fact that KME had lost nearly £700,000 in the six months to September 1978, its net liquid cash decline was only £7,000 – such was Bandell's skill in reducing stocks, sweet-talking creditors and obtaining money from debtors. The stock reduction had meant that KME was by then living hand to mouth on raw materials and had, on average, only three days' stock. This made production inefficient, but the blunt fact was that KME was only keeping going at all because of Bandell's talent. (Arthur Andersen were later prepared to offer Bandell a job, so impressed had they been by his integrity.)

The working party had been given the IDU analysis from May 1978. Officials had blotted out certain bits, but Marsden quickly found that they could be read if he held pages up to the light. There was nothing much to cavil at, he felt, except that he disagreed still with their pessimistic analysis of the prospects for radiator sales.

The working party discussed the prospects for the radiator market and in front of them appeared the departmental statistician who had been so rude about P.A.'s figures back in May. He had since revised his forecast for

radiator sales and, lo and behold, it was now almost
identical with P.A.'s May figures. Marsden said nothing.
When the man had gone, an embarrassed Brian Hilton
looked far from happy. Marsden quietly said, 'Remind
him of that May argument and tell him never again to do
what he did then.'

Ignoring the obvious

Some things hadn't changed. The leaders went, yet again,
to Manchester Business School and explained to the senior executives' programme why, although 'we've been
getting sound advice and we haven't completely ignored
it, it hasn't been implemented for a variety of reasons'.
The managers soon picked up one crucial factor.

Spriggs	We set up a council. We considered them to be a challenge to the stewards' committee and indeed to management. It won't differ in the future. The stewards will not give up their power but they still also want to adopt the normal shop stewards' role. A council would be possible, but it's got to be in the control of the trade union movement and have clear operating rules.
Jenkins	There are two well-defined roles in industry – unions and management. If there's a third body it will want to take power away from the union movement. If the union movement is strong it will kill management instead. When you've got three bodies, one will force its way in and cause a lot of problems.
Managers	That's your death-knell. You've just written your epitaph.
Spriggs	The stewards' committee has to be the government [of the enterprise] but they've got to take total responsibility for what happens. They can't sit back and bash the boss as though nothing had happened.

Managers   But you've removed management's power
              and not removed the power of the stewards
              as stewards.
Spriggs   The stewards have the power and that's how
              it will remain as long as there's a trade
              union movement.
Managers   We thought you'd removed one level of
              problem in having the cooperative. It's clear
              that you've added a layer of problem.

In one day's study the executives had diagnosed KME's
critical malady.

Another new structure

P.A. had revised its report to include an incentive scheme
on radiator production, but back at KME the convenors
continued to make heavy weather of P.A.'s recommendation that only 513 people be employed in the reformed
cooperative. They wrote to the working party, enclosing
P.A.'s updated report, but insisted on a staff of 591, thus
risking the working party seeing it as another ill-conceived
attempt to preserve over-manning. They were later persuaded to accept the P.A. figure so that their resistance
to economical manning couldn't be used against them.
'All right, we've done the usual tactic of analysing their
likely next move and going in on it,' said Spriggs privately.
'We're not ready as a nation for workers' control, and
with the experiences we've had daily in that factory, with
people outside sermonizing and moralizing, we'll have to
take a step backwards.'

Spriggs was unhappy about P.A.'s indication that Lewis
would have to go. 'It's dishonest for us to let that happen.
One man isn't responsible for it all. Even the best managers would be in a state the way we've been operating.'
It wasn't that Spriggs was insisting on the cooperative
principle – far from it. The Industrial Common Ownership
Fund had written to suggest a cooperative of 250 rather

than a risky private takeover employing 500. 'Fancy saying reduce the workforce to maintain the principle,' Jack reacted. He had more than once maintained that the cooperative was expendable if it was a barrier to further job-saving support from Government.

In between the bouts of strain, the leaders were becoming philosophical. 'If nothing else, we must go down in the annals of history. I don't think any other shop-floor people have had such an insight into politics and struggle as we have. Even if we fail, we've done more than anyone could reasonably expect of a rank and file organization.'

The convenors were still struggling to find permanent roles in the new set-up (cynics felt that they were struggling to specify jobs for themselves which the working party would accept) and had produced a new corporate structure (see Figure 4 on p. 291). There would be an upper-tier control board through which money and policy decisions would come. The convenors would be in the minority on the control board – the majority of whose members would be appointed by Varley – and which would be advised by a cooperative advisory committee of workers whose leader would be on the control board too. The stewards' committee would only be able to represent itself to the executive board, which would be appointed by the control board. It was not clear what Spriggs and Jenkins would actually *do*, though they seemed sure about the virtue of splitting themselves off from executive power. 'Whatever happens, we will have to put the workforce in a minority so the executives don't have to look over their shoulders all the time.'

Despite these gestures and assertions by the leaders, the working party seemed unimpressed by any plan which left Spriggs and Jenkins there to frustrate it. Consequently, the working party was increasingly against any scheme which put money into KME direct, even with the Department of Industry holding control. There was evident concern that the Department wouldn't be able to control the convenors, given the political bypass routes

Figure 4 The convenors' proposed corporate structure: October 1978

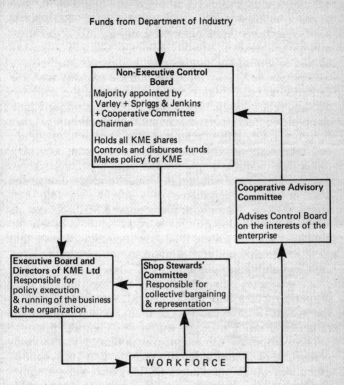

Funds from Department of Industry

Non-Executive Control Board
Majority appointed by Varley + Spriggs & Jenkins + Cooperative Committee Chairman

Holds all KME shares
Controls and disburses funds
Makes policy for KME

Cooperative Advisory Committee

Advises Control Board on the interests of the enterprise

Executive Board and Directors of KME Ltd
Responsible for policy execution & running of the business & the organization

Shop Stewards' Committee
Responsible for collective bargaining & representation

WORKFORCE

Notes
Civil servants agreed that Varley could, if he chose, appoint the majority of the Control Board to give Government control of KME's policy.
The Cooperative Advisory Committee would be of 10 cooperators, freely elected. Neither Spriggs or Jenkins could be on it.
The stewards' committee would be cut off from any links with the Control Board and would resume the normal collective bargaining role. Spriggs and Jenkins couldn't be stewards or convenors.
The Cooperative Advisory Committee would not become involved in day to day matters nor issues of collective bargaining.

which the two used unceasingly. The working party was
not impressed by the idea of the control board or the idea
of external trustees to control KME. They had several
basic objections. First, they believed that, if the business
was to be saved, any public money would have to go in
almost *in toto* at the moment of reconstruction. Second,
the convenors had by then lost much credibility with the
Department, with major creditors and with the bank, so
that any scheme which left them at Kirkby produced damaging side-effects to the scheme's acceptability. Hence
P.A. was repeatedly challenged over its plan to introduce
and take responsibility for an executive team at KME,
for, if P.A. produced a plan which Jack and Dick agreed,
it created a climate wherein the consultants were regarded
with suspicion – no matter how sound they felt their
proposal to be. As an insurance policy, KME's opponents
in the Industry Department were slagging Marsden behind his back and asking P.A. how it could *guarantee* that
Jack and Dick wouldn't interfere in any new plan, given
their ingenuity and commitment. Of course, P.A. couldn't
give a guarantee; the consultants' view was that, with the
proper structure and Jack and Dick committed to it, it
was worse to have the two of them ejected from KME
rather than inside using their four years' experience.

The whispering campaign even attacked P.A.'s competence and commitment to ensuring that its seconded
executives would succeed at KME, which was going beyond sense, for, apart from KME's fees, what advantage
could possibly accrue to P.A. if it were associated with a
half-hearted failure? The slur on P.A. was superfluous. In
short, the working party felt that external control could
not be made to work, even if the Government-supported
controllers held the purse strings.

The working party was, nevertheless, looking for a way
of preserving some elements of a cooperative. Unknown
to KME, it commissioned solicitors Slaughter & May,
who prepared an elaborate scheme which would give an
incoming owner 75 per cent of the shares in the new

KME, with the rest held by employees via a trust. It would have met the need for external control, some employee participation and the carry-over of some of KME's £4 million tax losses. The scheme didn't find favour with prospective purchasers, since Stelrad wouldn't employ Spriggs and Jenkins on any terms and Worcester wasn't going to run Kirkby on different lines to Worcester itself.

By early November the options had narrowed down to Worcester, which had submitted a detailed 26–page proposal for the takeover of KME.

KME knew little about the firm. They had visited Worcester's premises quietly and found pictures on the walls of Peter Walker, Tory MP for Worcester and ex-Secretary of State for Industry. The leaders believed that Walker was associated with Worcester and had received telephone calls from anonymous informers in Worcester to the effect that Walker was involved. Even Duckworth's initiative in visiting Kirkby was to count against Worcester. Spriggs was later to recall, 'I didn't like the way he dropped out of the clouds that day.'

The fact was that while KME believed that the formation of the working party had locked Government into a steely embrace, ministers had, for the first time, taken control of events. The convenors were alternately fretful and philosophical about their loss of initiative. 'We've done all we could; we've pulled every stroke in the book. You've got to decide what being progressive means. It isn't always to fight the management. You begin to appreciate the finer points of the commercial world and become less blindly committed.' Spriggs recognized that Government wouldn't give more money direct to the cooperative. 'We've had too many bites at that cherry. We can't bite our way through the stone.'

The flux round the working party now seemed intense and the leaders were not reassured when the expected date and manner of presentation of its report seemed to change daily. The convenors didn't know whether they were being led a dance but suspected that Williams was being rocked about by changing instructions from various senior quarters.

Finally, it was decided that the leaders would receive the report on the evening of Wednesday 15 November 1978, immediately after it had been considered by IDAB. The leaders would have little time to absorb it but could then have a stewards' meeting before the working party presented its report to the KME mass meeting at 8 a.m. the following day. The convenors and the working party would then fly to London immediately to join Alan Williams at a London press conference to announce the agreed solution, in time for the lunchtime news. That was a good sign for the convenors, for 'Williams won't want to be associated with a shambles. If there was nothing in it, he'd want the press conference in Outer Mongolia.' (Nobody at KME knew that if IDAB turned the working party solution down, Williams would have stayed away and Hague would have chaired the press conference in Manchester.)

The report emerges

The week of the report was busy to say the least. It didn't even start quietly. On Monday, right-wing Conservative MP Michael Grylls called for KME to be broken up and the bits returned to the private sector. The effect was probably counter-productive and more likely to stiffen the Labour Government's intention to help KME. That evening it was announced that Dunlop's Speke factory, a few miles from KME, faced possible closure with the loss of 2,400 jobs.

Elliott was trawling his contacts to build the story of the report's delivery and on Tuesday 14 November the *Financial Times* printed the recommendations of the report, which Government, IDAB and KME had yet to see. Elliott's comprehensive article named Worcester and detailed its plans to invest several million pounds in KME. Everyone was irritated by the story. Nobody knew where it had come from and everyone privately accused every-one else. Yet it was clear that Elliott had known of Worcester for a while and Spriggs accepted that he had probably let it out accidentally by mentioning 'a firm in the Midlands . . . near Worcester', he might even have said 'the Worcester firm'.

Elliott had eliminated the other runners and then looked up Worcester Engineering in the local telephone directory, and rung up to ask its finance director what was happening.

When the story broke, Duckworth was regretful. He hadn't realized how much trouble the press could create. As the media buzzed around, Elliott was able to tell the bemused convenors that the report would be finished that evening and would be submitted to IDAB, ministers and probably the Prime Minister in the morning. It would, said Elliott, be released at the press conference after the KME mass meeting the next day. It was nice to find that somebody knew what was going on.

On Wednesday Elliott was again able to keep the con-venors informed, ringing them in the evening as he re-searched his story for the day of the report, and asked had Spriggs heard that IDAB had still been discussing it at 7 p.m. and had eventually agreed the Worcester proposal?

Some IDAB members hadn't wanted to waste time or public money on this perpetually non-viable operation. However, the IDU had backed the Worcester solution as had Hilton, who had led the team presenting the working party's recommendation to IDAB.

The news failed to cheer the despondent convenors. 'After all,' said Dick, 'does any of it matter? Ministers only wanted a clear run at the party conference; they won't mind if the Worcester scheme fails now.' Silk pro-vided the only straw worth clutching since he had already tabled an early day motion in the House calling on the Government to put KME into the NEB. Given the Government's minority position to the Commons, the fifty MPs who had signed the motion knew that the Labour administration would face acute difficulty in trying to force such a move through the House. But it was a cheering gesture which was to be over-valued by the two leaders.

The IDAB meeting over, Hilton caught the late train to Liverpool to meet Marsden and the convenors. Discussions went on until 2.30 a.m.

The 7 a.m. stewards' meeting was a subdued affair. The working notes about cutting out tea breaks and forgetting 'scores' etc. were still on the blackboard from February (see p. 236). Only one of them had been actioned. It seemed a fitting background.

Spriggs told them of all the companies which had talked to the working party and which had then walked away. He complained about the 'carefully defined leaks, let out deliberately to give Worcester a head- start'. Worcester would employ 460 and doubtless would come in quickly to negotiate the terms and conditions they'd want with the unions, since they wanted the takeover cut and dried within two weeks. 'It's the job of the unions to get the best conditions for their workers'.

Steward John Murphy was worried that Worcester would run off with the business. He was told that the Government's £3 million shares would be in Worcester itself; that Worcester was taking a big risk investing millions in KME and since it had no radiator capacity of its own it couldn't make KME radiators elsewhere. It was true that Worcester would be getting 10 per cent of the radiator market, but it was also getting the chance to lose £1.5 million a year. Spriggs had seen the political writing on the wall. 'I'm probably the sickest person among you, but other MPs have lost factories too. How could we get them to fight for us if we turn down a £6 million plan?'

Another steward made his contribution. 'This is the biggest decision we've ever faced. We're not here to make a decision; let the mass meeting decide.' Spriggs was disgusted that the stewards might yet again duck their responsibility, but, before he could voice his feelings, Murphy chipped in again. 'We're here to give a lead', he insisted. And they did. The stewards agreed to recommend the Worcester proposal by twenty votes to four. The four dissenters wanted Government's £3 million to come direct to KME.

The steward's meeting ended. None of the stewards had asked to see the working party report. (None ever did. It was pathetic, Spriggs recalled later.)

The public address operator played Verdi's *Requiem* as the cooperators assembled to hear Spriggs give them the same outline facts as he had laid before the stewards. He told them of the stewards' recommendations, and added, 'I'm not pushing people to accept the scheme and the stewards have only recommended it after a lot of heart-searching.' There was, he said, no alternative. Hague expressed his regret that the scheme couldn't have been more palatable. The working party had tried very hard with both NEB and Government, but the NEB had said 'No' three times and Varley had declined to insist.

He told the meeting that KME needed more effective marketing but 'I'm impressed with the way you all work. There's not much wrong with the production,* . . . We commissioned a complicated document to show buyers how it could remain a cooperative even when they had taken it over, but nobody would accept it.'

Hague was referring to Slaughter & May's report which stated that KME's trading losses of over £4 million probably constituted KME's most valuable single asset and every precaution must be taken to preserve them for tax purposes, complex though the method might be. It contradicted the civil servants who had consistently pooh-poohed the suggestion that KME's tax losses were valuable to another radiator company. Their argument was that the Inland Revenue might claim that the losses were

---

* Spriggs later told him that he'd created a problem. 'They'll think they're all good workers.'

due to the drinks business. But even half the losses would
have been worth a net £1 million to a qualifying purchaser
like Stelrad or Myson. The Slaughter & May report was
not released publicly or given to KME.

'It is the first time,' continued Hague, 'that a KME
proposal has been backed by the Department and there
is substantial support in Whitehall which has never been
there before . . . Worcester might be able to develop the
business, and in ten years' time there might be more than
four hundred and sixty jobs.' There was murmuring, near
laughter from the cooperators. Ten years!

Hague also pointed out that Worcester wanted to continue contract work and Accadiair – not just make radiators. Hilton reinforced the point that Worcester would be
tied to KME and would be investing in new production
machinery.

Spriggs warned that if negotiations took too long KME
could become unattractive to Worcester and there would
be nothing left. 'We have at least brought some sanity
and some jobs.' But he also transmitted a more defiant
message. 'It's up to the trade union movement to negotiate as hard as in the past. They'll be negotiating for an
anniversary rise from the first of April and there should
be something above the statutory amount for those who
are going. Dick and I will sit down and squeeze everything
we can for them. We should sacrifice, but not grovel.'

'Jack's back in his steward's role and feeling a lot happier,' whispered Hilton. He was right.

Spriggs agreed with a questioner that the NEB taking
over KME would be ideal and 'the leadership will see if
at the thirteenth hour some sensible views can be brought
into the Cabinet. If we had a strong Minister . . . ' The
meeting accepted the Worcester proposal overwhelmingly. About twenty voted against, but were they voting
against Worcester or for Jack to have another knock at
Government?

The press conference

The meeting over, the working party and the convenors flew to London for the press conference where the report would be presented publicly. These arrangements had been made so that the findings could be presented by Government in an orderly way after the cooperators had been given the first chance to see what was proposed for them – but before every single thing had leaked out. Spriggs had a different view. 'Delivering the report at near midnight; having a stewards' meeting at seven a.m., then a mass meeting at eight, and then a mad dash to London for an immediate press conference is a classic technique for pushing people along.'

The report was introduced to the assembled reporters. Just as the leaks had suggested, it was scathing about KME's behaviour (though readers will find its judgements unsurprising, given the analysis of KME's various advisers throughout its life).

The workers' council, it stated, had ceased to meet after the first few months. 'KME is therefore not a co-operative in the sense that this term would be understood by the cooperative movement as a whole. Indeed, communication between "management" and the shop-floor in KME seems no better, and in some ways worse, than in most other companies . . . the leaders were also finding it difficult to transmit a sense of urgency to the workforce and to gain acceptance for unpalatable actions.' P.A. recommended (March 1978) that 'there should be a clear separation between the responsibilities of the directors and those of the remainder of the management team'.

The working party found that, between March and September, apart from the closing of the Constor and drinks activities, none of the recommendations in the P.A. report had been carried out. . . .

'In July 1978 P.A. prepared a self-financing incentive scheme for KME but it has still to be introduced.' Yet KME had a very good order-book for radiators, was turning business away and had next to no stocks of radiators.

The technical and marketing development staff was too small: 'KME never seems to have had sufficient marketing resources to obtain the orders it needed . . . or to have made a sustained effort to do so. . .

'KME has lacked decisive management. Unpleasant decisions have been postponed; forecasts have not been achieved. As a result management has lost credibility.'

The most damning paragraphs concerned the worker directors' role:

'KME has not used its status as a cooperative to develop a new organizational structure. The firm is managed on traditional lines with the directors acting effectively* as its senior management. The other managers do not take a full share in decisions; nor are they fully informed about internal and external developments . . .

'The shop stewards' committee, with the two directors, takes policy decisions, but the shop stewards are often in a difficult position. On the shop-floor, they frequently find themselves acting in opposition to decisions taken on the shop stewards' committee. KME has the worst of both worlds: it has failed to develop a new form of organization as a cooperative, but under workers' control its traditional, hierarchical structure is not functioning well.'

The working party thought that 'it would be unwise to assume that KME's performance will change in future unless external pressures ensure that it does'. The working party's strictures sounded familiar.

It had considered three basic options for continuation at Kirkby: receivership/liquidation, a cooperative or a takeover. The working party had rejected the first because it would only save a maximum of 225 jobs inside a purpose-built factory for Stelrad (which wasn't named). Furthermore, there could be no guarantee that a receiver or liquidator would accept Stelrad's plan as the best sol-

---

* This meant 'in effect'. If only they *had* been acting effectively.

ution for the creditors. This conclusion left the choice between a cooperative and a takeover.

The working party had considered funds coming direct from the Industry Department, but despite KME's proposal for control to rest with the Department, the working party sold the pass. Funds would have to be able to cut off promptly if the plan was not being carried out. (This was exactly the condition proposed by the convenors as evidence of their commitment to make a decisive change at KME). No monitoring process 'of the type we envisage' would work because 'the funds requested would have to be used almost at once'. Hence, they deduced it would not be practicable to fund KME directly from the Department. (The point about funds being used almost at once wasn't necessarily true, but it's what they said. The collective sigh of relief from the Department must have been impressive.)

The working party also rejected the NEB solution. 'The NEB has pointed out that it is not its policy, and consequently it does not have the resources, to engage in the management of its investments.' (The NEB's lack of interest could not simply be ascribed to torpor and incompetence. It had strong doubts whether KME could earn an adequate return on the funds invested and there was a basic logic in the NEB's anathema, since there were no signs that KME would act as a competent business except under duress. The fallacy in the NEB's argument was that it wouldn't have had to *manage* its investment – but merely to set the ground rules via its control of the resources which KME needed. The NEB, Hague and Hilton all felt that, whilst this point about management was often true, in KME's case the likelihood was that Spriggs' and Jenkins' ingenuity would quickly make the NEB's intervention inevitable.)

The working party's solution consequently involved a takeover by Worcester Engineering coupled to the end of the cooperative framework. Worcester was proposing to treble its turnover by taking on 460 of KME's employees to make radiators, presswork and Accadiair. Nearly £4 million would be spent on machinery improvements and a new radiator production line. The acquisition would give Worcester a sound base in the radiator market which would help to develop Worcester's business economically. Barclays Bank would finance Worcester, and Government would invest £3 million in Worcester itself, which would therefore be at risk if the Merseyside venture failed. Worcester couldn't amputate the Kirkby operation to save the parent company as IPD had done. The small but growing enterprise would take over KME as a going concern and so would assume liability for KME's creditors and the bank's overdraft. Overall, Worcester intended to invest £8.3 million in itself and KME. Government would give a regional development grant of £680,000 and an interest relief grant of £500,000.

The press conference was a lively affair. Spriggs had a knock at Williams, the working party and the NEB. He had been led to believe that if he attacked the NEB, Hague would back him up, but he was wrong. 'It's a sorry day for the Labour Government', he declared as he clashed publicly with Williams who said that neither Government nor the NEB agreed with his NEB proposal. The leaders and Silk made it clear to the reporters that they would still campaign for the NEB to take KME over. 'We will not impede the Worcester takeover but I hope we can persuade the Government to get the NEB in before Worcester finally signs.'

Spriggs' chagrin was deepened by Williams' statement that, although the cooperative had cost the taxpayer £5.5 million in aid since its launch, it had saved Government between £9 and £10 million in unemployment benefits. Spriggs and Silk looked at each other. It had been exactly what they had been telling Government – to no previous avail. What then, from the State's view, *was* viability – particularly since KME's demise would have immediately increased Britain's import bill, probably permanently? 'This only goes to prove what sort of social function a workers' cooperative can provide', said Spriggs. 'For every pound the Government has spent on us, we have saved it two.'

A *Daily Telegraph* journalist pursued a fascinating admission by Williams that IDAB had only agreed to support the Worcester plan on certain conditions, which he refused to disclose in case it jeopardized the deal. The convenors stirred uneasily. Soon after the press conference broke up, they had their fears confirmed. They became lost in the Department and bumped into Bob Cryer. One of IDAB's conditions, said Cryer, was that Stelrad should take an equity stake in Worcester. The convenors weren't surprised. Williams had told the press conference that the only alternative to Worcester was a liquidation which would save no more than 200 jobs. That could only mean one thing – Stelrad was still lurking in the background. This made sense from several angles. Stelrad could supply expertise and also provide a financial safety net for Worcester. The sum of £8.3 million was immense. Surely Worcester, even with its retained profits, couldn't afford to borrow £3 million from the bank and slot in another £3 million preference Government shares on its tiny equity base of £40,000. It would become more highly geared than a Ferrari.

Worcester's bumpy ride

These worries were all in the leaders' minds as they returned to Kirkby to ponder their next moves. They now had the backstop of Worcester and its Government support, which made it difficult for KME's critics to sustain the argument that there was no market for the cooperative's products. If private enterprise was prepared to come in, how could anyone – even the NEB – claim that Kirkby couldn't be viable?

Spriggs decided to try to get into the NEB to save the cooperative instead, although critics felt that his interest in the NEB route lay in the additional chance it gave for him and Dick to retain some power. The leaders' tactic carried the risk that Worcester would depart – without KME having reached the haven of the NEB. Yet, with the impending closure of the Dunlop factory at Speke, the politics seemed, on the surface, to be all moving KME's way.

The working party's* Worcester plan soon ran into trouble. Duckworth told Radio Merseyside's listeners what he proposed to do at KME. One of the listeners was Spriggs. It wasn't Duckworth's fault that Spriggs became irate, for the leaders – feeling proprietorially righteous despite the working party's devastating indictment of their competence – were looking for trouble, believing that Worcester could be treated roughly since it was too deep into the proposal to walk away easily.

The meetings between Worcester and the convenors soon became unrelaxed and the misunderstandings mounted with grim inevitability. The leaders wanted to know the position over the lease, the bank and the creditors. Duckworth wanted to talk about productivity, manning levels and incentives. Neither party seemed to grasp the reason for the other's worries.

The convenors were worried about their position as directors of KME, for their personal responsibilities ùnder Section 332 had been flung at them so often that they needed to know what would happen. Duckworth was concerned that Spriggs and Jenkins were undermining Worcester, though not intentionally, as they told the bank, BSC and King what Worcester was proposing. Duckworth told the convenors that it was nothing to do with them: if Worcester could get a better deal for itself with KME's creditors, it would.

Worcester had tried to induce Government to accept the burden of any undisclosed liabilities which could come to light in the depths of KME. Government refused – which only made Worcester suspicious of what might

* Described in the *Morning Star* as a 'burial party'.

emerge later. The convenors' concern was later amplified when KME's lawyers wrote that Worcester's takeover could be a fraudulent preference against any creditor left behind, since Worcester seemed to have no intention of taking over undisclosed creditors – which could lay Spriggs and Jenkins open to personal liability under Section 332 of the Companies Act. The lawyers continued 'the scheme seems wholly to be for the benefit of Worcester . . . so that first, they might carry forward and take advantage of any of KME's [tax] losses and that secondly, they avoid taking the responsibilities of undisclosed creditors'.

Hence, the convenors were suspicious of Worcester's intentions and the effects on themselves, while Worcester was suspicious of Government's reluctance to take on any liability and was telling the convenors to keep out of negotiations. It would have been hard to find a more potent device for creating mutual suspicion. But they did. It was Stelrad.

Duckworth confirmed that IDAB wanted Stelrad to be involved with his expansion plan at Kirkby, though he wasn't very keen on it. He didn't reveal what had already happened. (This was all explained to the author by Duckworth in 1980. The author had no contact with Worcester during the life of the cooperative.) Duckworth had gone to Stelrad's chief executive and said, 'We don't know enough technically on radiators, but you'd rather have us in there than foreigners.' This was true. The importers recruited good people and, once established, they were difficult to shift. 'You might prefer not to be involved yourselves', continued Duckworth.' The unions couldn't hit at Worcester but they could hit Stelrad.' (This was also true. After the September story about Stelrad, Spriggs had told Williams that he'd let Stelrad know that, if it took over, it would be faced with a strike.) Duckworth obtained Stelrad's blessing. The big firm wanted an option to buy KME, and with these assurances that Stelrad would pick it up from Worcester if things went awry, Duckworth was able to proceed. The Department's officials had jumped the gun though and, fearing that IDAB would turn down the working party's proposal, had, without speaking to Stelrad or Worcester, already put the Stelrad involvement into the scheme. IDAB liked it and made the idea a condition to be actioned in some form. 'We wouldn't have had Stelrad near Kirkby with us – it was dynamite', said Duckworth, 'but it was all right to link with them at a technical level – say ten per cent. We realized the Department was trying to help us to succeed. That's why our price kept going up.'

Meanwhile Elliott and Rohrer were both picking up the Stelrad story and the leaders felt that Stelrad's involvement would certainly explain Barclays' lending Worcester several million pounds. Perhaps, they deduced accurately, Stelrad had given a contingent promise to pick up the pieces, should Worcester fail.

Perturbed by the worries about Stelrad and the creditors, the convenors then found that Duckworth wanted to negotiate a new working agreement with the six unions while they, as convenor directors, remained on the sidelines. 'If I were him,' said Spriggs, 'I'd do a deal with us two and get us to announce and sell it as the only possible plan'. By sidelining the convenors at the start, Duckworth had upset them and the stewards. The convenors weren't going to be seen to have sold out and wouldn't be elbowed out of the negotiations. Spriggs was warned that KME could end up with nothing and that the convenors might push their luck too far. They, in turn, felt that Worcester was weak or fronting unenthusiastically for others and it might as well be brought out into the open. Once again they were trying to flush out further facts so that they could gamble from a position of knowledge.

A minister resigns

On 20 November, Bob Cryer resigned over KME. He had failed to persuade Callaghan to aid KME either directly or via the NEB. His responsibility for small businesses had been whittled away and he had also long been out of sympathy with a number of Government policies. Civil servants felt that his loyalties had been divided to the point where they were more and more reluctant to give him information for fear of its usage. In the early days he had been responsible for cooperatives, but now KME had proved the last straw. He had asked for the KME papers to read, and they had not been put in his box. In a cutting gesture, Callaghan did not replace Cryer, and his remaining duties were reallocated.

Spriggs felt that Cryer had given a lead, though it didn't necessarily strengthen KME's position. 'We may become a political football, and footballs just get kicked'. KME's favourite analogy was taken up by Elliott in the *Financial Times* the next morning where he tellingly described KME's history as 'a political own-goal . . . a political issue of a magnitude out of all proportion to its importance', because of its symbolic role in the tussle over Labour's industrial policy.

Elliott quoted Varley on the need to strengthen the cooperative's management. 'The NEB does not itself have the staff or resources to manage companies in which it invests', stated Varley. It was perhaps unfortunate that another article in the same issue of the *Financial Times* announced that the venture capital subsidiary of the Industrial and Commercial Finance Corporation was to begin to take part in the management of some of its investments because 'without participative management the odds against (ICFC's) success are very much increased'. This made the NEB look even more feeble than before and Varley was probably right when he continued that 'the major management problem in KME's present cooperative form would not be solved by an NEB acquisition'. It appears doubtful that Varley realized how crushingly insulting he was being about the NEB.

The NEB was coming under well-deserved pressure in

the North-West. Its regional board had made just one investment in the Merseyside special development area and only four others in the whole region.

The NEB soon launched an attempt to recover its assaulted reputation, by revealing that it was to improve the long-term management of its companies. 'The NEB's aim is to provide a framework for successful development of the company . . . a means of measuring performance against previous forecasts and a recorded commitment to action.' It was almost what the NEB had indicated it could not do for KME, just a few weeks earlier.

Suspicion and embarrassment

On 23 November, Duckworth laid his plans before the KME stewards. The meeting was not a success. There would be no extra severance pay beyond statutory amounts and the 260 redundancies were not negotiable. The general theme was that managers would manage and workers would get on with the work. The people from each union would negotiate the detailed redundancies. The results of his presentation were ominous. It stiffened the fight to save the cooperative, since nobody knew who would be redundant and Duckworth wasn't giving much money to the leavers. Mind you, it was no use Spriggs pretending that this was all Worcester's fault. He and Jenkins were already uncooperative.

Ignorance about who would be going could readily have been reduced by the convenors tabling their own 'shadow plan' for redundancies and going through the schedules, department by department. Worcester's submission had been based on the condition of selective redundancy – just as had been the convenors' intention earlier in the year. Duckworth may have felt that his providing 460 jobs should be enough cause for gratitude, but he was being seen by some as a hatchet man. 'If I'd wanted to lead a revolution, he couldn't have done a better job to promote it', reported Spriggs after the meeting. 'I've had to pacify the stewards and say we mustn't be seen to kill it.' It wasn't even clear that KME's managers were enthused by Worcester, though Bandell thought the takeover was a near certainty. Was Duckworth going to last? 'If I'd been him,' said Spriggs, 'I'd have walked out this morning.'

The climate deteriorated rapidly. Worcester was being tipped off by cooperators alleging that Spriggs was putting notices on the boards saying that Worcester was only a pawn in the move to obtain help from the NEB.

The leaders' resistance was being stiffened by the realization that there would be no executive positions for them in the new system, coupled to a belief that their political support was growing in Cabinet. Labour's National Executive Committee had passed an emergency resolution and would send a delegation to Callaghan to seek reconsideration of the cooperative's fate. The leaders were told that Varley and Williams seemed scared of something new slipping out. Stelrad had reported buoyant sales such that very strong demand was 'necessitating an increase in manufacturing facilities', so that KME's business prospects were evidently good.

Jenkins went to see Duckworth at Worcester, driven there by the transport manager Alan Johnstone who sat outside in the car while Jenkins discussed the convenors' futures with Duckworth. The two convenors knew that Worcester wouldn't have them on site because it felt that they would be disruptive. Jenkins suggested that he, Spriggs and Johnstone should be floated off to run a semi-independent transport operation handling KME's steel and radiators. It was not much different from a new P.A. proposal in which Spriggs would have become distribution and purchasing director with Johnstone under him. Duckworth refused, not wanting to be in the grip of the convenors in any fashion and not much liking the sound of the proposal. In the end, Jenkins negotiated non-executive consultancy fees for the two convenors and agreed with Duckworth that the mutual sniping in the press and television should cease.

Worcester later began to receive anonymous information from KME about a haulage company which did business with KME and whose directors allegedly were Mrs
Spriggs and Mrs Johnstone. A cooperator had told
Worcester that wagons went out at night with instructions
that they weren't to be stopped. There was no evidence
to support this allegation, only that wagons that had been
loaded and sheeted up the night before would be allowed
out, because the hauliers' drivers were reluctant to weigh
out again and perhaps have to unsheet their vehicles.
(These objections could have been easily dealt with by a
different weighing procedure. Worcester intended to
bring the CID in, if it took over, so that the stories could
be killed once and for all. KME had always been alive
with indiscriminate rumours, and indeed, Spriggs and Jenkins had instructed Lewis to bring in the CID after one
bout of rumours, but the police could find no evidence of
organized theft.)

The leaders visited Williams at his request, since he
wanted to check up on progress. They intended to ask
him to reconvene the working party to consider the NEB
option again. The meeting started relaxedly enough.
Williams was informed that there had been no letter of
offer from Worcester.

The convenors asked for the resumption of the working
party on the 'evidence' from Marsden and Hague that
they would have recommended the NEB if there hadn't
been political pressure. Williams became angry. He and
Varley *had* been prepared to recommend the NEB and
would have used all their powers; they hadn't said that
they *wouldn't* but that they *wished not to*. It was a bit
subtle as a defence.

Rohrer's new *Sunday Times* article was a thorough embarrassment for Government. It revealed that Varley and
Williams had accepted Stelrad's refusal to have the two
convenors remain at Kirkby and had approved secret
plans to sack Spriggs and Jenkins. Benn had been approached to find them 'quango' jobs. (This was utterly

naive of the Industry Department which had asked the ex-Lord Stansgate, known as a fierce critic of patronage, to place his friends. The Industry Department's reasoning was that the Energy Department had more such jobs in its gift, and after all, the convenors were Benn's embarrassing creations – there was justice in letting him sort out the wretched problem. The proposal had the added attraction of making a hypocrite of Benn, had he accepted.)

Williams backed Worcester again and said that 'no business has had more goodwill from us [than KME]. But how much more money do we have to pump in before they realize it is not going to work?' Spriggs accused the Government of chicanery over Stelrad. 'It is for the KME workers to decide on their leadership.'

The plan disintegrates

The exploding parcel had split into several pieces and now everyone had an explosive segment that they couldn't pass to anyone else; and the climate worsened day by day. The *Telegraph* revealed that Worcester was meeting commercial difficulties as KME's creditors tried to hold out for better terms, given the aid now on offer. Cryer twisted the knife in Williams and Varley. 'I am sorry that the hostile advice from the civil servants fell on ears too eager to listen.' The *Financial Times* printed the story of the convenors' jobless consultancy posts with Worcester. Hague told Marsden that he'd never have become chairman of the working party if he'd known that IDAB could veto its conclusions or put in conditions.

Spriggs was reported as declining to be 'bought off', whilst Duckworth complained about 'politically motivated' negotiations.

'Why don't you go into Parliament?' Duckworth had asked Spriggs. 'I do,' came the response, 'but I only get as far as the policeman at the desk.'

Spriggs felt that the trouble lay in Worcester not being

quite strong enough to work and not weak enough to ignore. 'We can make a profit,' declared Spriggs. 'P.A. showed us that. It's whether we've got the guts to do it – that's what you've always said, Tony. We would have done it one day. It's extremely regrettable that we didn't before.' Yet he was now resisting once again. Cynics at KME believed that Worcester was doomed as soon as the convenors realized that they would be stripped of power. The stewards and the workforce might be suspicious of Duckworth – but who was planting the suspicions?

There was a haze of confusion and suspicion obscuring almost all the facts, and the convenors didn't know what to believe. Hague had privately said that he didn't know whether Worcester was brave, mad, or both. The leaders learned from Duckworth that BSC could 'sing for its supper' and that Worcester might not now buy the freehold – though King had told them that he wouldn't grant Worcester a tenancy. It didn't much matter what was true and what was false by now; the climate of suspicion was not being improved by anything approaching candour or trust. The arguments raged inside the cooperative as to what needed to be done and whether Worcester was a good idea. Not one steward had asked to see the working party report – or even a précis of it. Nor had Lewis or Bandell. Nobody had.

The next KME mass meeting on 30 November was a tetchy affair. A motion from the floor called for negotiations to be broken off. The convenors persuaded the meeting to give a two-week deadline so that Worcester could answer the basic takeover questions.

Later that day the KME negotiating committee – two members from each of the six unions – met Duckworth and his works manager. The Worcester duo made it clear that they didn't intend to keep the convenors on site once they had taken over. Duckworth tabled a twenty-page document on working conditions, pay rates and incentive proposals. He was trying to clear the air, provide reassurance and make progress. Little resulted. KME believed that its creditors, bank and landlord were all dissatisfied with Worcester's plans; that the firm would phase out Accadiair and that Stelrad would own the business within six months.

Duckworth had tried to explain the Worcester plan, which put the firm clearly in the management role at KME. The negotiating committee ran to and fro consulting Spriggs and Jenkins repeatedly. Spriggs began to preach to Duckworth and the stewards about the ideals of a cooperative, but Duckworth reacted that he didn't think much of the job they'd done; he didn't agree with their policy and instead of paying people wages – and Worcester's were higher – they'd have been more secure if they'd invested in proper machinery, products and methods.

KME's negotiating group asked for union combine facilities with Worcester's own operations and asserted that they'd soon get Duckworth's employees in a union. 'They'll make up their own minds,' responded Duckworth, 'and negotiations will be independent; this is a separate factory.'

One steward opined that 'some people out there in the factory think you're the Messiah. We don't – we think you're the devil.'

'We're militant,' insisted the stewards,' and you're not used to dealing with militants.'

'Really?' replied Duckworth. 'You don't look very militant to me.'

A night to remember

They kept Duckworth talking all day, and he waited, having asked to walk round the factory without convenors or stewards so that he could talk to the people he'd be employing. Finally they said he could talk to the night shift at 11 p.m. It was a moment which embedded itself in his memory. 'As long as I live I'll never forget that night. We hadn't got thirty yards before we were each

surrounded by twenty or thirty people firing questions.
Some said we were a bunch of crooks, a rip-off. Others
were talking about production rates and conditions. I
wasn't totally put off by that – they'd been boiled up,
there was no doubt about it. We felt there was a decent
bunch of chaps there if only you could get to them, but
as long as Spriggs and Jenkins were around they would
manipulate us and them and the business would go. The
welders seemed to be dead keen on our incentive productivity scheme even if they were belligerent that night.
I thought I'd got on well with them, but it's difficult when
someone's saying things behind your back. When we left
we decided that we'd give it another week and then get
on with running our own business. Our works manager
– a socialist – had wanted to keep the place going and
save jobs; he'd have been works manager at Kirkby and
we'd have put one or two other people in quickly. After
the experience that night he said we were wasting our
time there.'

Williams tried to head Spriggs off by suggesting that
the agreement with Worcester should include all employment conditions, but not commercial negotiations. But
the convenor's suspicions about deeper plots were accentuated by the news that Ford's engine plant at Bridgend
was now apparently getting £147 million in grants. The
Industry Department had previously stated the aid to be
£75 million. There was always some hidden agenda, mut-
tered Jenkins, and why did a tiny firm like Worcester
keep coming back to KME for more punishment? If the
convenors were in the way and Worcester was serious,
wondered Spriggs, why didn't Duckworth tell the
negotiating committee, 'Chase these two, it's your only
chance'?

KME badly needed a leak from Stelrad. (It never came.
Stelrad was watertight.) Jack rejected the author's suggestion that the Worcester deal should be tentatively agreed
with the condition that Stelrad was never to be involved
in ownership – unless it controlled the whole of Worces-

ter, which would mean that Worcester couldn't sell KME off to Stelrad.

Exit Worcester

Worcester cancelled the meeting with Accadiair, whom it had yet to meet. Duckworth was tired after the KME trip. The convenors felt that Duckworth was jumping from issue to issue without resolving any of them. All issues were interdependent, but one had to start somewhere. Was the obvious place the workforce? The convenors wanted Worcester to clear itself with landlord, creditors and bank before it began to negotiate all the internal matters. Worcester felt that it wasn't worth finalizing those if the internal climate was unresolved.

It was all suspiciously deadlocked on 7 December when Williams announced that Worcester had pulled out – exactly a week after the meeting with the night shift. Duckworth accused Spriggs of manipulating the workforce and obstructing the commitments made to Government by KME. The convenors believed that Williams would be roasted by his ministerial colleagues for being seen to have botched a solution yet again. Nobody at KME realized that their rejection of Worcester had, in fact, made Williams almost totally fireproof.

Worcester looks back

Throughout the life of KME, Worcester was the only enterprise solidly prepared to put money into the Kirkby venture. It might have been taking a big risk. Nevertheless, in 1980 Duckworth looked back without much doubt:

'There was and is a market there. The merchants had said there was room for another maker. They've been let down by Thorn and Myson before. The most significant factor was that there was a lot of Government money available at no interest and then low rates.

'I went to Schlatter in Switzerland to look at the latest equipment and felt we could install a new production line with back-projection welding which cuts the labour force dramatically and which you need because, on radiators, there's always an air of discontent when you have guys with a reasonable skill who don't like the repetition and who know they should be doing something better. All the makers have had troubles in that area. It seemed to me to be the opportunity to be first with a very automated line. I like to feel I have the courage of my convictions and, unlike lots of British management, we were interested in automating into volume business.

'The trouble was that the new line would take eighteen months to build. Meanwhile we would continue with the existing radiators – there's a good market for premium radiators like Toprad – and we'd use natural wastage to take the workforce down and a bonus scheme to keep output up. They weren't well paid, and we were going to raise people's base pay and the good chaps could have earned £10–15 a week on top. My experience is that bonus schemes get better as people learn. At that night meeting the welders said it was on.

'We felt that the market would remain buoyant and, if not, we'd have delayed commissioning the new plant or shut down the Toprad line because the new radiator would be much more competitive and so we'd be in a position to fund generous redundancy. But we wouldn't then be seen as good employers and we wanted to run the two lines because I've never made anyone redundant and I didn't want that on principle.

'We'd have been coming on stream about mid-1980 and we would have picked off the imports. There's been a million radiators a year coming in, and it's not economic to shift them all around Europe.

'It was all fairly sound from our point of view and I was convinced that we could make it pay in the first twelve months, and we'd the Stelrad backup. We weren't paying anything for the assets and we'd have done a deal with

BSC – not so sure about Nat. West. – and we'd have sold or leased the office block which you couldn't build now for £1 million. King kept pushing us and knew that there was a lot of money about, though he was his own worst enemy and we knew he was under a lot of pressure. Worcester was making £400,000 profit that year – and we did it again in 1979 – and we felt we could put in the new gear and be ahead of the opposition, cut the overheads and get the production costs down.

'The resistance of the workforce was the only real risk. They can mess up any firm if they want to, and they'd been told that they'd been badly treated and ripped off by previous employers. But they'd failed themselves. They'd had a go and spent money employing people instead of getting the product right.

'Their leaders were playing from a position of strength, as though they had a good business to sell. I suggested to Hilton that a man be put in to manage the takeover because we were negotiating with two people we weren't going to employ. He had a word with the minister, but Government felt it couldn't do that. They had them down to London on occasions, and I said to Hilton, "I don't know what you're saying to them, Brian, but they come back more determined than ever."

[The visits to Williams in 1978 were confirming the leaders in their belief that Government and officials were concerned, and so they deduced that the NEB option was strengthening. In addition, Westminster, Whitehall, industry and media sources were all disbelieving about Worcester's commitment to proceed. 'Even if Duckworth and Spriggs had got on together,' one well-placed source was to recollect, 'I wonder if Worcester would have proceeded?']

'The trouble with a maverick like Spriggs is that you can't plan. I'd told him that I had a future and he hadn't and that if he put us on the map with his people we'd respond to it. "We don't have to be here," I said. Spriggs replied that if Worcester was the only way, he and Jenkins would walk away to save the jobs, but he didn't give the impression that he really would.

'Jack thought he could pull it off again, but Williams and Varley were adopting Tory beliefs and the criteria of business. "Is it viable? Has it a long-term future? We're not just here to prop up jobs," they were saying.

'Spriggs is a very cunning, very capable guy, but he's totally incapable of running a competent company. He's got a lot of energy when he gets on his feet but not when he needs to get down to all the little things you need to run a business competently. He and I never raised our voices to each other. We never fell out in the way reported. I don't think he honoured his commitment. I don't dislike the guy.

'Some people felt I'd got a fever to go in there because, if you've built up a business like Worcester, you don't give it away easily. I'd rather they said that we must have set up a really good deal for us to get involved. We believe that we had.'

16. Final battles: 1978–9

- The last application
- Worrying rumours
- Receivership surfaces again
- Clutching at straws
- The final assault
- Waiting for the end

Worcester's withdrawal was a mixed curse to the convenors, who felt that Duckworth's departure was embarrassing evidence of their own intransigence. They persuaded themselves that KME could gain from the situation by exploiting its political support and that Williams should be pressed to reconvene the working party.

Meanwhile, there were recriminations between KME and Government. Spriggs blamed Worcester for making no concrete takeover proposals. Williams reminded people that Spriggs' first public comment on the Worcester plan had been to say that it wasn't what he wanted and that he would campaign for a different proposal. It was clear that Williams felt that Spriggs had ratted on his commitment to abide by the working party proposal.

Williams was invited to address the next mass meeting at Kirkby and, to KME's surprise, he agreed. Duckworth was also to be invited by Dick to speak. Spriggs was offering them both the chance to talk directly to the workers, confident that his own authority would be backed by the mass. (But Duckworth didn't come. Jenkins never invited him!)

KME's mass meeting on 11 December was lively. Introduced to the strains of 'Ride of the Valkyries', Williams was heckled sporadically as he revealed what had been going on to the assembled cooperators. He defended the Government's position without apportioning blame, admitted that he had tried to find jobs for the two directors and pointed out that the working party had been unanimous in backing a plan which would have saved 460 jobs.

The effect of his speech was disappointing. He had accepted the invitation without hesitation, not wanting to flunk a meeting and feeling that he had behaved more honourably and openly than KME and so had nothing to conceal. Robust as it was, his speech changed nothing, though Spriggs said afterwards, 'Alan can certainly hand it out.' Spriggs spoke next, obviously concerned to counter the impression that he might have been misleading cooperators by filtering information. Some cooperators thought that he made a fool of Williams in his speech. Whilst Spriggs urged the workers to turn out every radiator they could, the cooperators 'refuted' any suggestion that the leaders were responsible for the breakdown over Worcester. The meeting, reported *Labour Weekly* showed that 'KME was more than its critics' pretence of an idealistic venture kept afloat to satisfy a handful of political dreamers.'

A debate in the House produced a Tory demand for KME to be put into receivership, whilst further debate continued within the KME leadership. The Department had told them of an entrepreneur named Lowell who was interested in putting £750,000 into KME, who wouldn't need Government support and who would be willing to keep the cooperative structure so long as executive control were separated off. Lowell felt that his case hadn't been fully considered by the working party, but since his technique was to come in only when everyone else had given up and since he hadn't put in a proposal to the working party, this was scarcely surprising.

Spriggs was advised to draw up a plan to sack spare cooperators by the time Parliament reassembled in early January – and to do it, not talk about it. As it was, there was no political interest, but if Parliament reconvened with workers helping to save the place and the import threat still there, a political chance could be created, he was told. He and Dick couldn't be allowed to smash yet another new plan, so he was advised to ditch the dual role of convenor director and either support a rescue plan, or go. Spriggs agreed. KME would put in an application on the basis that a new external board would control its funds. There would be an incentive scheme so that 513 workers could turn out the required number of radiators, while 260 people would have to leave on the basic statutory redundancy pay. He was now agreeing the condition which he wouldn't earlier accept from Worcester.

The leaders were wary of Lowell, who wanted to discuss his plans with P.A. If P.A. thought his ideas sensible, then negotiations could start. Wasn't this sensible, the convenors were asked, because it kept Lowell off KME's back and used P.A. as a filter for his plans? 'No!' claimed the leaders. 'Lowell can then go to Government saying he's agreed with P.A. and it's only us two in the way. We don't want to be in the secondary bargaining position.' They made it clear that they wouldn't be pushed aside.

There wasn't time to investigate Lowell's ideas, and his entry would only give the officials a chance to prevaricate, they felt. KME's application should go in alone. If Lowell only came in when everyone else had gone 'let him stay at the back of the queue'. 'What queue?' Spriggs was asked. 'Lowell *is* the queue. They'll never help KME without some private risk money being there.'

The last application

Despite this self-evident truth, on 13 December 1978, KME applied for a loan of £5.8 million. One million was required for working capital, £1.3 million for the freehold and £3.5 million for plant and machinery, including a new radiator line. There would be a completely new corporate structure; P.A.'s managers would be brought in, workers would be sacked and money should be advanced only against KME's specific performance of its promised plan.

The officials were wary of any more applications from the beleaguered cooperative for, while there was a requirement to consider any proposal, there had to be an end to the number of times KME could cut and come again. 'I've been to IDAB eight times,' said Andrewes mournfully.

The ensuing debate at KME was punchy but, as always, unproductive. The main problem was the corporate structure and how an investor would fit it. It was no use just tinkering with the constitution – it was a problem of behaviour. The 1971 Industrial Relations Act had shown that you couldn't get people to behave with a piece of paper. If the convenors reverted to the shop-floor they would rip the place apart. Anyone coming in to manage the place might as well put his arm in the mincer. The only alternative was for the two convenors to go, or else join management unequivocally. But could they? Would they? KME had to find a structure which, because it was inherently logical, would work – even if people changed their minds under pressure.

The omens were discouraging.

'Even if I swore on fifty Bibles, the shop-floor wouldn't believe me,' concluded Spriggs.

'They'd believe your intentions, but not that you'd carry them out. Maybe you should go on the top external board with service contracts and signed, undated resignation letters.'

'That's political dynamite,' asserted Spriggs. 'Williams has already been burned over that.'

'Everything is political dynamite now.'

'Maybe we have to discuss the price of our going if we're in the way,' mused Spriggs.

Once again it was all or nothing. The notion of choosing one single role was too unbearable to face.

There was no sympathy at Westminster over the convenors' failure to sort themselves out. Callaghan had been blunt. 'How can we help people who won't keep promises and won't help themselves?' There were official minutes in circulation in Whitehall ('dirty notes' they were called) about absenteeism, fiddles, card schools and people working elsewhere. Silk received a stewards' delegation from the factory which complained that they'd never had a cooperative or proper democracy and, although Jack had done a lot, the place was run on poor political lines.

As the cooperators realized that the departure of Worcester had sharply depressed their chances of jobs and good redundancy money, resentment towards the stewards and convenors was growing apace.

The leaders faced their fifth successive stressful Christmas. Peace and goodwill were not in evidence.

At least P.A. was still backing the KME application. They had updated their plan and had furnished Hilton with the career details of four P.A. staff who might be seconded as chief executive to KME. All were impressively experienced, and P.A.'s reputation would be attached to their performance at KME. The commercial director would also come from P.A.

P.A.'s proposed new organization structure showed two new worker directors in a minority on the policy board – which would include KME's chief executive, the commercial director, Jenkins as personnel director and Spriggs as distribution and purchasing director. Bandell would not be on the board but would report to the commercial director. There was no place for Lewis. Spriggs and Jenkins would not be eligible for election as worker directors or as convenors. Their new restricted role would be solely as managers. It wasn't exactly specified what their responsibilities would be. Jack had chosen his transport and purchasing job because 'it's a very active role and I'll be out of direct contact with the workers'.

The leaders attempted to involve the Cooperative Development Agency by trying to ask its chairman, Lord Oram, to act as non-executive chairman of the trustees who would control KME's funds under the new proposal. They couldn't even get to speak to him. Lawrence, the CDA director, said that he would strongly recommend that Oram should not become involved and his own recommendation would, he said, carry weight. The bad Samaritans of the cooperative movement were still passing by on the other side.

The author suggested that he, Silk and Williams should get together privately as three Labour Party members – not as minister, MP and professor – to try to find a way out. There would be no record that could come back to haunt them. The convenors thought it a good idea. So did Silk: 'It should have happened long ago.'

The effort to involve Williams privately failed. He didn't feel competent to advise on a corporate structure. This wasn't the point of the projected meeting. If Williams didn't want to even explore the options confidentially, then the deduction was obvious. He wanted, or had been ordered, to kill the cooperative. Neither he nor Silk ever sought out Marsden or any other analyst to try to create workable proposals. Although Williams frequently made contact over matters by routes outside the ministerial or officials' channels, when it came to KME, he recalled: 'It never occurred to me.' This was strange. However, politicians had many other problems on their minds. The winter of discontent was scarring Britain with strikes and shortages and Government was drifting helplessly towards a general election it could scarcely fail to lose.

On 19 January 1979, Dunlop announced the total closure of its Speke factory with the loss of 2,400 jobs. In the face of gruesome trading figures, the firm was reducing its tyre-making capacity. Once again, wrote the *Liverpool Post*, Merseyside had taken the brunt of corporate closures.

There was another meeting with Williams on 24 January, the day before KME's £5.8 million application was due at IDAB. Williams was worried about the lack of private sector finance which would be needed to meet the criteria. His other worry was that the current radiator shortage would cease once the competition's new capacity was in operation. KME wouldn't then be missed.

Marsden pointed out that KME was now fully price-competitive and still winning orders. Furthermore, some of its customers had received rough treatment from Stelrad and Myson in the past and wouldn't want to be in the pockets of one or two suppliers. Sankeys were said to believe that the market would be short of one million radiators in 1979.

The meeting had been lethargic, though Marsden had been asked to state what, in P.A.'s view, were the snags in KME's new proposal. He was worried about the use to which the answers could be put. After a vigorous attack on the officials and politicians in the *New Statesman*, officials had contacted P.A. to see what could be done to 'correct' the impression that they and P.A. were at loggerheads.

Worrying rumours

Williams took Spriggs and Jenkins aside after the meeting. There had been aspersions cast by people about KME, not just about people going over the wall, but about the activities of the transport operation. What about Tolyn Ltd – a transport firm which had Spriggs' wife and Johnstone's wife as directors and which traded with KME? Spriggs was ruffled and reacted sharply, insisting that no favours had occurred. There was no evidence of any unreasonable behaviour, though it was later to emerge that in the period 1977 onwards Tolyn had received £120,000 of KME's dispatch department's expenditure of £900,000, though its business had always been won at competitive prices. Spriggs had speedily terminated the naive involvement of the wives who had resigned from Tolyn in September 1977 – neither ever receiving a penny from it.

Meanwhile, Williams knew that if the story leaked out to a Tory MP or a newspaper there would be a problem.*

Receivership surfaces again

The KME party left the Industry Department, ferreted around and learned that every paragraph in the paper going to IDAB was negative – what KME had not done, the market, viability – it was all there. Spriggs rang Hilton and suggested that he tell these facts to the Minister. Williams would be fed up, they felt. There was no hiding-place from KME's scrutiny. They were right; for a long while the Department had known that there was no such thing as a 'safe' paper on KME.

One day, said Spriggs, someone was going to resign from IDAB. 'What's the point of sitting there letting civil servants and bankers run the country?' Just as the IDU's paper was going to IDAB, the bank agreed tentatively to consider the case for a new conditional loan. It seemed there might be some private sector finance from National Westminster.

There was a complete smother on news from London and KME's leaders spent an anxious weekend wondering what had happened. Elliott's article in Monday's *Financial Times* told them. IDAB had rejected the application.

Rohrer found out that IDAB had instead recommended that Government should give financial assistance, not to KME, but to the *receiver*. Williams and Hilton were hopping mad about the exposure, believing it to come from IDAB's Harry Urwin, who himself believed that the officials had leaked it all. The whole thing was degenerating into a barely competent farce.

Williams wanted to see the convenors. Apparently, if the EI Cabinet Committee said 'no' to KME's proposal,

---

* Spriggs was normally philosophical about the endless rumours. 'I've lived with this for years. Your back becomes stronger and the knives bounce out.'

that was the end, but if it said 'yes' it then had to go to full Cabinet. The odds were really stacked against KME if the committee had powers to reject but not to accept.

The leaders feared that the receivership route was being proposed in order to expel them from the cooperative. If P.A. managed the business for Government and the receiver it would save jobs and imports. How could MPs resist if the alternative was to take another risk with the convenors' wily squirming?

The *Guardian* wrote that the attempt to force the co-operative into receivership and strip the worker directors of authority had infuriated Labour MPs. Plessey, it was reported, was to make a further 800 redundancies at Liverpool, and unless rationalization occurred, 3,400 would go later if the place were closed. Williams counter-attacked with the announcement of the new GEC–Fairchild micro-processor plant at nearby Neston with the gain of 1,000 jobs, but reporters felt that he was distraught and that the story didn't come across well.

Williams met the leaders on 1 February and opined that it was all over. He put it to them that KME should go into voluntary receivership. Government money was available for the receiver and Government would try to save as many jobs as possible.

Spriggs claimed that the IDU's case to IDAB had been cut and dried before the bank had agreed to give conditional backing to the P.A. plan. The officials counter-claimed that the bank had not gone far enough and had only offered to give sympathetic consideration to a loan in 1981, but Williams disagreed with them. The bank, he said, had gone as far as it could and couldn't be expected to offer more so far in advance of an unknown situation. Williams seemed far from relaxed and agreed to have a further meeting on 5 February – after KME's mass meeting. The convenors kept quiet about a letter they had sent to Lowell appointing him as KME's chief executive if Government refused aid. It was a last-gasp weapon in the battle for survival.

The vote at KME was crystal clear. The mass meeting unanimously rejected voluntary receivership or liquidation. This was promptly signalled to the Department. Callaghan, the leaders learned, had said that he didn't wish KME to be on the Cabinet's agenda. Why were the officials revealing this, mused Jenkins – were they trying to clear themselves?

Clutching at straws

The Merseyside group of Labour MPs was reported as being near revolt. The moderate Eric Ogden had suggested considering 'whether we continue to support Government in the lobbies' and ministers were bracing themselves for a rough ride as the weekend press kept up the pace of disclosure. Monday's *Guardian* published an article setting out KME's case and questioning the Government's commitment to socialism. It caught the eye of ex-MP Robert Maxwell, head of Pergamon Press and one-time supporter of the defunct *Scottish Daily News* cooperative. He rang the author to express interest in rescuing KME just as the cooperative team was assembling for yet another meeting with Williams.

Lowell accompanied the KME party but there was little time for any synthesis of ideas and he and the convenors were still relative strangers.

The question for KME was – who were their friends? Nobody knew what Lowell was after or how he would act at Kirkby. Maxwell was a mixed blessing – his past record was impressive in a variety of senses. Williams now seemed embarrassed at the resurgence of KME's case after his categorical statement that it would not go near Cabinet again. Silk was annoyed because he had been sharply criticized by Callaghan for not knowing what was going on, and he wouldn't be at the meeting – something had come up. It was inauspicious.

However, Williams and the officials were friendly.

Spriggs opened up. 'We're not producing a new proposal – it's a variation.'

'But Jack,' responded Williams jovially, 'I expect you to be able to produce an instant new proposal from your pocket. You've never failed us yet!'

Williams must have felt that Lowell and Spriggs were saying different things and they were, indeed, working out their positions in the meeting. However, in view of KME's track record of ingenuity, Williams could not rule out the chance that there was a master plan which made it tactically useful for KME to conceal something by confusing the issue. This was flattering. The fact was that Spriggs was still wary of Lowell and neither knew even roughly what the other would really accept.

Williams circled round the problem. 'The situation is nebulous and will only be clarified when Government aid is known, but we need it the other way round. We can only consider aid when all the other elements are clear. The PAC would have a field day if we gave money against this uncertainty.'

Binning backed him up. 'Your new plan for £¾ million aims to avoid the hoops you haven't managed to get through with your £5.8 million proposal. But it can't. It isn't £¾ million you want. It's £¾ million now and perhaps two or three million pounds later.'

Lowell claimed that with his £¾ million and no Government money KME would be viable even if he withdrew his money after two years. 'In my rescue creditors could be hurt and staff disappointed by the redundancy terms. It's not an elegant solution. It's a desperate solution.'

Spriggs began to distance KME from Lowell. 'Government would think we'd gone potty if we change from £5.8 million to a prospect of £¾ million or even nothing. Like us, Government must want to see a final solution now. We've been in intensive care too long. I want Cabinet to consider the KME application for £5.8 million less the £1.3 million for the lease. We can't put Mr Lowell's part in. It's too vague.'

The meeting ended. Neither Williams nor the officials had been unfriendly or had tried to divide Lowell from KME to show up the disunity. Yet once the debate resumed privately in the waiting-room, it soon became clear that the two were miles apart.

Lowell denied Spriggs' charge that he would abandon KME but, he said, 'You've got to take decisions this week and sack the two hundred surplus people.'

Jack jumped up in a rage, put on his overcoat and started to leave. 'We'd never have agreed in there if we'd known that. We should have gone to Cabinet alone. We can't sack them. We won't do it. They must have their entitlements earned over the years.' He was extremely angry.

'You can't give it them,' continued Lowell. 'You haven't got it. Your promise to them is worthless if Government doesn't give aid. When will you sack them?'

'When Government refuses aid,' said Spriggs.

'But what about my £¾ million, won't you accept that?'

'No!'

Lowell repeated that if he could get speedy agreement with creditors there could be properly funded sackings, but no *ex gratia* payments. 'I will fund for the future but I won't pay for the past.'

The leaders finally conceded that if Government refused aid, people would have to be sacked without extra entitlements. The meeting concluded with Lowell departing to contact the creditors, but with no agreement over the substance or timing of further meetings with KME. Everyone was bad-tempered – partly because they were frozen. Due to the winter's strikes, the building had long since run out of heating oil. Jack had been right to put his coat on.

Back at KME, the convenors were far from flattering about Lowell who told the leaders that he wanted to discuss their personal positions. 'We knew it,' they said, 'everyone gets worried about us. We've been sieved more often than flour.'

In the end Lowell departed. He had not presented any solid proposal to the Department or to KME and the leaders told Hilton that Lowell had been offered the job of chief executive and the P.A. plan in its entirety. They pointed out that it hadn't been KME's fault he had withdrawn – not wanting to give the IDU a chance to gloat over another Worcester episode and then use it to deter other suitors. Lowell had a different perspective. He had been reserving his position, yet he felt he'd been clear to the convenors on many basic points, but they hadn't been prepared to listen. There had been no point in pursuing matters when faced with the convenors' discouragements and disinterest. 'They always talk about politics and not about management. Every time there is another prospect they talk politics. They're only friendly when they've got no option.'

KME had moved nowhere, though the Lowell episode had bought a little time. Perhaps Maxwell would be the more logical, more experienced mystery man. The problem was that Maxwell had eaten bigger men for breakfast, but he had a public reputation to maintain and couldn't afford another cooperative failure. Maxwell urged the leaders to bring a fully worked-out plan to his headquarters at Oxford. 'I don't want to prolong it if there's nothing to be done. If there *is* something, I want to do it immediately.' It sounded impressively purposeful.

KME's stewards were being kept in ignorance of these liaisons, with Spriggs placating them by saying that if the backers were named, they would walk away.

Spriggs and Jenkins visited Maxwell secretly at Oxford on 9 February while Marsden went to the National Westminster head office in London. The trio travelled as far as Euston together and the leaders didn't discourage co-operators from assuming that they, too, were going to the bank. They told Hartland that they were going to London to collect their CBEs!

The meeting with Maxwell was friendly and very businesslike. Seated at the end of his long boardroom table

Maxwell looked no older and just as ebullient as he had a decade earlier. His interest in KME was, he said, two-fold. First, he had been involved in the *Scottish Daily News* cooperative. 'It looks as though you have made all their mistakes and you didn't distinguish between the jobs of directors of a company and the jobs of shop stewards.'

'We were advised a long time ago that we were walking on hot coals trying to combine the two roles,' replied Spriggs.

'You're the largest cooperative and it would be very damaging to the country if you went under. We need to move towards workers running their own businesses – cooperatives have an important role to play. In Yugoslavia they are very toughly managed. They don't keep surplus workers, and the workers boot out management if they aren't good.'

Maxwell's second motivation was that, as KME had lasted so long, they must have learnt a few things, and the demand for radiators must exist if Feroli was interested.

The leaders told him that P.A.'s action plan could create breakeven at Kirkby. Two hundred redundancies, better management and better prices should do it, provided the radiator output held up with fewer workers. 'It either needs Stakhanovite efforts or a self-financing productivity deal,' asserted the author.

'Forget Stakhanovite efforts,' reacted Maxwell, 'people want to be able to touch some benefit; it needs to be a self-financing deal which puts money in people's pockets. They're not politicians.'

Maxwell took them to lunch via the scenic route which zigzagged through the two hundred people in Pergamon's main office. It was an impressive reminder of the scale of his operation. After lunch Hilton returned their telephone call. He'd been lunching with a receiver. 'Are you putting a receiver into the Department?' asked Spriggs. 'It seems easier than putting him into Kirkby,' responded Hilton.

Spriggs read the confidential press release to Hilton. It

had been drafted so that an agreed statement existed just in case there was a leak. Maxwell informed Hilton that he was anxious to get an assurance from the Department that they would *welcome* his intervention. 'Hilton may have instructions from Varley to kill KME,' said Maxwell. 'Even with my influence it could stall. They're cunning sods and pretty ruthless.'

Maxwell warned the leaders not to raise false hopes back at Kirkby. As they prepared to depart, Maxwell added the word 'exploratory' between 'positive' and 'discussions' in the press release. Dick pondered privately: 'Do I detect a move back to caution?' The leaders returned to Euston and caught the 5.30 train back to Liverpool. At 6 p.m. the whole press release came over the Press Association and Extel news tapes.

It appeared that the *Daily Mail* – already knowing of Maxwell from KME's Commons friends – had confused him with Lowell, and Maxwell felt it best to release the correct story. The leaders were sanguine about the leak since they felt that it reduced the chance of Maxwell risking his reputation by messing them about. If it went sour, he could only protect himself by blaming the leaders for blocking agreement. 'I'm past the stage for blocking things,' sighed Spriggs. 'Callaghan will think two real nutters have got together.' Others were not so confident, and Maxwell's projected involvement was the joke of the evening at the *Financial Times*. Its staff recalled his abortive forays into Tinlings and Aston Martin and forecast that he would abandon Kirkby within seven days.

It was six actually. Maxwell cancelled his meetings with the Industry Department and would now only come in after a receivership. He wrote to Spriggs, saying: 'No good purpose would be served in our meeting with Government, unless and until you and your colleagues have called in the receiver so as to crystallize the previous debts.' He enclosed a report by auditors, Coopers & Lybrand, who had told him that £1 million would be needed just to put KME back on its feet. They had found no fault with KME's figures, but their central conclusion was blunt. ' . . . the position has already been reached when a receiver should be appointed'.

The convenors were disappointed but quickly became reconciled to a receivership. They were now following an unconscious pattern in which they repelled each unacceptable condition and then accepted it as their own next move, but too late to retrieve the departed suitor. They had done it over the manning levels, sackings, redundancy pay and now receivership. A step-too-late was their accidental decision rule. What they now had in mind was a 'cosmetic' receivership in which the old company would end and a new pre-agreed enterprise arise immediately, if not effortlessly, from the wreckage. This, they seemed to remember, was exactly what had happened with Cork in 1974 with the agreement of King and of KME. And hadn't Williams had a receiver standing by at the time of the abortive Stelrad deal? Surely the fact that Stelrad would only be managing the business for a receiver did not disguise that Stelrad was to be the eventual buyer?

There were no alternative suitors, though KME had to deal with yet another 'Bootle millionaire' who rang up and claimed to have £2 million available in cash. This one turned up an hour late for his appointment. He'd had to wait for a bus.

The final assault

Since receivership was inevitable, the leaders decided to take the initiative. They went to see Williams. Despite the grim situation the atmosphere in the Department's tenth-floor waiting-room was jaunty. 'The flag's flying over the Lords. The bar must be open.'

Silk couldn't come to the meeting, and nor would Maxwell be there. Dick was cynical about Maxwell. 'First, he was going to rescue it; then he wanted a lifebelt; then he wanted a line on the lifebelt; then he wants a boat; and now he wants someone to pick him up. We've seen it all before with other people.'

The meeting was opened briskly by Spriggs but it quickly became tortuous. 'A receivership could be attractive to us but we'd want it clear. We know that you, Alan, have felt we've agreed in the past, and then it's been upset. We're not just going into receivership on the off-chance; it would be open house for anybody.'

There was a long, legalistic discussion which boiled down to the Department insisting that one couldn't pre-arrange the acceptance of an offer by the receiver. It wasn't possible to exclude the chance of a later, better offer by closing the bidders' list. But, argued KME, 'that's just what we did in 1974 with Cork through your John Lippitt. It never went on the open market.'

The leaders didn't press the comparison with 1974. In fact they behaved very discreetly, not even making comparisons when Metal Box's name crept into the conversation. The Department's lawyers were insistent. It wasn't possible to pre-arrange the outcome of a receivership, and Government could not be party to KME's plan.

The leaders asked for a recess. Williams guessed why.

The convenors returned within minutes to state that they wanted their own application for £4.5 million to go to full Cabinet. It had always been on the cards that they would take a chance on the hopeless political climate. It would then be seen to be Government which had killed the cooperative, not them. 'It's sad,' said Jack, 'because we believed we'd made a step forward.'

Williams explored the nuances. 'You're not taking this route because the Department is obstructive but because we, legally, can't find a way to guarantee what you want.'

'Government can find a way within the law,' retorted Spriggs.

'No,' said Williams. 'Government, more than anyone, has to be legal. There is no instruction at any level of Government to do differently. We cannot completely control the situation and be legal too.'

'Can you, Alan, make the Cabinet committee aware of our offer?' asked Spriggs.

'But you wanted it completely confidential.'

'Cabinet matters are confidential, aren't they?'

Williams smiled at the neat response. 'Whatever happens, none of us will ever forget KME,' he concluded. Everyone grinned wryly.

The meeting over, the convenors pondered their position. 'If we can't get a sensible arrangement with the receiver, we'll revert to being union convenors,' said Jack. Dick agreed. 'It would be nice to go back to being what we prefer.'

Waiting for the end

The subsequent meetings at KME were quiet affairs. The stewards supported the leaders' actions, and there was no backing for the steward who proposed that KME should go into receivership. The mass meeting also backed the platform – a fact immediately transmitted to Williams. One radiator worker suggested laying off non-working and non-productive people to conserve money, but there were only two votes in favour. Also rejected was a proposal to make the spare people redundant. Nobody, it appeared, was ready to do anything to improve KME's position, and nor would the leaders encourage them to do so. If the convenors had picked up either proposal they could probably have got a response – but they didn't, even though, as Spriggs said afterwards, 'It was clear that the people were ready for an action plan if only it could be arranged.' He still seemed to feel that an outside intervention would save the leaders from taking any action themselves.

Spriggs claimed that sackings would have brought liquidation sooner and that there had been no money to pay people off in the spring. He was deceiving himself. Observers agreed that the real problem was that redundancies would have left Spriggs feeling destroyed as the champion of saving people's jobs.

Outside KME, nothing stirred. With the imminent commissioning of Stelrad's new capacity, Metal Box was rapidly going cold on the idea of rescuing Kirkby. Feroli rang up with another tentative scheme and so KME made a half-hearted attempt to get the Cabinet decision on its latest application deferred for another week. The trouble was that the cooperative had struggled to get on to the Cabinet agenda and now it was struggling to get off. It scarcely looked credible.

In the event, Cabinet did consider KME at its normal Thursday meeting on 22 February 1979. Williams had reported on the position, and whilst two or three Cabinet ministers expressed doubts, it was clear that the leaders had exhausted all their goodwill. The long list of fundings, failures and missed targets showed Cabinet members that there was nothing that could be done to save them any longer. The application was turned down. That afternoon, Callaghan told the House that the best way to save the cooperators' jobs was via the receiver. The Tories cheered.

Callaghan's statement to the House had been recorded and taken back to the Department where Williams phoned Spriggs to tell him the news. With his officials present, Williams played the recording over to Spriggs. 'Now,' gloated Williams, 'you can do all those terrible things you've been threatening.'

'What terrible things?' asked Spriggs, trying to keep some dignity in the humiliating circumstances.

'Sitting in, that kind of thing,' said Williams.

'Alan, I'm not going to say anything – you've got too many people around you – but I think you'll live to regret what you've said.'

It is hard to avoid feeling sad that Williams could have behaved in this fashion, though KME had been a sore trial to him for many months.

Later, Spriggs was gloomy. 'There's nowhere for us to go – there aren't any escape routes now. The House is shut next week while they're off campaigning over devolution. We'll go under the carpet. The International Socialists will march up and down in Kirkby and maybe four plonkies will take a bit of notice.'

Williams complained again about the breakdown of the Worcester plan. Spriggs resolved to stop attacking Williams, since it just gave the minister the opportunity to remind everyone about Worcester once more. The embarrassment was that Williams had a point. Jack felt that Government's problem lay in fearing that KME was full of gimmicks. 'But what we did, we think was politically normal.' The question was whether Silk would be at the next meeting with Williams. 'If he's going to kick a few tables over, that's the place to do it. But he's not, is he?' The meeting with Williams was inconclusive. The Department was talking to a number of firms but none would come in before a receivership. Silk wasn't there.

Birds Eye was again threatening closure; Lucas was sacking 100; Osram were to close in St Helens with the loss of 160 jobs. Plessey were considering sacking all 4,200 workers if the 800 redundancies couldn't be agreed. At the Mother's Pride Aintree bakery 350 jobs were at risk in the wake of the bakers' strike; Akzo would close in Kirkby with the loss of 100 jobs; BICC were about to announce their closure in Kirkby with 500 jobs eliminated. The area was going downhill at breakneck speed.

Government was on the run too. At the beginning of March it was mauled in the devolution referendum. Wales voted no by four to one, while Scotland had a wafer-thin majority in favour. Devolution was dead again.

The leaders contacted all their main competitors, but there was little interest in buying the enterprise. 'They're all waiting for the corpse,' gloomed Spriggs.

The end was very near. The mass meeting on Monday 26 March adjourned, but the bank said that it would have to pull the plug out at 5 p.m. the next day. Instead, the

Tuesday mass meeting agreed unanimously to go into immediate voluntary liquidation. It retained dignity as well as avoiding the unpleasantness of falling out with the bank, which had been very patient and supportive. The liquidator, Bernard Phillips, had been present to hear the decision. All the employees were sent home. Apart from the few whom Phillips would employ temporarily, they were now all unemployed. It was the symbolic end of KME.

The date was 27 March 1979. One day later the Labour Government was to lose its vote of confidence and call the May election. It was the first time a government had been forced into an election by a Commons vote since 1924.

17. Vanishing point: 1979

- **The Indian rope trick**
- **Victorious Tories**
- **End of a dream**

There was an epilogue. Would you have expected otherwise with an enterprise as tenacious as KME? Everyone blamed everyone else and the following morning's press was full of it.

Spriggs blamed Callaghan and Varley. 'The Government has been terribly hostile to requests for a new initiative from the Department of Industry. The Minister has spent too much time putting forward reasons for not creating new initiatives, rather than reasons for them. Government is always saying that it cannot afford to get involved in saving jobs in private industry – it had a chance to save jobs in its own company and it turned it down. Civil servants have made it their business to discredit any plans we have put forward, and Eric Varley is the prisoner of those civil servants. We are terribly upset and cannot believe that a Government which is supposed to be socialist can take this action. We admit we are not lily-white – we have made mistakes – but KME could have made it with more help.'

Williams had a different story. It was a 'history of lost opportunities'. He again pointed out that 460 jobs could have been saved by Worcester. KME had received Government aid four times and each time had promised it would be the last occasion.*

Williams also said that there were four lessons to be learned from this 'unfortunate situation'.

---

* This last point was untrue.

1 The work done before setting up a workers' cooperative was vital.

2 Cooperatives must never be established from what were clearly sinking ships.

3 High priority must be given to using professional managerial experience, especially in policy making.

4 There must be a willingness to take tough decisions. Although P.A. had recommended a year earlier that redundancies were essential, no jobs had been axed.

The *Liverpool Daily Post* claimed that 'It was another nail in Merseyside's well-studded coffin.' Spriggs had dominated its destiny, it wrote, but his unrelenting tenacity could have played a leading part in the cooperative's downfall.

The *Financial Times* said that, having come from industrial failure, KME had been unable to shake off politically orientated, anti-capitalist and anti-management attitudes. The leaders had been loath to take tough decisions, especially about redundancies. 'In some ways this is not surprising because the two convenor directors won their reputations on their past ability as shop stewards to save jobs when former owners wanted to sack workers.'

KME, said the *Financial Times*, had never been a true cooperative and there had been no real worker participation in the management. Its closure should not be taken as proof that worker cooperatives are doomed to failure, but it did illustrate the problems of attracting capital and management and in taking the sort of commercial decision needed to make profits.

The *Guardian* praised the CDA and neatly juxtaposed two philosophies. They quoted Williams. 'No business had had more goodwill from us, but how much money do we have to pump in before they realized that it is not going to work?' 'It's not enough,' the *Guardian* contradicted him, 'to take an unviable company, hand it over to the workers, inject a large dose of public money, hint that there is more to come and then hope for the best. Neither, having done so, is it enough to condemn the 'cooperatives' for their commercial failure.'

The Westminster atmosphere was fevered, for it was the day of the Labour Government's crucial vote of confidence.

Spriggs said that it would be fine for Merseyside's MPs to protest about unemployment 'but never let it be said that we at KME are taking a selfish line for the cooperative alone'. He was asked if, in the light of the Government action, he would still support the Labour Party. He took the opposite tack to the Dunlop workers, then campaigning against Labour in the Liverpool Edge Hill bye-election. He would work for Heffer and for Labour in his own constituency and would support Silk. 'We might need a change of leadership though.' It was a shrewd political stance. Petulance would have cost him sympathy.

The day ended dramatically. The Government lost its vote of confidence and the next day's Edge Hill by-election converted a Labour majority of 6,171 into a Liberal majority of 8,133. The Labour vote dropped from 13,025 to 4,812. Quite apart from the national influences, the rotten conditions in Edge Hill and the devastation of Merseyside's job base had created their effect.

The Government and KME were now both effectively dead. A general election was called for 3 May 1979 and Parliament was dissolved.

KME's liquidator was finding little interest in the business even though the Department had circulated everyone who could conceivably be interested. 'The only people they haven't spoken to are Woolworths,' quipped Spriggs.

The leaders told a stewards' meeting that prospective buyers didn't want to deal with any of the people on site (i.e. they wouldn't negotiate with Jack and Dick), and there was a heated debate about trade unions and representation. 'We'll stand by our principles of organization,' said Spriggs. 'If necessary we'll get nowhere and see the place full of seagulls.'

Under pressure from the stewards the convenors admitted that there was little alternative to the buyers' conditions and 'if that's what the membership wants we'll pull away and finish tonight'. They were gambling with their reputations again – not much of a gamble if the previous history of the workforce's acquiescence was anything to go by – and risking the collapse of every negotiation.

Stewards complained that they had been given only two minutes' notice of these matters, and the temper of the meeting was not improved by the arrival of some embarrassing news. Professor Douglas Hague had been appointed Margaret Thatcher's economic adviser and speechwriter. 'Who appointed him? Alan Williams? Hague must have decided which way the election will go.'

'We believed we were getting an independent chairman – it was two to one against us before we began,' claimed Jack. Afterwards, he agreed that the Government defence would be clear if KME kicked up a fuss. 'I agree they'll say it was a three-nil job, but Marsden isn't going to be backed into that corner.' The Industry Department said stiffly that Hague 'was seen as an independent chairman'. KME's chagrin never came to anything.

There was a poignant exchange at the end of the stewards' meeting. 'Why,' asked a steward, 'has KME failed?'

'The trouble,' he was advised, 'was that we couldn't create a structure to manage ourselves effectively.'

'But you can't blame the people,' he reacted. 'The Dunlop and Triumph failures weren't the fault of the people – it was the management.'

'But here at KME, the people *were* the management.'

The mass meeting didn't last long. 'While we are together we can still fight. The question is whether we go for individualism or collective responsibility based on the leadership of your choice.' It was unanimously resolved to remain as one body and deal only with employers who would negotiate with the workforce's representatives. Spriggs and Jenkins were still in charge.

It made no difference, for the situation was weakening day by day. The trade adjusted itself to KME's obliteration. Stelrad was reported as offering to buy every Toprad which merchants had in stock, if in return they would then stock Stelrad. Demand wasn't quite so buoyant now, and new capacity would soon be commissioned. The market might not now support the same investment as in KME's recent plans – not that Government had believed KME's case anyway. Worcester seemed uninterested. Myson looked round, but only to see if there was any worthwhile machinery to buy from the liquidator who, in a fit of optimism, had written to the TGWU and AUEW asking if their pension funds would invest £1 million to save KME. The answer was no. The liquidator had also been in touch with fifteen firms advised by the Industry Department, but none were interested, and Callaghan's Commons statement now looked hollow. Receivership wasn't saving jobs. The election campaign was in full swing, and oblivion was fast approaching.

The leaders became reconciled to KME's remaining assets being sold under an auctioneer's hammer, though the workers didn't know this, because Phillips insisted on confidentiality so as not to prejudice a sale as a going concern or risk losing the workers' cooperation. The convenors had agreed with him.

The Indian rope trick

KME's formal creditors' meeting was well behaved – indeed quiet. Phillips was surprised because there were usually attacks on the directors at such meetings. The history of the company was quickly told. The estimated loss for the 1978/9 year would be £1.07 million after crediting the £207,000 paid by Government during the working party period. The bank would recover all its money, and preferential creditors would be paid. Unsecured creditors, principally BSC, might get half their money depending on the sale of assets. The Government's money would be totally lost.

There had been no offers for the business but, the liquidator reported, within the last hour he had received an approach from KME's worker directors. Spriggs outlined the situation. 'Since there is no offer, we, the workers of KME, are prepared to bid an amount of money for the business to continue on a portion of the factory. We would start up on radiators only with about three hundred people and then sit down to negotiate an agreement with Accadiair. Press shop work would be gradually built up too.'

Any Government aid, he continued, would be secured and controlled from outside with Government appointing the chief executive and financial director and with the worker directors serving the chief executive and therefore not in control. This would secure the business, satisfy the creditors and save jobs on the site.

The convenors' plan was to offer the liquidator £500,000 for all the assets and pay him, over twelve months, out of their profits, with the Government putting in the money initially for working capital and for plant and machinery. It wasn't clear how anything akin to private capital would be injected. In fact the scheme was KME's version of the Indian rope trick:

The leaders and Phillips visited the Department to discuss the plan for the cooperators to buy the business out of its profits. Hilton had shown masterful control in keeping a straight face at the creditors' meeting as Spriggs had unfolded his plan for corporate levitation, and now the officials insisted that they were anxious to analyse the new scheme, even if election conventions forbade a decision during the election campaign. The visitors told them that Stelrad was offering fourteen weeks delivery and was also importing radiators from France. Thorn was giving twenty-six weeks delivery and was having quality problems. Tricentrol was importing radiators; MARC were reporting imports sharply up and a Danish maker was trying to recruit KME's entire sales team. The import problem, said the IDU blandly, was not really a consideration.

Victorious Tories

Thirty million Britons voted on 3 May 1979 and Labour was well and truly beaten at the polls. The Labour vote was fractionally higher than in October 1974, but the Liberals were one million votes down and the Conservative vote had risen by over three million to give them a forty one-seat majority in the House.

Silk scraped back with a majority of 858, Alan Williams by only 401. Bob Cryer struggled home with only 78 votes to spare, and even Benn's majority declined from 9,373 to 1,890.

Sir Keith Joseph was appointed Secretary of State for Industry. Lord Trenchard was made Junior Minister. 'With a viscount and a knight, it's a royal department now,' said Jenkins. 'All it needs to complete it, is the Queen to go in as a typist.'

On 23 May, the last day on which the auction could be postponed, Jack rang Hilton. There was embarrassment at the other end, but the answer was no; ministers had decided that KME's application to carry on alone did not meet the Industry Act criteria.

Once again the information was let out for, by early evening, Elliott had the whole story, including IDAB's advice – which was more than KME knew. It was in the press before KME had received the rejection letter. Nobody could have got the information save from inside the administration, and it showed that it hadn't just been Benn, Varley and Williams leaking stories.

End of a dream

The stewards' meeting two days later was a muted affair. Sitting on auction lot 600 (twenty four stacking chairs) were the convenors and fourteen stewards. They agreed that there would be no point in a political fight or in occupying the factory. 'We'd have to be prepared to fight for five years and it wouldn't swing a single vote.'

The meeting petered out, though not before the stewards voted to donate the social fund's £8,000 to the Royal Children's and Alder Hey Hospitals. 'Even if we could distribute it to our members we wouldn't want it.' (This is an endearing Merseyside quality. Ford workers at Halewood had recently been awarded £100,000 in back pay. They donated the lot to a Liverpool medical research project.)

The mass meeting was assembling in the main canteen. As usual, the public address system was playing popular music up to the point when Jack rose to speak. The music man had selected 'The Impossible Dream'.

Jack gave people no false ideas of the prospects before KME – though the bleak situation was clear already to most cooperators – but he still had to head off the fantasy that there was a pot of money somewhere. 'It's an easy job for a shop steward to tell people what they want to hear. We can't offer that to you today. We'll get to the point next week where we either have to take up the cudgels or let the auction go ahead and go about our business as private citizens.'

'We had the chance to change society. It's something this country needs. We did offer it. We've been let down. We've let ourselves down in many ways.'

The meeting was told that although the rejected proposal did meet many of the conditions which were required, the new Government 'is not going to help people like us. Government is starting to take the most expensive economics lesson in history. We'll pay the price. They'll learn the lesson.'

But the strength of the phrases couldn't disguise the emptiness of the prospects. After the meeting, people hung about having long, depressing chats.

'The £3.9 million wasn't enough, that was the problem.'

'It was Lewis who messed it up.'

'No, it was outside here, not us; not Jack and Dick.'

'It *was* us – we are the biggest crowd of pinheads in town.'

'I didn't want stewards wearing two hats – I want them to fight the boss.'

'What boss?'

Ex-steward, George Wright, was particularly outspoken. 'They all thought there was a big bag of money and that Jack and Dick could just go back to Government and keep getting more. The day Jack said it was all over they were like people who had been battered. They just didn't believe it.'

'The trouble was,' said Alan Johnstone, 'that they never knew about profit and loss; that if you don't produce it's a loss. They didn't know it was a fact – and we never did anything to change that.'

Spriggs reflected, 'In a cooperative, we should have had more improvization and cooperation. They'd have given more under private enterprise. For example, the inspectors would never take the place of a man who'd gone to the toilet. They'd stand there and see the press stop. As Dick always said, the biggest enemy was inside. You know one weekend there was murder here. We ran out of welding gas on Thursday and had to tell the people there would be no weekend. They asked if they could scrub the floor – anything. In the end the steward had to admit that they'd already done their Friday work and their weekend output. They'd have come in at the weekend and done a few radiators for Monday and read the papers on overtime. Working to a finish is a disease. You find it everywhere. Some people have to lose their jobs before they even wake up to the problem they've got.'

'Some of them don't believe it's finished now. The International Socialists say that we went into a cosmetic liquidation to get everyone out of the gate. Perhaps they think Dick and I are sharing out the spoils. There are even people saying that since tax was taken out of their wages and it wasn't paid, someone's got it. They don't realise KME used it to buy stuff and pay wages to keep the place going. They don't seem to know what making a loss means and where the cash goes.'

The final mass meeting was held on the last day of May 1979. It had a quiet, dispiriting sense of decay, even though six hundred people had turned up. The Government was blamed for the cooperative's failure, but nobody suggested a march or an occupation. Indeed, no resolution to carry on the fight was put to the assembly. Jack told them quietly that their jobs were lost and reiterated that they should look for alternative employment – though with 20 per cent unemployment in Kirkby this wasn't much of an alternative.

He would stay in the factory for a few days in case any negotiations came to something. There would be no purpose in calling a further mass meeting. The leaders were trying to end the sad struggle with poise and dignity. They didn't want to capitulate or to have the platform rejected so that the media could show that people were disunited.

Jack was somewhat overcome with emotion at the end of the meeting. It was a bitter end for him and Dick. The dream hadn't worked. They knew that much responsibility for failure lay on their shoulders. Yet they also knew how rancorously Government had treated them and how little the cooperators had really put into making the place work. 'I've learned over the years,' said Jack privately, 'that what they needed was direction, discipline and education.' It was a statement which would have warmed the hearts of many managers.

The auction at KME soon proceeded but was halted in mid-sale just before the big presses were put up for sale. An American machinery dealer (Joe Epstein) had paid a £200,000 deposit for everything unsold. He hoped to restart production and then sell it as a going concern. If that failed, he would sell the machinery.

That same evening one shop steward from KME's long departed drinks operation rang the factory gatehouse to check that the auction had stopped. Did that mean he should start on his old job again in the morning? It indicated the level of comprehension which Jack and Dick had had to put up with in the KME stewards' committee.

Epstein's action had demonstrated what the convenors had long suspected – that the factory's machinery was valuable in spite of the IDU's constant denigration of its worth. They went to the Industry Department with Epstein, who told Hilton that the KME presses would still be working when everyone present was dead and gone. Hilton looked at his colleagues, said Spriggs, as if to ask where the Department had been getting its information, if the principal machinery wasn't worn out after all.

Epstein eventually held a second auction in October 1979. It raised about £1 million. His profit before expenses was £500,000. Before the auction there had been an approach from the minister for prosperity and progress for the Mentmore Maharishi – the 'World Government of the Age of Enlightenment'. The visitors were, said Spriggs, very professional and asked intelligent, commercial questions. If KME were taken over there would be meditation during working hours. Spriggs wasn't sure whether this would entail 'practising flying and becoming invisible – though that should suit us; our people are good at becoming invisible.' Unfortunately, it was the visitors who vanished.

Once empty of machinery, the factory was guarded by a handful of ex-KME personnel, all employed by IPD as the landlord. King also employed two ex-cooperators to supervise the place and show it to prospective buyers. The two were Spriggs and Jenkins. They were still there in September 1980 when King sacked them all, having failed to let or sell the factory. It remains empty.

18. Refutations, judgements and conclusions

This analysis restrains itself to a three-part sequence. First, there are some refutations of common fallacies about KME; the chapter then moves to judgements on the actions of various key figures and institutions; finally, there are some conclusions and recommendations for the future.

Part 1: Refutations

Refutations are necessary if only to deter the naive and the biased from writing a simple-minded slogan as an epitaph for KME. And it's easy to see who will be buried beneath the gravestone. It could only be Spriggs and Jenkins. How easy, how neat it would be to shovel all the dirt over them and claim that, but for their actions, the cooperative could have succeeded. This would be perverse, since it is only too evident that, but for them, the cooperative would never have happened at all and, but for their relentless, politically embarrassing tenacity, KME would never have lasted half as long as it did. Besides, burying Spriggs and Jenkins would let too many others steal softly away from the scene.

Fallacy 1 *It wasn't a 'real' cooperative. That's why it failed and that's why we can ignore it.*

This view was favoured by the traditional cooperative movement, including the Cooperative Development Agency. Yet it fails on the CDA's own definition of a cooperative as 'an enterprise owned and controlled by its own workers'.

KME was owned and controlled by its shareholder/co-operators, who were always held responsible for its actions. Indeed, it was precisely the claim that the cooperators controlled their own destiny which enabled KME's critics to walk away, disclaiming responsibility for the wreckage.

KME's critics claimed that it wasn't properly structured and didn't observe 'cooperative principles'. But it did. Membership was open to all and there was democratic control and reasonably fair distribution of wages, though the element of education in cooperative and business matters was sadly lacking.

Secondly, who is to say that Spriggs and Jenkins would not have dominated *any* structure? There is a limit to what can be achieved in adjusting people's behaviour by structuring an organization in a particular way. Resourceful leaders can often mould an organization's working practices almost regardless of the ostensible structure. The convenors had saved the employees time and again. Why should observers feel that the grateful followers wouldn't have remained passive under any system?

After all, KME could have changed its control style as it was. The mechanisms were there; the means existed. They just weren't used. It seems doubtful if KME's story would have been changed by alterations to the cooperative's constitution alone. Indeed it might have put prospective backers off. Banks, officials and ministers almost invariably look for strong leadership.

Nevertheless we must not just dismiss the abuse which came KME's way from the traditional cooperative movement, despite the movement's apparent delusion that it owns the idea of cooperation and has some right to tell the rest of us if we have permission to apply the word. The fact is that KME was not the kind of cooperative one would hope to have seen and it would have been so much easier to back a cooperative whose members were committed to the simultaneous development of an effective community and a competent business.

However, there is nothing inherently undemocratic about KME's equal voting rights leading to control by an autocratic élite. People sometimes voluntarily choose strong leadership and centralized authority. The convenors' dominance was repeatedly legitimized in votes and elections.

Democracy is only risked when such leaders manipulate the constitutional arrangements to make it impracticable for the followers to dislodge them. True, KME's leaders were advantaged by their holding office, as is a government or sitting MP. But KME's elections continued; stewards were changed by their members; mass meeting votes took place; it only needed 50 of the 750 cooperators to feel strongly about an issue and an extraordinary mass meeting could have been held to change things; the cooperators didn't have to remain disorganized and ignorant of the business position. The limited participation of the mass of KME's workers was no more undemocratic than are local government elections, where the bulk of the populace habitually refrains from going anywhere near a voting station. At important mass meetings to vote on big decisions, at least KME's cooperators turned up.

The real charge should be that KME's leaders were ineffectual at developing constructive participation and made no real effort to overcome the ambivalence of many cooperators towards the extra personal responsibility which would have resulted. Nor were the leaders ever forthcoming with the information which could have helped the cooperators to become involved.

Fallacy 2 *The cooperative never had a chance. It was underfunded and sabotaged from London.*

Yes, it was underfunded initially, and some officials' attitudes were strongly negative as, later, were those of certain politicians. Even so, KME could have turned towards profit if *any* of the survival needs had been tackled with anything approaching competence inside the cooperative. The cooperative and the business could both have made impressive progress, to the point where even an unenthusiastic government would have been hard-pressed not to back them further. As it was, the poor labour habits, the rotten pricing and the new product failures cost KME at least £500,000 a year unnecessarily.

The second underfunding was the result of KME asking to be underfunded as much as by Government letting it occur. Furthermore, it was the cooperative's perpetual refusal to countenance the actions proposed by everyone who ever advised it which led directly to the commercial failures and to the near universal belief outside that the cooperative would never voluntarily take steps towards rectifying its commercial deficiences.

Fallacy 3 *No matter what they had done towards business efficiency, they would still have been killed off.*

This secondary defence of fallacy 2 rests on the belief that if KME hadn't looked like a suicide prospect, officials and politicans would have taken more vigorous action to murder it. The claim does a disservice to both officials and politicians because there is only partial evidence that the Whitehall/ministerial axis was actively destructive from mid-1976 onwards. True, it was unhelpful. Ministers lacked any socialist perspective worthy of the name. There were no positive steps taken to nurse the cooperative back to health. However, there was a basic sympathy over the saving of jobs, and KME was regarded, in the words of one well-informed source, as a 'hospice patient' to be relieved from pain in its self-induced terminal illness.

Before 1976 it was a different story, but once the disgraceful behaviour over KME's 1974 application and the vilification of Benn had spent themselves, Part had retired and Carey been mollified by Varley's espousal of the officials' own line, then matters became calmer. Admittedly, Varley had refused to recognize, let alone rectify, the original underfunding by granting the undercapitalized business extra monies early in 1976, but that, too, was perhaps part of the anti-Benn campaign, coupled to an over-readiness to associate himself with his officials and his Treasury colleagues.

As Benn pointed out, the Treasury, the cooperative movement and Labour's right wing were all hostile, feeling that 'KME would give cooperation a bad name' – an outcome which, much of the time, they certainly did their best to arrange. It was unfortunate that Williams persistently rejected KME's plea to be rescued from its policy-making agonies via a Government-controlled re-structure of the cooperative.

That said, there is evidence that by 1978 ministers and officials wanted a solution which would save jobs on a sensible, permanent basis, though not necessarily via a cooperative and almost certainly without any room for Spriggs and Jenkins to continue what were seen as their wrecking tactics. There was, therefore, a lengthy period in which the product market and the political climate would have supported KME's survival relatively amiably.

Fallacy 4 *There wasn't a business there and so KME shouldn't have received backing because it was bound to fail.*

This was untrue, for several of KME's products had a sustainable market position. The radiators were good products, and there was nothing wrong with Accadiair that better pricing, credit control and product development couldn't have cured. Contract presswork would also have been a good market if only KME's internal efficiency and commercial skills hadn't been so inadequate. Only the 1981 recession and competitors' new radiator capacity have put a question mark against KME's long-run survival chances, had it seized its chance to become more proficient.

There *was* business there. The cooperative was simply mediocre at exploiting the opportunities and instead made life unnecessarily difficult for itself. First, it made the classic mistake of the underdog and persistently under-priced its products, believing that it needed to do so in order to obtain business. Using a cheap price to shift goods was about the limit of KME's marketing strategy. The cooperative thus depressed its own revenues and the general market price level too, because KME's competitors felt impelled to keep their prices down. Of course, customers gained from the lower prices of goods, but this was not the motivation for KME, which was slowly growing weaker as it failed to raise its prices to match its costs. The radiator industry's criticism of KME's pricing policies was not so much that they were unfair as that they were unintelligent.

Second, the cooperative always subordinated business efficiency to the goals of maximum employment, maximum wage and minimum restriction of the workforce.* These goals were not ignoble and, as Benn recalled, it really was a 'right to work' campaign, a fight for every man day. Nevertheless, the resulting costs were substantial and KME's actions only maximized benefit to the cooperators in the short run. The long run was always left to take care of itself, usually by the application of political force.

KME had several chances to develop a sound business and an effective form of self-government. It failed because it muffed them.

Fallacy 5 *KME wasn't worth supporting because the cooperators didn't put any money into it.*

It is true that the cooperators didn't put much money into KME. They didn't invest in its capital beyond their £1 stake and nor did they guarantee any loans to the cooperative; but one way of putting money into a business is

---

* A tendency noted in Yugoslavian worker cooperatives operating in a much more supportive social climate.

to take out sub-normal payments for your work, and they did a little of this.

Varley challenged the leaders over the workers' failure to invest in KME, comparing the Kirkby enterprise unfavourably to the *Scottish Daily News*.* KME's battered ex-IPD workers had been laid off for two weeks out of six throughout KME's formation period and had latterly received a basic wage of £43 per week. Where Varley thought the Kirkby cooperators were to find any significant sum to invest is hard to say, but few things so reveal his ignorance about the situation he was declining to help.

It was undeniable that a larger investment by the cooperators – had they any money – would have improved the political climate and the commercial view also, since it is always easier to back people who are evidently willing to back themselves. Although Britain's trade unions have been reluctant to encourage workers to 'buy their own jobs', some experts see a capital subscription as absolutely fundamental to a cooperative, often basing their view on the experiences of the Mondragon cooperatives in Spain, where would-be cooperators have to invest some £2,000 each, if necessary borrowing it from the associated bank. This entry filter was not available at KME, since its impoverished workforce already existed. Nor was there a bank to lend unsecured sums to Kirkby's would-be cooperators. Perhaps out of their debilitating background in one of the most socially deprived areas in Britain, KME's cooperators should have sprung, armed with understanding, commitment and funds. Had the cooperators been selected to ensure financial, political and social compatibility, it is likely that KME would have been more effective as an organization, but as it was, the issue of subscriptions was not so much a fallacy as an impossibility

---

* The SDN cooperators had invested their redundancy pay (which KME workers did not have) and so created a double jeopardy such that, when the paper failed, they lost both their jobs and their capital.

and, I submit, of limited relevance too. If KME's coop-erators had been investors as well, the cooperative, as structured, might have ripped itself apart even faster rather than settle down to more competent behaviour.

Fallacy 6 *We could not interfere. It was an experiment.*

This was a repeated defence by Williams and his officials to excuse their standing-by and letting KME expire through its own self-destructive inadequacies. As Wil-liams said, 'I'm a great believer in letting people find their own solutions if they can.' But what if they can't? KME got as far as defining the necessary solutions but just couldn't bring itself to implement them. That was to the leaders' discredit since they really wanted Government to take the hard decisions for them and, as Williams pointed out, 'A minister who puts himself into the position of forcing sackings is going beyond his job. It's a managerial decision, and if they couldn't do it, they didn't deserve to be in charge. They can't always find fall guys and I wasn't going to be backed into a corner with no line of escape. It was their own responsibility.'

His view had some merit, hard as it was. It was true that one part of the experiment was the testing of the ability of untrained people to pull themselves up by their own bootstraps. Nevertheless, it is inane to think that any experiment has to run its full course even when it is obvious that it will fail.

We can only be grateful that the Industry Department does not undertake medical research or defence devel-opments. As your teeth and hair fall out due to their drugs, and as the experimental planes crash out of the sky, they would stand supinely by, chanting, 'We cannot interfere. It is an experiment.' There were few elements in the KME story which were as depressing as the know-ledge that once the cooperators had been thrown into the deep end, had splashed about and wasted their strength and begun to drown, Williams' response to their cries for help was to watch their feeble grasp slip from the side of the pool, tell them to learn to swim, and then look around for someone else to rescue them.

It should be obvious that when an experiment goes seriously and permanently wrong, for identifiable reasons which can be rectified, you adapt it to learn more, rather than continue with a doomed waste of time and resources. Yet, that assumes one thing; that you want the experiment to have the best chance of success. I do not accept that Varley, Williams and the officials were so ignorant of scientific experimentation that they believed that they could not intervene. They chose not to intervene.

Fallacy 7 *Workers cannot manage and KME's failure proves it.*

The cooperatives' history certainly shows that the workers did not manage particularly well – if one assumes that their overriding goal was business efficiency. I would argue that they didn't manage very sensibly even if the goal was maximum job-preservation in the long run. However, their goal emerges as maximum job-preservation in the short run and, at that, the leaders' skills were far from paltry.

KME's fiercest critics expected the cooperative to collapse quickly in a welter of self-indulgence, mutual distrust, confusion and anarchy. It didn't. The cooperators at least kept station, so that their poor management controls remained no better and no worse than they had been five years earlier. There was also the question of their risking existing levels of competence. One basic reason for KME's failure to improve its systems was the leaders' fear that innovation would put at risk the mechanical efficiency of the systems which it did possess. It is not unusual for people to cling to ingrained habits when the situation seems highly threatening. The result is that, to avoid the risk of decline, improvements are eschewed.

Nevertheless, it was never clear that KME's key figures

really understood the differences between good and bad management. Good management loses few opportunities to improve systems, efficiencies and welfare, knowing that advances can only be made by never-ending attention to all the individually minor improvements which make up day-to-day progress.

Spriggs and Jenkins had little interest in management methods, preferring to rely on the grand political strategy and some misty, commercial master-stroke which never materialized. Lewis didn't give the impression of being up to the task of performance analysis, though Bandell thought that Lewis was quite a capable chap – an opinion shared by few others among the story's main figures. Bandell himself was simultaneously self-effacing and aggressive. Unwilling to challenge the financial and managerial consequences of the convenors' indifference to commercial performance, he wouldn't be persuaded to create pressure by writing a monthly commentary to go with the vast (and largely ignored) accounts. As Ward said, 'He should have been standing there saying, there's no way we can do those figures – and look at all those variances.' But Bandell went along with KME's implausible budgets and refused to revise the accounts to make them more comprehensible as instruments for action. He claimed that the weekly figures gave people 'all they needed to know', which is not a view which any of KME's advisers shared. Bandell dismissed Cowe's 1977 report on KME's financial systems and the criticisms of the MBS executives (some of whom were finance directors of public companies) saying, 'I've seen more consultants' reports than you've had hot dinners.' John's central asset was his integrity and loyalty to the enterprise. Without his skill, KME could have sunk as early as 1977. Yet I know of no major investigation or report ever generated inside KME to try to spell out its operating deficiencies. Similarly, the cooperatives' search for new products was laudable but badly handled. In the end, KME's management gave up, and by 1977 the management culture was one of strategic fatalism.

It is unfair to say that workers can't manage, because that assumes that they are trying to do so in terms which business people would normally adopt. There was a sense in which the cooperative didn't coherently try to do so, and the story shows that, if you put untrained, unsupported workers in charge of a tricky situation, which no professional management has previously cracked, they may behave in an unbusiness-like manner – particularly if their commitment is to a different goal. KME kept itself afloat for over four years in the most unpromising circumstances. In warding off redundancy, the cooperators managed better than almost any other group outside Fleet Street and the Civil Service itself.

Fallacy 8 *Only liberate workers from their shackles and tremendous progress will occur.*

This view of the potential of a sturdy working class, presently cowed and socialized into drably limited behaviour by capitalist exploitation, is best summed up by militant Marxist, Peter Taaffe, who wrote, 'Through a democratic socialist plan of production, run under workers' control and management, unemployment and poverty would at last be wiped out, and undreamed-of prosperity could be achieved within a short period.'*

The goals are noble; the means raise doubts. The galvanizing effect is evidently expected to emerge through arousing and tapping the latent energy and talents of workers. At KME, the pent-up power of the workers remained largely an illusion, partly because the cooperators' motivations and latent skills were never developed by themselves or their leaders. In the end, it wasn't very clear that much potential force existed, let alone that there were ready ways of energizing it. The KME story

* *Guardian*, 21 January 1980.

illustrates the difficulties of inducing workers to accept heavier loads of responsibility even when self-interest would seem to be a powerful driving force.

Reluctance to accept more responsibility may be prudent, in that it reduces short-term stress, but it can be ultimately self-defeating when it leaves the workers' fate in the hands of others. Stoical acceptance then becomes the workers only practical reaction to their leaders' judgements. These dilemmas of responsibility and leadership range far beyond KME. There is plentiful evidence that many intelligent people – responsible within the family and community – just don't want to take responsibility for decisions in their work enterprise too.

One can seek to explain these phenomena as the consequence of people being socialized as serfs; but this scarcely accords with the resourcefulness of the Kirkby workforce's challenges to management over the years. More to the point, a lack of curiosity and initiative might be an initial reaction to controlling one's own employment, but KME went on for nearly five years, and they'd had a preview of self-management issues three years before that. Even so, one might accept this excuse more readily if the workers had tried hard and stumbled, but their persistent organizational inaction was depressing. Perhaps the stress at KME created its own collective lethargy.

The indifference wasn't universal, and like most communities, KME included people prepared to commit themselves to responsibility and to seek challenging goals which they could pursue with enterprise and energy. KME's cooperators included, I judge, a fair share of willing, would-be committed people. The breakdown arose from the lack of mechanisms for linking their commitment to goals, and from their ignorance, which was fostered by the leaders and accepted, far too readily, by the cooperators.

Leadership in organizations is frequently concentrated in the hands of a few. There is a core of activists –

managers, union officers, politicians and the like – who shoulder above-average responsibilities and duties and who are surrounded by a larger group who seem content to acquiesce in their own roles as individually – and sometimes collectively – uninfluential followers. Just consider the active numbers of unionists, political party members, community leaders and the like. Taaffe's own organization remains tiny. The question which recurs is not 'Why do leaders do as they do?' but 'Why do the rest let it happen?'

Some analysts have a simple answer. The market economy is seen as an impassable obstacle to effective workers' control and so 'islands of socialism in a sea of capitalism' are to be deplored and will inevitably fail. Yet nothing at KME was so inherently flawed that success was impossible.

Whilst the Left sees a market economy as oppressive and the Right naively claims that worker democracy and business efficiency are incompatible, both are united in a wish to enhance liberty and enterprise at the expense of stifling bureaucracy. The key question is whether participation can add to efficiency – and there is some evidence that it can – and is the addition big enough to justify the risks and burdens of investing in developing new relationships?

There is little in our history to suggest that collective endeavour through the State would solve the problems of alienation and impotence. Advocates of state socialism rarely spell out the shape of the hazy utopia which is to replace welfare capitalism and which will, they hope, both deliver the goods and be benign.

Although worker cooperatives may be a pre-figurative form of grappling with capitalism in capitalist terms, to be followed by a socialist era, if worker cooperatives can be made to work effectively in a mixed economy, capitalism will have adapted and the advent of state socialism will be deferred. Worker cooperatives may pose more of a challenge to Marxist analysis than to capitalism.

Part 2: Judgements

What should we now make of the conduct of the various parties which were associated with KME, now that the easiest excuses have been challenged? Readers will make up their own minds from the story, and there would be no need for this section were it not for the flattering self-image of some of the key actors.

Collinson, P.A., and the National Westminster Bank

Let us start with those who come out of the story with reputations enhanced. The list is short. Only Len Collinson, P.A. and National Westminster seem to emerge with clear credit – Collinson because he behaved unselfishly, offering experience, commitment and integrity in a situation which would scarcely give him an easy time or offer him any great advantage. Spriggs and Jenkins were foolish to push him out.

P.A. behaved honourably too. It would have been so easy for their consultants to shrug their shoulders at KME's failure to implement their plan and to distance themselves from the floundering cooperative. Instead, P.A. stood by KME, and although it might be claimed that Hartland was over-enthusiastic about the prospects, this could scarcely be said for the highly experienced Marsden – though this didn't prevent the NEB from trying. Though socialists tend to assume that management consultants are simply agents of capitalism, consultants do have a creditable attachment to sense and efficiency, as P.A.'s commendable loyalty demonstrated.

The bank, too, behaved supportively in trying circumstances, though it is fair to say that it faced an increasingly limited choice. In one sense, its fated role was awarded at the moment it took KME's account at the very beginning of the cooperative. Once it had accepted KME's funds, how could it refuse help to a worker cooperative, with the Labour Government committed, in words anyway, to consider nationalization of the banks? Would

National Westminster want to provoke Labour's left with such an act of bias? When the cooperative needed funds, how could KME be treated differently to any other commercial enterprise? The assets were there as security, assuming Government couldn't really ask for them back; nearly £10 million had passed through the accounts; the management's figures were demonstrably honest and competently consolidated; and the cooperators had, it seemed, a plan to turn round the improving business. The die had been cast and National Westminster was firmly embedded in it. Nevertheless, the bank showed considerable political flair in agreeing to an overdraft for KME early in 1976, because it smartly pulled the rug from under Varley, then making his first shabby attempt to sink Benn's cooperative by trying to cast the bank in the role of reluctant villain.

The bank took a similar view when asked for extensions to the overdraft, even though the convenors had stretched their view of KME's survival chances to unconvincing limits. National Westminster made it clear to the working party that it wasn't going to rock the boat, no matter what it cost. Given the politics of the situation, it is hard to see what else National Westminster could have done. To its credit, it did not go round undermining KME or initiate any of the abortive attempts to sink the cooperative in favour of a return to private enterprise. It did not seek to curry favour with the City by stamping on this upstart challenger to capitalism.

True, National Westminster was KME's preferential creditor and so could expect to recover much of its money from the debris. In fact, it recovered all its monies, including interest. Nevertheless, the cooperative had many reasons to be thankful that the bank had behaved as it did.

The working party
The working party also behaved creditably in pressing and difficult circumstances. Its members made extensive

efforts to protect KME's cooperative structure, to maintain the maximum number of jobs and to salvage what it could from the badly performing business. Doubts arise on two counts. The first relates to their avoiding pressing Varley over the NEB. He had every reason to feel pleased with their work. However, they did have a potent reason for their behaviour, though it was just a little too pat, a trifle too elegantly circular. Even if Varley had been willing to face the political flak of a prospective mass resignation of the NEB's members – and there are limits to the heroism required of any minister in such circumstances – the NEB might have messed up KME. The NEB wouldn't have behaved viciously; it might simply have been unable to give KME the attention which was needed. This wasn't just the view of every member of the working party, but of the author and the convenors too, although the convenors, perennially optimistic, felt that once inside the NEB, their political skills could have quickly averted any such accident.

The second doubt arises over the working party's attitude towards KME being funded from the Industry Department. The working party felt that, even though Spriggs and Jenkins were virtually begging to be released from their intolerable bind, they would resist being forced into actions they hadn't taken voluntarily. The working party also felt that any money promised by Government would have to go in, *en masse*, at the beginning of any rescue. Had the rescuer not been Government, one could confidently describe this objection as nonsense. Anyone else would have talked with KME's bank, suppliers and customers and come to a scheme of arrangement over the future of the business – just as Worcester had intended to do. Provided that all interests were parties to the agreement and provided that Government used some arms-length device like a board of trustees, there seems no reason why Government should necessarily be more exposed than any other rescuer. Otherwise the implication would be that, once Government proposes any rescue by any route, its money will be beyond recall or control by any monitoring process or legal provision.

The working party's final objection rested on their weary belief that Spriggs and Jenkins, tenacious and ingenious as they were, would subvert any agreement secured by control from the Industry Department. It is a tremendous tribute to two shop stewards from Kirkby that it was feared that they could turn an apparently defenceless Government department upside-down and shake the money from its pockets.

Nevertheless, the track record of the convenors' cavalier treatment of promises did exist and the working party held the view that a system of external control divorced from effective management control inside KME would lead only to continued disappointment over the cooperative's performance. The working party was attacked for its caution, and there are Labour MPs who look at the combination of a management consultant, a well-placed civil servant and an adviser of Mrs Thatcher and feel that no more needs to be said. On balance though, it is clear that the working party tried hard to correct KME's deficiencies and performed its tricky task with as much sympathy for the cooperators as could be mustered out of the inhospitable climate which had developed.

National Enterprise Board

In the case of the NEB there is little to add to the story except to note that the new institution has had to struggle unceasingly to find a stable role in public life. It has been criticized for being too timid and also for excessive risk-taking, whilst always being a repository for Government's uncertainties about its own industrial policies.

It is true that it rapidly became a disappointment to its promoters and its interventionist role was soon reduced in scale. Yet the NEB could only be as adventurous in its commercial judgement as the Cabinet would allow it to be. The fact that it was hostile to KME and undermined the cooperative's declining credibility must not obscure the fact that its members were appointed, and its policy framework determined, by the Labour Government. Over the years, the NEB has come more and more to resemble an outpost of the Industry Department.

Cooperative Development Agency
The CDA can be over-criticized too. They were bad Samaritans over KME to be sure; their behaviour was regrettable. Nevertheless, the CDA had only just been formed as a result of all-party support for a proposal which could scarcely have been more modest short of doing nothing.* The CDA's need for credibility would not have been helped by an immediate association with a controversial and commercially declining cooperative. Opinions about the calibre of the CDA vary from the derisive to the quietly approving and there is evidence that, as it matures and faces the need to justify its re-financing after the initial three years, the CDA is gearing up to take a more incisive role in cooperative develop-ment. This would be welcome, for the CDA has been firmly linked to the traditional cooperative movement, and one of the paradoxes of recent years has been that movement's defensiveness compared with the more vig-orous, new cooperatives largely associated with young, middle-class activists. The agency's director was also an export from the Department of Industry – a depart-ment which has well understood the Roman Empire's control system of maintaining loyalty and minimizing in-dependence by colonizing the top posts in its associated territories.

---

* In the bastion of market capitalism, the US Congress has founded a Cooperative Development Bank plus a national network of technical and advisory offices and voted $300 million over five years as the bank's investment fund. Britain's CDA has no investment fund and a budget of £900,000 for three years.

Robert Kilroy-Silk

Silk intermittently worked very hard for KME. Wary of the hot potato bequeathed him by Wilson, he soon found that KME's leaders were neglecting lifelines of assistance whilst claiming all the credit. Yet as the difficulties mounted, Silk was being pushed to support a venture which was clearly being mismanaged – sometimes being phoned several times a day and asked to put pressure on ministers, whilst having to cool down his Commons colleagues in case publicity revealed KME's true state.

Robert saw the officials and Williams being constantly abused from Kirkby as they tried to help. He had to face criticism in his constituency that he was only interested in KME. Spriggs should have known that Silk would pick up the signals of mismanagement, for cooperators and constituents came to him knowing nothing of what he and the leaders were doing. Robert would ask them what they thought of the ministers' views: 'What ministers? What views?' 'Those at last week's meeting.' 'What meeting?' Robert could see that no matter how outsiders tried to help, the leaders weren't going to change. Like all the officials and politicians, Silk gradually became fed up with Spriggs.

Mind you, it wasn't just the leaders. A steward's delegation visited Silk in 1978 to complain about Spriggs and Jenkins. Silk tried pushing them, saying, 'But you're all stewards – why don't you do something?' He feared they wouldn't – and he was right. He faded towards the end, unwilling to mislead Government or cooperators, for, by then, there was nothing to be done. KME had lost most of its cash, much of its impetus and all its political credibility. It had become a laughing stock in the House.

I believe that Silk could have played a more positive, more resourceful role in pressing for the reconstruction of KME but, that said, few people outside politics grasp the range and persistence of conflicting pressures on an MP's judgement and time. It is the only job where the person has to be prepared at any time to show some knowledge and views on any subject under the sun. Such diversity is the enemy of competent concentration. MPs tend to back campaigns which are deftly handled, and the rest tend to slip from view.

Tony Benn

Tony Benn is one of the most vivid politicians of the age. Managers often hiss at mention of his very name. Few of them have read any of his speeches or can tell you accurately what he stands for; but they hate him, one of the most vilified, traduced figures in Britain, despite the fact that Harold Wilson – far from a friend – accepts that he has been one of Labour's best administrators. Many of his themes were initially derided and yet have become accepted wisdom. He coined the word 'deindustrialization' in 1975 and, wrote Peter Jenkins, 'his warnings have come true with a vengeance'. Yet it makes little difference to his reputation, for as Paul Johnson has written, 'if we could dismiss his message as false, we would find him much less offensive. So we ignore logic and reason, and take refuge in abuse.'

There seems to be one sound reason for this widespread distaste. Benn appears to be full of contradictions. He is seen as a state centralist for supporting planning agreements, yet he is also passionately in favour of the dispersion of power. He is alleged to be single-mindedly driving for personal position whilst he pursues policies which ensure that governmental power eludes him. He could so easily have used his talents to become the darling of the trade unions and the Parliamentary Labour Party but, instead, has sought the applause of those who despise the pragmatism and fudging of politicians in office, whilst remaining in office himself. As a senior minister he outraged his colleagues as he distanced himself from Cabinet's less edifying actions, despite his nominal responsibility for its collective will.

I have great admiration for Tony Benn, yet to my regret, I find myself ambivalent over his erratic effect on affairs. His impact continues to be imposing but not always constructive, for his major defect seems to be an optimistic simplicity in public which goes beyond sense. He is careless about issues of choice and romantic about the motives and energies of the working class.

He is aware of the impediments to socialist progress, but on a platform the optimism takes over. 'Capitalism and democracy are incompatible,' he has said, ignoring the evidence before his eyes. I'm not even sure if he doesn't welcome the vilification of his ideas. If they were applauded, he might have to find a strategy to implement them, and this is where there is a persistent hole in his policies. If only he and his acolytes had been competent at planning specific policies which would command electoral support, he might have become Britain's most effective agent of political change. Indeed, perhaps he is, for as I write in the early summer of 1981, Benn's interventions are reconstructing the face of British politics almost week by week.

He seems anti the trade union establishment and supports independent, local, community-based, rank and file individualists in their fight with the centralist establishment of the trade union movement. Benn is on the side of the grass roots. Cooperatives are essentially anti-state corporatism, as Stephen Yeo has pointed out,* and Benn sees that market socialism might well incorporate the trade union movement in capitalism – but from the bottom up and not via the union hierarchies. If, as Middlemas has observed,† trade unions are now incorporated in the State and both respond to and seek to control their membership, unions will feel queasy about the growth of cooperatives with their inherent threat to existing trade union structures. Benn has few allies at the top of trade unions.

* See *Capitalism, State Formation and Marxist Theory*, ed. P. Corrigan (Quartet, 1980).
† See K. Middlemas, *Politics in Industrial Society* (André Deutsch, 1980).

Benn's self-reliant, community-based groups of self-controlling enterprises are quite like the CBI's view of small businesses and, indeed, like that of the Thatcher Government. He disagrees fundamentally with his right-wing Labour colleagues who have seemed more willing than he to assume that narrowly based centralism will become benevolent once the existing élite has been replaced by themselves. The positive side of Benn includes insight, compassion, courage, tenacity and, in half contradiction to my complaint of over-optimism, he has that inspiring belief in mankind which we are all the worse for discounting ourselves.

Yet he can mislead people. He has made much of the fact that, when he returned to the Industry Department in October 1974, he was accidentally given a brief marked 'For an incoming Labour Minister – except Mr Benn'. He uses this incident to imply that his officials were machiavellian in preparing three briefs. Yet there usually are three; one for the new Minister if the opposition wins the election, one if the Government wins the election and appoints a new Minister, and one for the previous Minister if the Government wins the election and reappoints him to the same post. It's perfectly normal; for why fully brief the reappointee if he was running the Department only a few weeks earlier? Benn may have got the wrong brief, but it does not reveal any plot. So is Benn ignorant of such procedures despite his long history of ministerial office, or is he trying to kid us?

Where KME is concerned, Benn must have our almost unqualified sympathy. He had overcome ferocious opposition within his department and was even blamed for his officials' inadequacy. Civil servants told me later that it was Benn's fault that the cooperators mistakenly thought that £5 million was the funding limit in 1974. Perhaps the Department of Industry was empty of officials on the day Benn needed their advice on the matter. Where Benn is culpable is over his failure to ensure that an adequate management system would be set up in KME. True to his beliefs about workers' sense, he left it instead to the cooperators to work out a reputable democracy for themselves.

What ensued is a blot on the two convenors' record. They let Benn down. He had placed faith in their response to his backing and they corrupted his purpose by concentrating power in their own hands. Benn would not say so, but he was upset at the way control at KME became a travesty of his original wish. Benn may have been too trusting in 1974, but the price he paid through KME's behaviour was excessive.

He had tried to find a new way to bridge the gap between capital and labour and his enthusiasm had been dashed by the behaviour of the civil servants and the convenors. He deserved better of them all.

Tony Eccles

I came to KME believing in the fundamental right for people to be able to control their own destiny and their own working lives and that, offered responsibility and the chance to exercise self-control, workers would grow in self-confidence and self-reliance. The first belief remains; the second now seems more problematic than I had hoped.

In retrospect, I should have been more alert to the leaders' obstinate refusal to face up to the issues which confronted them but, even so, I tried very hard to shift their behaviour. The trouble is that the role of the adviser is essentially powerless. Early on, I thought that clear exposition of the logic of the cooperative's needs would be enough to induce changes. As the organizational failures mounted, I became increasingly frustrated by the leaders' behaviour. I remained loyal to them, hoping that they would eventually see the light. Only once did I try to play the ends against the middle, when the stewards complained that they didn't know the business position. I incited them to rise up and force Jack and Dick to give them all the facts; but instead, they ran away. I offered to talk with any individuals or groups in the factory, but few were willing and the discussions got nowhere – possibly because the individuals didn't know whether to trust me. All offers to KME of outside help were refused and the 1977 survey was suppressed. By mid-1977 I had become convinced that only an external force would change anything in KME and so I began to push for external conditions to be applied by Government. The leaders knew that I was becoming depressed by constantly seeing no result from my sporadic haranguing of them. They said that they would understand if I faded from the scene. I stoutly insisted that I didn't fade, but I now see that I did so unconsciously, gradually distancing myself from the leaders' doomed policies whilst continuing to help them as much as before. Over the years, there were probably one thousand meetings and phone calls. I ended up as a more detached observer of a fascinating story, chastened and saddened by the experience and much more cautious about the scope for workers' control. However, my detachment related only to my judgement that KME would keep on failing; my desire and endeavour to help it to succeed wavered not one iota and KME's eventual failure grieves me still.

Many of the cooperators were sceptical about my role. On the one hand, as Chaplin found, 'most workers trusted Eccles as someone with the cooperative's interests at heart and with experience no one in the cooperative could match'. Against that, cooperators were concerned about what I was getting out of it – particularly when I was doing it for nothing, a worry that I felt reflected on them more than on me. As the standing of Spriggs and Jenkins fell, suspicion of me grew, since few knew what advice I was giving – though the stewards knew full well that I had consistently advocated better management skills, self-governing work groups, the creation of a policy-making control group and the opening up of information and discussion to and with every department. No steward could reasonably claim that he couldn't know exactly what

I was saying and doing at any stage, had he cared to listen, let alone to ask. As the prospect of KME's collapse grew, so did a little mixed bitterness. 'It's all right for you, you'll still have a job. You're doing all right, you come here in a suit. But you've been straight in what you've said.'

I was criticized from outside KME for proposing that KME's drinks operation should be shut down and 150 cooperators sacked. It would be, I was told, a return to free-market managerialism. But since there were no signs of alternative products and every indication of persistent losses, it seemed to me, as a believer in the merits of a mixed economy, grotesque to assume that 750 people should be employed on work for 600, since in the end, of course, it meant employment for none. And what if there'd been 1,500 people or 15,000 – is employment to be immutable regardless of the state of the firm? In a market economy open to international trade that could only result in even greater unemployment, and in a planned state the consumer would pay directly or indirectly for an inefficient use of resources.

From time to time someone would ask me why, if I was so committed to the cooperative, I hadn't come to work there. I had indeed considered offering myself as works manager and, if I hadn't changed jobs at the beginning of 1976, I might have taken a sabbatical year to do so; but I doubt if it would have been of much use. The people who asked were always given four answers. First, that I would have made unpopular decisions which would have been rejected. Second, that I would have become trapped inside, and the convenors would have turned the cooperators against me if I had challenged their view of the world. Third, that I was of more value to KME as an outsider when assisting Jack and Dick with Government, and fourth, that it was painful enough paying my own expenses and cutting back on other activities to work with KME – I couldn't afford to take the drop to a KME salary too; and (though I didn't tell them this) I couldn't see how KME's people could benefit from turning my own and my wife's lives upside-down when they would scarcely make any serious effort to find out how to save themselves, let alone to do it.

Conversely, my resignation would have been a threat of no magnitude. The leaders would have explained it away. So I plugged on, largely wasting my breath, hoping that the cooperators would finally wake up to their plight, listen, and pull themselves together. The situation was rather like dealing with family relatives; there are times when they infuriate you but you just can't abandon them.

There was no basis of power for me at KME. The leaders didn't want to share power (and if they'd offered any to me, divorced from the cooperators sharing it more widely, I'd have refused); the stewards didn't want to take the responsibility; the workers didn't really want to know; the council had collapsed; the management had surrendered; the officials and Ministers were of little practical help; the CDA wanted KME to go away, and the unions pretended it had gone away. Wherever I looked, there was nothing to use as a lever.

KME's people
The behaviour of the cooperators, the stewards and the leaders was all intertwined, for there was an identity of interest between the workers and the leaders who had saved their jobs for nearly five years. This should not be underrated as an achievement, but it does not prove that the leaders both inspired and reflected the workers' aims. Rather the convenors dominated the cooperative, whilst asserting that they were merely reflecting the popular will. In so far as the popular will existed, this was initially true. Nevertheless, the leaders must be the central focus of analysis, since they created the deterioration of KME's three operating phases (shown in Figure 5 on p. 377), for, whilst the workers may have been unenterprising and the stewards confused, the leaders' behaviour was the main cause of this sad sequence.

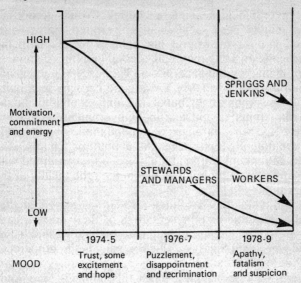

Figure 5 Morale at KME: 1974-9

	1974-5	1976-7	1978-9
MOOD	Trust, some excitement and hope	Puzzlement, disappointment and recrimination	Apathy, fatalism and suspicion

The leaders had characteristics which were vital to KME's formation and external image. Without them – particularly Spriggs – the cooperative would never have happened. His unrelenting tenacity was vital.

Unfortunately, the skills which are required to promote solidarity in the face of management initiatives may be quite inappropriate once the initiatives all rest with the employees. A shop-floor culture which is collective, oral, reactive and which deduces from experience is quite different to a managing culture which is individualistic and takes initiatives based on analysis. The leaders were never very interested in factual analyses, and their antipathy towards normal management systems, which was shared by many cooperators, made them rotten at running the business. Little of their energy was spent on this task, and everyone outside became fed up with their obstinate refusal to take charge competently.

This might not have mattered if the leaders had instead created a charter for the professional managers so that

effective management of the business could occur; but
they didn't. They simultaneously rejected the management role for themselves and refused to give it to the
managers. In fact, they had a cavalier attitude towards
both managers and supervisors. The leaders' intelligence
is not in doubt, for they had a good capacity to acquire
skills and knowledge, but it was only exercised on the
narrow fronts of outsmarting Government, killing off
threats to their centralized power and massaging the press
to promote KME's image. As a political scientist described President Carter, they 'were more concerned with
the appearance of doing well than with the quality of the
work done'.

Until it was too late, they refused to accept that they
had a dual role as representatives of the workforce and
promoters of organizational competence. 'There is no
dual role,' said Spriggs. 'This company is the property of
the unions.' Yet the stewards and convenors wouldn't
accept the responsibility which this implied. Nor would
they reconstruct the organization.

The result was a gaping void at KME. The managers
didn't have the power to exercise control; the workforce
had neither the information nor the structure to do so;
the stewards had little inclination to accept the responsibility; and Jack and Dick insisted they weren't in charge,
whilst constantly demonstrating that they were. Yet they
could easily have improved matters. The leaders started
off with vast amounts of a commodity which many managements would dearly love – the trust of the shop-floor.
By the end, it had almost all evaporated. They had blown
it away, for their behaviour was in continued contrast to
that needed by KME's circumstances. This criticism could
have been avoided if it had been clear that the leaders
were committed to social goals of subsidized self-management and were indifferent to the goal of business success.
Yet if the leaders were interested in self-management,
they weren't much good at promoting it. The key question
is whether the leaders were accidental autocrats who used

democratic systems in the quest for power. The unavoidable answer is 'yes'.

A good leader helps his associates to grow, views his subordinates optimistically and seeks their advice whilst using his strength to nurture them and help them to become stronger. With the possible exceptions of electrician Ralph Peacock and John Bandell, I cannot think of anybody at KME who grew in stature as a result of the convenors' leadership. Far from it; they were all diminished by the experience of seeing their self-esteem consistently eroded. The leaders were basically distrustful of the cooperators, critical of every steward, supervisor and manager; they interfered in details, withheld information, withheld responsibility and only involved others to endorse what had already been decided. Some of this was justified; most of it was not. The widespread demoralization and eventual apathy were entirely predictable.

Like many managements, the leaders wanted the workers to be resourceful but not to challenge existing power structures or to threaten them as power holders. It was also part of their old need for solidarity. Spriggs had said, 'I want complete support. I don't want majority decisions. I want everyone to agree the policies.' So all policies had to be agreeable by definition. Given the workers' ignorance of the cooperative's trading, it wasn't surprising that they would only give backing to a low level of organizational competence which wouldn't threaten old working habits.

The result was deadlock. The cooperators would do less and less to increase their endeavours when faced with a leadership which undermined every single attempt to broaden the base of responsibility in KME. Spriggs and Jenkins repeatedly claimed that the workforce's behaviour justified their poor opinion of the cooperators' sense of responsibility. It was impossible to convince them that it was the inevitable result of their own behaviour and that they had never seriously investigated, or invested in, an alternative. But that would have required the leaders to put their own power on the line. Unwilling to try, the convenors were stuck with having to accept the workers' power to veto initiatives, and so the leaders' own power became of no avail. They became powerless paternalists. All they could do was to face the outside world, bluff their way through and bang the table with Government whilst making optimistic promises that they could not bring themselves to deliver.

KME failed internally partly because it had lousy constitutional arrangements which the leaders refused to rectify, and so there was nothing to stop Spriggs and Jenkins from accreting all power to themselves. In one sense they shouldn't be blamed for this any more than one would blame a gas for filling a vacuum. It was their misuse of that power which was so costly, as well as being an affront to the ideals they were trying to embody. The convenors liked power and authority but couldn't use them constructively and resisted any and every power-sharing reform, since they believed that they would be sharing power with people who couldn't cope. There was some truth in this, but people were not being helped to cope. If there was ever an implicit challenge to their leadership primacy, they would habitually polarize the choice and indicate that they would only work on their own terms, and then only when they were sure of the decision going their way. As one steward said, 'Jack's anti-authority, unless he's got it.'

Stewards at KME also had another explanation for Spriggs' unwillingness to hold effective discussions on the running of the business. He was very good at one-to-one meetings, clear-sighted and fast on the uptake. He negotiated well where it was clear that he was the leader of the two parties at such meetings. He was also excellent at communicating from the platform to mass meetings; indeed, one defence of the workers' acquiescing in his leadership was his ability to mesmerize mass-meeting audiences. He could talk their socks up and down.

Yet he lost something when talking with informal

groups where his authority role was unclear, as would occur in policy-generating groups faced with uncertain choices. The dynamics of such groups are out of any one person's control. He avoided them.*

It wasn't that KME's leadership was malevolent. Indeed Spriggs was, if anything, too benign, since he could scarcely bring himself to press for actions which were not acceptable to an ill-informed shop-floor. Once the cooperators had rebuffed the early de-manning plan, the leaders became fatalistic about the chance of encouraging the workers to more knowing behaviour. Despite constant warnings, only after years of trading failure and organizational confusion did the leaders begin to revise their view of their role – and then only with the utmost reluctance and when it was too late.

The harshest judgement on Spriggs came from Williams, whose abiding memory was of a project which could have saved hundreds of jobs at several points and which was 'run into the ground by bloody-minded obstruction. Hundreds of jobs were sacrificed to the vanity of one man.'

Some will agree with Williams – including some cooperators – though there are ameliorating circumstances to excuse much of the leader's behaviour.

The leaders had two sound excuses for their own actions – the workers and the stewards. The workers were a decent bunch of people who wanted a job and a wage. They hadn't really asked for a cooperative and its accompanying turmoil. They had some initial enthusiasm that things would be different in the cooperative in an unspecified way – perhaps happier – and there are commentators who claim that only the leaders' behaviour caused the optimism to wilt. Yet the enthusiasm wasn't translated into a positive drive to face up to KME's needs. The

---

* Author's note: I have a kinder explanation for Spriggs' preference for one-way and one-to-one meetings. He is almost deaf in one ear, which makes informal group meetings a misery for him.

wages improved and so did performance, but cooperators seemed strangely incurious about their prospects, leaving more and more control in the hands of the two leaders. It wasn't unlike the trust which they had placed in King.

There were some energetic people to be sure, but they still left much to the leadership, and as they became unhappy, they did little but opt out and sit around moaning in an utterly ineffectual manner. The people who took against Spriggs and Jenkins couldn't even plot competently, despite their opportunities to gather the votes of the dissaffected, and depression might have occurred even if the leaders had shared power, for, as Ralph Peacock put it, 'It's difficult to tell a man with a welding torch still in front of him that he's part of a new system.' One excuse for the lack of commitment could be that the pressure for production drove out any chance of building consensus, but the lack of consensus actually *depressed* output, and nobody could see the afternoon card schools and go away continuing to assert that there was no slack time to create commitment. It wasn't a trade-off between production and democratic growth. The latter was simply avoided.

I have sympathy for the workers at KME, but as we recall factors like the craftsmen who would never countenance any change to their self-important traditions, we clearly cannot load all the odium on to the leaders and the stewards, or just blame social conditioning and external pressures. The 750 cooperators had nearly five years in which to make their mark on their own working lives.

It is hard to avoid feeling sorry for the stewards, as well as resentful of their response to the pressures placed upon them. The stewards' committee never made any serious attempt to share power with the convenors or to campaign for changes in the cooperative structure. Individual stewards did try to represent the business needs to their members; some were replaced for their pains and others instructed to represent their members' interests directly. Underbriefed and ill-prepared, the stewards weren't able to convince themselves, let alone their members, that the cooperators owned and controlled the business and that, as representatives, the stewards had to look at the business needs.

The business implications were unnerving, and it is no wonder that the stewards recoiled from seeking information and extra influence. Responsibility would have been inescapably theirs. Otherwise they would have been forced to re-structure the enterprise and give the business control to some other body – the council or the management – to free themselves for traditional collective bargaining.

Several stewards both understood and tried to shoulder the dual responsibility, but the stewards' committee was never united on the matter. Some stewards would back anything proposed by Jack and Dick. They were known disparagingly as 'the nod squad'.

Other stewards constantly sought the easy way out by pushing responsibility on to the powerless managers. 'It's management's job to manage' was a recurring theme, even though it was patently obvious that the convenors held all the power. Faced with the dilemmas of responsibility, the stewards let Jack and Dick rule. As the stewards lost confidence in KME's business skills, they became more and more reluctant to get involved in the mess. Indeed some observers feel that the convenors left the organization deliberately vague in order to maximize their own power, and that the stewards connived at this.

One manager said afterwards, 'Jack and Dick should have said that the stewards' committee was the controlling body. Then people would have fought for positions and couldn't then have denied their responsibility for the business.' I wonder. The leaders became scathing about the stewards at the end, saying 'they include a lot of weak-kneed people who've got to blame us'. They were right, but the stewards' positions were difficult. All their previous experience had been in traditional firms where the stewards try to influence management decisions. Lacking this source, KME had a desperate need for a body which would take responsibility for generating initiatives. Neither the convenors nor the stewards would walk forward. They couldn't move from the role of adversary to the role of controllership.

Opinions will vary about the relative weight of responsibility for KME's decision-making inefficiency to be borne between workers, stewards and leaders, but if reformation from inside was impracticable, what of the outside?

Department of Industry

The Industry Department officials might have played a more positive role. Much of their behaviour has been detailed in the book and perhaps some analysts will use it to generate yet more heat in the perennial argument about the power and tactics of the Civil Service. The ways in which the Civil Service coordinates and maintains its strengths so as to affect ministerial actions are being increasingly documented elsewhere and it is not this book's purpose to give perfunctory coverage to an important and complex topic.

Nevertheless, there are three elements which must be faced. In the battle over Labour's industrial policy it was inevitable that civil servants would be placed in a difficult position, given the split between Wilson and Benn. Technically, all Permanent Secretaries are appointed by the Prime Minister and so owe him their first allegiance. Despite this and despite any provocations which came the officials' way from Benn, their behaviour towards him was still a disgrace. After 1976, the officials went out of their way on occasions to ease KME's path, but they never really engaged in any sustained positive attempt to help KME to reorganize itself. Perhaps they were under political instruction; perhaps they felt that KME would never change and that their effort would be wasted. Not for a moment do I believe that they lacked the skills to help. They were sophisticated, intelligent, politically sen-

sitive and generally impressive. Nor did they lack for
confidence. Lippitt believes that officials have a mission:
'There should be more interchange [with industry] not
least because the Civil Service probably contains a disproportionate share of the country's talent.'

Leaving aside the issue of the relevance of that talent
to the tasks, his view raises a question: To what end is
that talent used? The blunt fact is that, outside the debating arena, intellectual confidence is of little help. When
the debate is over, it is competent action which is required. Yet Government's control and monitoring role at
KME was less than would have been exercised by a
capital-providing bank, and officials didn't seem to agree
that the institution which puts up the money has a responsibility for influencing the development of the enterprise. Indeed, officials took the opposite view, implying
that if they intervened, Government could become the
unlimited liability banker for what ensued.

This is still puzzling, for either Government can control
the use to which its funds are put, or it cannot. The
statements of Sir Peter Carey and John Lippitt to the
Public Accounts Committee do not provide conclusive
evidence one way or the other, largely because they
seemed to be saying contradictory things. Over the purchase of the business from the receiver in 1974 they simultaneously claimed to have done everything possible to
get the best price for the cooperative; to have done
nothing, since they had been unable to intervene without
breathing down the cooperators' necks; and thirdly, that
they were completely helpless to intervene in the face of
the receiver's excessive valuation. The committee was
unimpressed, concluding that the Department could have
justifiably taken a more positive attitude.

The Civil Service cannot have it both ways. Either it
didn't have any ways to help the cooperative effectively
– in which case monitoring is little more than passive
surveillance to ensure that illegalities do not occur – or,

if it was trying to help the cooperative, it went about it in a funny way, and our opinions of its competence would have to be downgraded.

Opinions are mixed. Benn describes Lippitt as 'a savage critic', although Lippitt did make an effort to help, telling Lewis in January 1975 that action plans and contingency measures should be prepared, management should be strengthened, accountants engaged, financial controls strengthened and the schemes agreed with the shop stewards. He felt that KME didn't listen to his views, and concluded that he was wasting his time, not fully appreciating the depth of their business ignorance.

What is clear is that there was no love lost between Benn and his officials. When I met Lippitt with Spriggs and Jenkins, his was clearly an adversary position. But then so was Varley's. All in all, mitigating circumstances do exist for some of the officials' behaviour early on, but even so, it was not the Civil Service's finest hour.* Later on, there was grudging respect, even affection, for Spriggs. To the last, Spriggs underestimated the officials' sympathy and overestimated his political backing.

Eric Varley

The actions of Varley are best passed over quickly since they had one constant strand. His behaviour was consistently unedifying and, as Silk put it, 'Varley was never any help at all,' though he did give aid after a fashion. He did, after all, for an extraneous reason, give KME the wrong amount of money at the wrong time – and claimed the credit. In the course of a critical review of Benn's

---

* Even in 1981, time had not mellowed them. Some continued to claim that Benn had simply and cynically used the Kirkby workers for political ends, despite a decade's evidence of Benn's unwavering support for workers' control.

   Some civil servants still object to Benn having treated cooperatives more favourably than traditional businesses. But if experiments are to be judged only by the standards of what already exists, politicians would have precious little to do in the promotion of social initiatives, which is, after all, one of their main functions.

book *Arguments for Socialism*, Varley had the nerve to write, 'I shall always remember how proud he [Benn] was to announce on behalf of the Labour Cabinet, that the Kirkby cooperative [KME] would receive financial support, and how disappointed he was that he had to tell the Commons that the cash was on a once-for-all basis – a pledge that I broke when I became Secretary of State for Industry and gave it more money.' Of course, he didn't give it more money when he became Industry Secretary, for, as chapter 7 shows, he was critical, obstructive, and refused to rectify the underfunding of the improving business in 1976. Despite the IMF's insistence on cuts in public expenditure, more than a year later he and his Cabinet colleagues chose to ignore the basis of his own earlier refusal, as well as the cooperative's shift from an improving to a deteriorating performance and a year's evidence of KME's malfunctioning; but then the fresh money was given to counter Merseyside unemployment, not because it would work. The Industry Department officials knew it would be insufficient and when Silk inquired about its adequacy, he was told, 'Let's say it will get you through the next election.' A ministerial friend of Varley has an even more jaundiced view of motives over the change of heart between the 1976 refusal and the 1977 grant: 'Eric was standing for party treasurer again that year and didn't want it to fail before a certain date.'

Varley had entered the House as a left-winger, but his subsequent career has been an impressive support for the old political adage: 'To get along, go along'. His ability to turn his skills to any policy and do what those above him want, clearly ensures that he will remain in high office. He has been popular in the Parliamentary Labour Party and is evidently a competent administrator. He may well be a socialist too, though throughout the KME saga the best that can be said for him is that he was a master of disguise. But he'll survive and prosper. In 1981, the Labour Party and the TUC set up a committee to prepare a new industrial strategy to fuse centralized planning and shop-floor worker democracy. On it were Benn, Booth, Heffer and Atkinson. So was Varley.

Alan Williams

We should have more sympathy for Williams. Under instruction, unavoidably set up as the minister responsible, he was constantly embattled in Cabinet Committee as either Benn and his allies would reserve their position or, if he were giving KME money, the strongly negative Treasury axis would reserve its position instead.

Williams' officials thought well of him. 'He was an ideal minister in many ways. He could look at the politics, look at the facts and he could take decisions.' Given his talent, charm, intelligence and evident skills, I, respecting and liking him, had hoped that he would admit that he had been pushed into his actions; but he couldn't agree. 'I wasn't forced to do anything. Eric was informed at every stage and we were in agreement.'

In my judgement, the actions of Williams and Varley can only be a source of regret to the Labour movement, though their behaviour was not out of line with the Labour Government of 1974–9, a Government which latterly seemed to its left-wing critics to lack ambition much beyond that of remaining in charge. In the end, it was not persuasive in either of any government's two basic leadership roles.* It could neither win support for its transactions, nor for its role in transforming the political climate by inspiring people.

The transactional role is of bargaining and exchange, and by 1979 Labour's one central claim to competence in this area, the bargain with the trade union movement, broke down over the 5 per cent pay limit. At the same time, the Labour Government offered little impression of merit in its transforming role, that is, there was little to arouse, engage or elevate people's commitment to a vision of worthwhile, principled goals. The KME story is an

* See James McGregor Burns, *Leadership* (Harper & Row, 1978).

analogue for that period, and Varley and Williams emerge as no more uninspired and uninspiring than the rest of Government.

The Labour Party's later aggression over policy and accountability is entirely understandable after that 1974–9 experience. Williams felt that KME offered an important lesson over the re-selection of MPs. 'Spriggs would take the fight with Labour ministers to the constituencies.' Some party members would see that as entirely appropriate. Fortunately, new Labour leader Michael Foot has recognized the basic desire among Labour Party members for a synthesis of transactional and inspirational skills. On the day of his election to party leader he said, 'The art of politics is to bring together the integrity of one's principles with effective action. You have to do both at the same time. To say that you can only do one is not an appropriate approach to politics.' Over KME, Varley and Williams seemed less than impressive with either.

Lord Salisbury's 1881 dictum will serve as my last word on the ministers, officials and the convenors. 'Those who have the absolute power of preventing lamentable events and, knowing what is taking place, refuse to exercise that power, are responsible for what happens.'

You may think my judgement to be severe on the officials. The *Telegraph* leader, reproduced on p. 390 comes from a different political perspective from my own, yet reached the same broad conclusions.

Part 3: Conclusions and recommendations

The democratization of work has a long and difficult road ahead, not just because of the resistance of existing power holders, but because of the ambivalence of workers and their organizations as they try to cope with the twin pressures of efficiency needs and workers' aspirations. The issues weren't different at KME, it was the approach which was different. The differences between KME and

THE DAILY TELEGRAPH

FRIDAY, SEPTEMBER 22, 1978

135, Fleet Street, London, E.C.4.

Tel: 01-353 4242. Telex: 22874/5/6.

Classified Advertisements: 01-583 3939.

CO-OP ON A STRING

MR ERIC VARLEY is one of those Ministers who usually espouses the cause of common sense, and usually loses the argument. So it would be wise to expect that his Department's decision to refuse the demand from the Kirkby co-operative for another £3 million from the taxpayers will in due course be overturned. There is a willing commercial buyer for the Kirkby factory once the co-operative has gone into liquidation. There would be substantial redundancies, but that is because the co-operative employs far more men than it needs. Under the terms of the 1972 Industry Act another £3 million subsidy would require Parliamentary endorsement. It should be refused.

That said, the Kirkby workers are deserving of sympathy. They have been at the receiving end of a classic tale of political manipulation. When their original employers put the factory into liquidation in the early 1970s, Sir Harold Wilson, their local M P, thrust them into the arms of a property company which promptly went bust. Then they were taken up by Mr Wedgwood Benn, who endowed them with £¼ million to launch their co-operative. They say that this sum was quite inadequate for the purpose. Of course it was: for while the Treasury cannot always veto Ministerial ventures into entrepreneurship, it can mess them up.

When Mr Wedgwood Benn moved on from the Department of Industry, his former civil servants embarked upon a great crusade: to destroy every trace of his tenancy. The Kirkby co-operators can be forgiven for feeling that, even if their prospects were really as glittering as they pretend, the fact that they were sponsored by Mr Wedgwood Benn would, in the eyes of the Department, seal their fate. So what has happened at Kirkby — and at Meriden and the *Scottish Daily News*— does not prove that co-operatives cannot succeed. What it does prove is that co-operatives which look to Whitehall to finance them are just asking for trouble.

a conventional manufacturing company were mainly those of degree.

What then is required for worker power to be more effectively deployed?

Workers need more knowledge and understanding, notably of business issues, if they are to take charge competently. Lacking authentic information and the ability to understand its implications, workers can scarcely make informed choices or participate intelligently in the central decisions of the enterprise.

As James Madison put it when debating the US Constitution: 'A popular government without popular information, or the means of acquiring it, is but a prologue to a farce or a tragedy; or perhaps both. Knowledge will for ever govern ignorance, and a people who mean to be their own governors must arm themselves with the power which knowledge gives.'

Lacking the knowledge and comprehension to become involved effectively, KME's cooperators relied on their leaders, whose reluctance to inform people was matched by the workers' disinclination to find out. Faced with the workers' incomprehension, the leaders became anxious, debate was inhibited, conflicts were suppressed and so problems incubated with destructive effect.

The issue of business understanding arouses mixed feelings among socialists, unhappy at the thought of becoming associated with business managements. Yet the need for expertise is critical in the face of complex problems, and it is saddening to see how vulnerable are workers to market conditions, largely because the ethos which binds them collectively is so antipathetic to management and to business. The result is an inadvertent blind trust in the fates which leaves too many workers to wake up to the problems only when the roof falls in.

Such behaviour is not intelligent, and a workforce or its unions who protest that a factory closure is a shock are often merely advertising the weakness of their monitoring of the business. Unions have a long history of reacting to management initiatives, but this is scarcely enterprising enough in those turbulent times. The need for business expertise was well summed up by a worker cooperator at the Institute for Workers' Control conference in 1975: 'It's absolutely essential. Without it, workers' control is meaningless. You don't know what you're controlling.'

On the left, there is a view that management expertise is deliberately mysterious and they demand that it be 'demystified'. Yet there is nothing inherently mysterious about management. The techniques used are simply those which try to detect patterns in events and to discern sensible choices of action so that judgements can be made, often in situations of intractable complexity. Management isn't mysterious; it's just difficult.

Nor is it a process which can be wished away; for the act of coordination has to be carried out in some fashion, whether it be by a centralized élite or by being distributed throughout a non-hierarchical collective. Problems of organization are not dissolved simply by being dispersed.

Whether the organization is a hospital, a ship or a business, its resources have to be marshalled to carry out its tasks in the face of dilemmas. Only those with little experience of managing seem to believe that management is simply an authority form for suppressing spontaneous natural efficiency.

The issue of dispersing business decisions throughout the workforce is a challenge to advocates of worker power. There is little evidence that the bulk of workers are yet interested in the grand strategies of business. Study after study shows that workers are interested mainly in what affects their everyday worklives and workplaces. People tend not to intervene in grander affairs if they believe that the power holders are trustworthy, constructively motivated, competent and well informed – particularly if they feel that their own contribution wouldn't be relevant or helpful. The democrat may bridle at this, but what if the people choose to be interested only in their local situation and prefer to let the leaders lead? Are we the ones pushing 'democracy' on to them in the name of their own interests?

One answer to this is that the followers might become interested in sharing power and responsibility if only their lack of confidence and experience didn't inhibit them. We cannot be sure, and perhaps the diffident workers have a point. The task of making effective decisions in a complex organization which faces uncertain conditions whilst also being decisive, participative, power-constrained and accountable, is pretty tough. However, a survey by Ursell *et al.** has shown that a sample of shop stewards strongly approved of participation, were less partisan than managers about business versus union needs and wanted participation, not just to gain more power and responsibility but to solve everyday problems, increase efficiency and reduce conflict. But their enthusiasm for participation was prospective and does not prove that they would continue to support it if they were to experience KME's traumas.

KME certainly scotches the simplistic view of worker participation – that if you provide the opportunity, people will readily blossom. Participation is stressful and not just for the reasons of role confusion which racked KME's stewards and convenors. As one KME steward put it, 'No one on the shop-floor wanted genuine involvement because it would have meant challenging your mates.' This accords with other findings and, as Martin Lockett has argued,† the idea that people are more satisfied as a result of participation seems to be believed more by those who haven't been close to the experience. People's interests may be enriched by participation, but partly in the direction of feelings of vulnerability. Furthermore, satisfaction may be lowered as a result of enhanced expectations which are not being met. Boring work may still seem boring even if you own the means of production.

* *Industrial Relations Journal*, Vol. 10, No. 4, 1979.
† *Democracy, Participation and Satisfaction* (Imperial College, June 1979).

Add these discouragements to the need for business skills and it is clear that building confidence and inducing people to take responsibility will not occur quickly even if the workers are willing to be organized to that end. Meanwhile the business may languish. Even after the investment in participatory systems the resulting decisions may be of poorer technical quality (i.e. they won't be the best to reach the goals which the participants are seeking) than those made by the most able, experienced and best-informed leaders.

This brings us to the question of control structures and the issue of representation procedures. If there is a need for high-quality decisions to achieve the cooperative's targets, and if some cooperators remain reluctant to participate in business decisions, what should the cooperative do in the meantime? There will be a transitional phase pending full involvement by all cooperators, but the transition could take years of sustained efforts to enhance the management skills of the cooperators so that they can run their own affairs effectively and democratically. Some, indeed, will never want to become involved and will continue to behave instrumentally towards their work-lives.

The inevitable conclusion is that control will have to be exercised by representatives of the workforce, notably those who are more technically skilled and fully briefed, for even if all the cooperators were interested and knowledgeable, many management decisions are multi-faceted and cannot be reduced to simple choices to be made by mass meetings or via polls. Representative democracy may be unavoidable except for major policy decisions, even when the organization is strongly egalitarian. Yet the decision to have representative leaders will cause a further concentration of influence since those with the most information and power will tend to control agendas and limit the options to be considered.*

* *A Model of Decision Making for Worker Cooperatives*, A. Thomas and C. Cornforth (Plunkett Society, Oxford, 1980).

The need for expertise, speed of decision on day-to-day matters and a representative system all imply that the cooperative – unless quite small – would need to have leaders with some executive authority, and so executive power would become concentrated even though the leaders would be ultimately accountable for their decisions to the whole workforce. Once executive authority is to be invested in the hands of a smaller group, then it becomes practicable to employ professional managers if the cooperative chooses.

Should it so choose? The problems in a new cooperative are much like those of any new business, except that in a new conventional business its founder(s) usually have a clear prior idea of their purposes and the power to pursue them. As the CDA's director has observed, 'The establishment of a successful industrial enterprise as a cooperative needs at least as much organizational care, managerial competence and commercial realism as the establishment of a conventionally constituted enterprise.' Unless the new cooperative is tiny, the chance that professional managers will be employed is very high.

Whether or not professional managers are employed, one searing lesson of KME is that power and accountability need to be clearly located and delineated if the organization is to be effective – whatever its goals. KME's drift into centralized power was ineffectual on any grounds since it didn't lead to competent management and, for the workers, the operating climate was little different from that of a traditional enterprise. Indeed the erosion of the unions' collective bargaining role meant that the workers' influence over events became more tenuous than it might have been in a traditional enterprise. At first, some cooperators had felt that 'we don't need unions now we're in a cooperative' but later, many workers became critical of their unions' emasculated role, believing that they no longer had any effective representation over genuine grievances for, as Figure 2 (p. 106) shows, whether the grievances went via the management or the stewards, they always wound up with the two convenors.

Nor were the unions effective at raising people's wages, for no wage bargaining occurred. I have often wondered what KME would have done in the absence of incomes policy, where the cooperative would have been forced to choose its wage rises. My guess is that the leaders would have proposed that everyone receive an increase which matched inflation or the 'going rate' of rises, and that no serious dissent or discussion would have occurred.

As the leaders overmanaged KME democratic forums, the process of democracy became debased and their ability to call for effort, flexibility, obedience and commitment was impaired as the workers withdrew their support. Lacking a logical framework to spread power and responsibility, the cooperators had little opportunity or motivation to become involved or committed to the goals and policies of the enterprise. Yet they did have substantial power because of their ability to veto the initiatives of KME's leaders. This was ironic, for one of the criticisms of modest forms of worker participation is that such schemes give 'the illusion of involvement without the reality of power'.* KME's style of operation turned this on its head, since the shop-floor cooperators had the reality of power without more than the illusion of involvement.

The key dimension behind all these organizational pathologies was structure – the way in which the cooperative arranged its affairs. KME demonstrated that if you start off with an ineffective decision-making structure and neither the power holders nor external forces will make a move, then you cannot take the one vital decision – the decision to change the structure. Structure is a central component of organizational competence, not an unimportant afterthought. Goodwill and hard work are not enough. It isn't just a matter of relying on the integrity

* *The Right to Manage*, W. Daniel and N. McIntosh (PEP, 1970), p. 125.

and skills of a few leaders and hoping that the organization can muddle through; sometimes it can be, but to rely on that is not an act of strategy, but one of faith.

It isn't that one structural form is best, but that, for a given circumstance, some structures are systematically and demonstrably better than others. There are limits to the number of ways you can run an organization unless you are utterly indifferent to the goal of economic efficiency, and it isn't clear that we are so rich in resources that we can afford to fritter them away through inefficiency. This doesn't mean that there are no left-wing ways to run a company, but it doesn't help when left-wingers applaud ineffectual methods just because these ways seem to be anti-capitalist. Socialists should be as interested in operational competence as anyone, and the cooperative structure, at its best, should have made KME easier to run.

It wasn't easier to run; and the reasons are painfully obvious. The convenors and stewards just couldn't cope with the twin roles of workforce defender and efficiency promoter. They were trapped by their historical roles, and as one steward put it wistfully, 'We're used to fighting the management. It is hard for us and our members to realize that we are the management'. The powerless managers thus became the scapegoats for failure and when that became too implausible to sustain, the focus of blame shifted on to Jack and Dick as the stewards scurried for cover. The stewards can't be blamed for being ambivalent about their roles as workforce representatives and policy makers, and, unprepared, they were in a poor state to take the initiative even if they had been united on what action was necessary. The duality of power between workers and management was internalized within the shop stewards and it tied them into anguished knots. Under stress it was no wonder that they reverted to representing their members to an elusive image of 'management'.

Too late to matter at KME, the two convenors and I

developed a solution which has possibilities for resolving the contradictions which bedevil proposals for worker directors and which have turned experiments – such as the Post Office and British Steel Corporation – into unfortunate experiences. Before it is proposed – and it has surfaced in the book before – a brief analysis of trade union attitudes to cooperation is necessary.

The British trade union movement has been equivocal about workers' control and has oscillated between a desire to hold on to its adversary role in collective bargaining arrangements and a half-hearted wish to extend its power into the citadel of management – the boardroom. Even so, there has been ambivalence about the shared responsibility which would inevitably ensue if power were shared. In 1977 the TUC backed away from the Bullock Report's espousal of worker directors and asserted that 'collective bargaining can be extended greatly to increase trade union influence over main policies. The extension of worker representation on policy boards or committees should not be used as a means of frustrating the processes of existing collective bargaining machinery.'

Others are not so sure. Tony Lane wrote in the *Guardian* (15.9.80): 'there is a recognition [in the trade unions] that the old ways can be pushed no further and that there have to be new and better ways and that these must connect with efficiency and company strategic planning'. His implication is that unions will not escape some responsibility for business decisions and their consequences – even if they extend power through collective bargaining – let alone if extension occurs by other methods of power equalization.

The fork on which the unions are impaled is that they exist to protect their members' livelihoods, but the route by which that objective is best achieved in a mixed economy is not clear to them. The choice is that of independence versus absorption into a business framework; between a narrow definition of a defensive role and the murky risks of a more confusing amalgam of roles. These are difficult choices to make. Giles Radice MP has summed it up: 'All unions agree that the problem [of industrial democracy] is how to devise a system which preserves union independence while genuinely increasing employee influence over industrial decision-making.' 'Increasing influence' would imply increased responsibility for business policies and decisions – exactly the point from which many unionists recoil.

KME offers a solution to this problem, but before we can reach that point, further union problems should be briefly discussed. Why is it that unions have been so ambivalent about cooperatives – sympathetic in principle but pessimistic, even antagonistic, in practice. The answer is chilling.

Worker cooperatives offer a major threat to the existing structure of British trade unions, for the common cause between cooperators suggests the need for union integration, not the multiplicity of occupational unions which presently exists. Because enterprise-wide union amalgamation is far more relevant to workers' control than the messy tussles between multi-union factions, combine committees ought to have a bright future. Yet they are often discouraged by union hierarchies.

I have argued* that an extension of industrial democracy will create a matrix organization in which a new axis of company-based and industry-based worker amalgamations will arise. This will cut across the present union movement of occupationally based unions, though these will remain to represent sectional interests against oppression, both from employers and from other workers. Both axes would become equally legitimate.†

This development would make the trade union movement more sophisticated, more complex, trickier to op-

---

* 'Industrial democracy and organizational change', *Personnel Review*, Vol. 6, No. 1, 1977; and *Trade Union Behaviour towards Workers' Cooperatives* (Plunkett Society, Oxford, 1981).
† 'Sit-ins, worker cooperatives and some implications for organization', *Personnel Review*, Vol. 6, No. 2, 1977.

erate and conceivably more unruly as contending power groups gravitated to the two different axes to pursue their struggles. Add to this the fact that unions are far less powerful than is popularly supposed, witness their inability in 1979–81 to mount any serious resistance to a huge rise in their members' unemployment, and it is scarcely surprising that the growth of worker cooperatives is an unappealing threat to the existing precarious structure of the union movement. Although some people see the trade unions as the natural institution to help workers' self-management, unions will express polite support whilst remaining operationally opposed to cooperatives unless a structure can be found which maintains union legitimacy.

Wilson has claimed that Benn's company planning agreement proposals were downgraded in 1974 in part because union leaders, such as Jack Jones (TGWU) and Hugh Scanlon (AUEW), were opposed to shop stewards being given more power within enterprises. Yet the unions' consistent theme for many years has been that extensions of industrial democracy can only legitimately occur through developments in the single channel of union representation. KME demonstrates exactly why the role confusion which results from that approach ensures that, in the short term at least, their policy simply will not work. What is the point of roping in union-based worker directors if they are promptly immobilized in anguish like KME's stewards? The aims of collective bargaining and overall guardianship of the enterprise are not automatically synonymous, indeed they are sometimes opposed when fights occur between immediate needs and longer term considerations. If you accept these points, then the traumas over worker directors and the TUC's retreat back into collective bargaining are explained.

The final problem is one of union competence in business management, for unions have set their faces against the acquisition of business skills in case their members might become more sympathetic to management's case.

Indeed, the declared union policy is that management training will only be sought when all their representatives are properly trained as representatives. In effect, this means 'never'. The TUC seems to prefer to wait years for its own projected workers' university to be founded rather than use the extensive facilities which already exist throughout the country's educational system. It seems doubtful whether this isolationist stance is in their members' interests. KME's cooperators had little idea about the way a business really works and the stewards had alarmed Hague by claiming that to sell more goods 'all you need is contacts'. Their view of marketing strategy seemed limited to wishing that they had 'a go-getter to bring work in'.

Putting together the problems of this antipathy towards acquiring management skills, the insistence on a single channel and the limited inter-union integration at the workplace, we have a huge obstacle to the progress of workers' control. Indeed, I now see these long-standing policies of the TUC and the Labour Party as major impediments to the growth of worker cooperatives – or perhaps even to any serious attempt to democratize work. There needs to be a different way of reconciling the twin needs for employees to have business competence and also good representation.

In contrast to the Bullock Report's questionable attempt to integrate these two roles, the requirement is for a *separation* between the workers' role in promoting the overall health of the business enterprise and the mechanism by which collective bargaining intersects with the management of the enterprise. By rejecting a two-tier board system, Bullock tried to integrate policy making with policy execution, thus putting worker representatives in the unstable position of KME's stewards. Separating these two roles is just what occurs in local government so that councillors can 'represent' voters to council officials without feeling over-confused or finding that they are negotiating directly with themselves.

The structure reproduced in Figure 6 (see p. 403) might help to overcome these problems and would in my view have worked at KME. Indeed, it was the one towards which the convenors and I moved during KME's life (see chapter 15, p. 289).

The essential strength of this two-channel proposal is that whilst it could, one day, lead to the resurrection of the single-channel representation system, it doesn't, in the meantime, petrify industrial democracy into present collective bargaining arrangements for the years that it will take union members to prepare themselves for shared control and responsibility at board level.

Other analysts are more optimistic and, whilst agreeing on the potentially debilitating effects of shop stewards' role confusion, nevertheless conclude that the multiple pressures can be absorbed in a single channel route.* I suspect that their equanimity is more appropriate for industrial democracy issues in a previously traditional organization with an existing and recognizable management and would not fit the more stressful circumstances of a sizeable worker cooperative.

A sensible structure is vital and, as KME showed, in its absence none of the other organizational needs could be nurtured competently – neither resourcefulness, commitment, enterprise, learning, responsibility, nor even enjoyment – and it was so sad and unnecessary, for there are no unalloyed heroes or villains in the story. No easy scapegoats exist, for everyone had some logic on which to base his actions and, despite my criticisms of Spriggs and Jenkins, they emerge as remarkable figures. The problem wasn't just Spriggs and Jenkins. The issues were systemic; and they will remain so unless the trade union movement and the Labour Party change their stance, for it is evident that the role confusion for the workers' representatives will remain intolerable until workers feel

---

* See M. Marchington and R. Armstrong, 'Employee participation: problems for the shop steward', *Industrial Relations Journal*, January 1981.

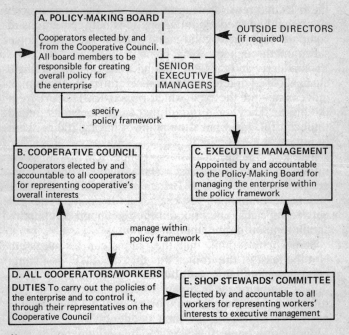

Figure 6 Proposed cooperative structure

A. POLICY-MAKING BOARD

Cooperators elected by and from the Cooperative Council. All board members to be responsible for creating overall policy for the enterprise

SENIOR EXECUTIVE MANAGERS

OUTSIDE DIRECTORS (if required)

specify policy framework

B. COOPERATIVE COUNCIL

Cooperators elected by and accountable to all cooperators for representing cooperative's overall interests

C. EXECUTIVE MANAGEMENT

Appointed by and accountable to the Policy-Making Board for managing the enterprise within the policy framework

manage within policy framework

D. ALL COOPERATORS/WORKERS

DUTIES To carry out the policies of the enterprise and to control it, through their representatives on the Cooperative Council

E. SHOP STEWARDS' COMMITTEE

Elected by and accountable to all workers for representing workers' interests to executive management

Notes
The key feature is that the stewards do not have to absorb the role conflict of representing two potentially adversary interests and that they neither control the business nor represent directly to the Policy-Making Board, or to the Cooperative Council. They deal only with the company's executive management.
 — the Policy Board (A) may have a majority of cooperator members if it so wishes
 — the Policy Board (A) can be amalgamated with the Council (B) if the Council and the cooperators feel it can cope with the policy-making role on its own
 — the Council (B) could appoint the management executive (C) directly and eliminate the Policy Board (A)
 — once the shop stewards' committee (E) and the cooperators *can* cope with the dual role, then the stewards' committee could be amalgamated with the Council (B)
So if (A) and (B) can be amalgamated, and if (B) and (E) can be amalgamated, then (A), (B) and (E) could be amalgamated and the shop stewards could control the policy of the business. It is what KME tried to do, and failed. The figure, as it is, seems much more manageable.
 There are variants of this scheme too. For instance, a Cooperative Council sub-committee might be formed to deal with discipline and absenteeism, instead of the management carrying out the Board's policy.

much more secure and have a more sophisticated view of the risks and rewards of multiple roles. The trade unions risk being bypassed by amalgamations between unions at company and factory level as workers seek their own salvation through combine committees, whilst both the Labour Party and the TUC still back the policy of a single channel of worker representation through the union movement – of the type which ripped KME apart from the inside. They seem to feel that the unions must retain total control; but what's the point of having 100 per cent of not much?

The key conclusion is stark. Unless KME is an aberration, industrial democracy and sizeable worker cooperatives will not work in Britain whilst worker attitudes and trade union policies remain as they are. The gap between socialist rhetoric and the likelihood of effective action remains depressingly wide.

Some people think that the unions can be bypassed. Not the least of the ironies was that, as KME was dying, people became entranced by the highly successful Mondragon cooperatives in Spain, where unions have had no role at all. Mondragon's supporters applaud the workers' need to raise capital for their cooperatives, but lacking Mondragon's bank, this says goodbye to any large, capitally intensive cooperatives in Britain if Government funding is unavailable.

Yet the State has a role to play, for as the Mutual Aid Centre's European research concluded, the speed at which cooperatives develop is very closely related to the environment created by the State through tax concessions, and from impetus arising from laws – as in France. Given that 'a lack of working-class contact with the business of managing assets and taking risks' could be a major barrier to an entrepreneurial and upwardly mobile class of skilled people,* unless the Labour Party and the TUC do change

---

* C. F. Pratten quoted in *Britain's Economic Performance*, eds. Caves and Krause (Brookings Institute, 1980), p. 142.

their view, then perhaps worker cooperatives will be more likely to flourish as a result of commitment from a reformist Conservative Government. The only alternative, unlikely if the last ten years' experience is any guide, is that a ground swell of energy and organization from the shop-floor will force unions into more flexible patterns of activity. Under the impact of recession, there are some signs of local initiatives by workers, trades councils and local cooperative development agencies. They will need all the help they can get.

I would like to feel that KME's story will not be used as evidence of the stupidity of encouraging cooperatives for, despite its oddities, that should not be the lesson. As Oscar Wilde wrote, 'the truth is rarely pure, and never simple'. According to American evidence, seventy-five companies which were scheduled to be shut down and which instead were purchased by their workers have done consistently better than under the former owners.*

It would have been hard for the people at KME to succeed even if the external climate had been helpful. As it was, a backward-looking union movement, a confused cooperative sector, an unhelpful Government and Civil Service all combined to let the workers at Kirkby gradually maul themselves to economic death. The challenge had been overthrown and traditional patterns of organization had been sustained. So Britain retains a destructive gulf between capital and labour; there are class disparities and hostilities, and a resistance to enterprise, innovation and productivity – not universal, but far greater than seems logical. A successful KME might have helped a bit. Yet as we recall this attempt to find a place in the market economy between private capitalism and state centralism, we can see that powerful interests combined to thwart it. Looking at Britain's industrial landscape, in what sense can we describe their victory as a success?

* K. Frieden, *Workplace Democracy and Productivity* (National Center for Economic Alternatives, 1980).

Perhaps their antipathy was intensified because KME's life was mistimed. Since it originated from Benn, it arrived smack in the middle of the Labour Government's internal argument about industrial strategy. In some ways Varley and Williams were victims of these pressures from Labour Party sensitivities. Indeed, what else explains the amazing series of meetings and Government actions over what one observer called 'this potty factory and its big-headed shop steward'. As John Elliott recollected, 'The world wasn't ready for KME, Meriden and the like – not the Whitehall world, the union world or the business world – so it was despised, hated and feared. The press made much of it, for the death of Bennery was always journalistically appealing, and people in Whitehall and Westminster were prepared to gossip about KME because, unlike British Leyland, it wasn't important; it wasn't felt to matter.'

I believe that it did matter, both for its jobs and for its chastening lessons. The abuse of its life will become muted as years go by and it will be recollected as a pioneering and courageous event in which 750 decent people, led by two larger-than-life figures, fought against tremendous odds – not just from outside, but between and within themselves. I salute them.

KME bibliography

Chaplin, Paul. 'Dreams and realities: worker cooperatives in the mixed economy: the case of KME', unpublished MBA dissertation. Manchester Business School, 1978.

'Workers' attitudes at KME' (tentative title), CRU Monograph No. 4. Open University, in press 1981.

Clarke, Tom. *Sit-in at Fisher Bendix*, pamphlet No. 42. Institute for Workers' Control, 1974.

'Industrial Democracy: the institutionalized suppression of industrial conflict', in *Trade Unions under Capitalism*, ed. Clarke and Clements. Fontana, 1977.

A comparative study of three worker cooperatives, final report. Social Science Research Council, 1978.

'Redundancy, worker resistance and the community' in *Jobs and Community Action*, ed. Craig. Routledge & Kegan Paul, 1979.

Cowe, Roger. 'Financial information systems in worker cooperatives', unpublished MBA dissertation. Manchester Business School, 1978.

Eccles, Tony. 'KME' in *The New Worker Cooperatives*, ed. Coates. Spokesman, 1976.

'Industrial democracy and organizational change' in *Personnel Review*, Vol. 6, No. 1, 1977.

'Sit-ins, worker cooperatives and some implications for organization' in *Personnel Review*, Vol. 6, No. 2, 1977.

'Control in the democratized enterprise' in *The Control of Work*, eds. Purcell and Smith. Macmillan, 1979.

Trade Union Behaviour towards Workers' Cooperatives, Plunkett Society, Oxford, 1981.

Lester, Tom 'The crumbling coops' in *Management Today*, February 1979.

Williams, Ellis. 'Is it all at the Coop?', unpublished BSc dissertation. Loughborough University, 1976.

Ralph Peacock has also drafted a book on KME. Chris Bond wrote a play on KME also called *Under New Man-*

agement,* a title taken, as with this book, from the sign hung over the factory fence by the Kirkby workers during the 1972 sit-in.

General bibliography

Bank, J., and Jones, K. *Worker Directors Speak.* Gower Press, 1977.

Benn, T., Dell, E., Hattersley, R., Rees, M., Rodgers W., and Williams, S. *Policy and Practice: the experience of Government.* Royal Institute of Public Administration, 1980.

Beynon, H., and Wainwright, H. *The Workers' Report on Vickers.* Pluto Press, 1979.

Blumberg, P. *Industrial Democracy: the sociology of participation.* Constable, 1968.

Brannen, P., Batstone, E., Fatchett, D., and White, P. *The Worker Directors: A Sociology of Participation.* Hutchinson, 1976.

Bray, J., and Falk, N. *Towards a Worker-managed Economy.* Fabian Society, 1974.

Burns, J. M. *Leadership.* Harper & Row, 1978.

Campbell, A., Keen, C., Norman, G., and Oakeshott, R. *Worker Owners: the Mondragon achievement.* Anglo–German Foundation, 1977.

Caves, R., and Krause, L., eds. *Britain's Economic Performance.* Brookings Institution, 1980.

Chaplin, P., and Cowe, R. 'A survey of contemporary British worker cooperatives', unpublished paper. Manchester Business School, 1977.

Chiplin, B., Coyne, J., and Sirc, L. *Can Workers Manage?* Institute of Economic Affairs, 1977.

Clayre, A., (ed.) *The Political Economy of Cooperation and Participation.* Oxford University Press, 1980.

Coates, K. (ed.) *What went wrong?* Spokesman, 1979.

---

* Performed at the Everyman Theatre, Liverpool, 1975.

Drulovic, M. *Worker Management on Trial*. Spokesman, 1978.

Elliott, J. *Conflict or Cooperation: The Growth of Industrial Democracy*. Kogan Page, 1978.

Garrett, J. *Managing the Civil Service*. Heinemann, 1980.

Greenwood, J. *Worker Sit-ins and Job Protection*. Gower Press 1978.

HMSO. *Report of the Committee of Inquiry on Industrial Democracy* CMND 6706 (The Bullock Report), 1977.

Jay, P. *Employment, Inflation and Politics*. Institute of Economic Affairs, 1976.

Kaufman, G. *How to be a Minister*. Sidgwick & Jackson, 1980.

King, C. D., and van de Vall, M. *Models of Industrial Democracy: Consultation, Co-determination and Workers' Management*. Mouton, 1978.

Labour Party *Worker Cooperatives*. 1980.

Lindblom, C. E. *Politics and Markets*. Basic Books, 1977.

Lockett, M. *Democracy, Participation and Satisfaction: some implications of worker cooperatives for industrial sociology and organization theory*. Imperial College, 1979.

Middlemas, K. *Politics in Industrial Society*. Deutsch, 1979.

Oakeshott, R. *The Case for Workers' Coops*. Routledge & Kegan Paul, 1978.

Paton, R. *Some problems of cooperative organization*. Cooperatives Research Unit. Open University, 1978.

Sedgemore, B. *The Secret Constitution*. Hodder and Stoughton, 1980.

Sennett, R. *Authority*. Secker & Warburg, 1980.

Thornley, J. *The product dilemma for workers' cooperatives in Britain, France and Italy*. Cooperatives Research Unit. Open University, 1979.
Workers Cooperatives. Heinemann, 1981.

Vanek, J. (ed.) *Self-Management: Economic Liberation of Man.* Penguin, 1975.

Walker, K. *Workers' Participation in Management: problems, practice and prospects.* International Institute for Labour Studies, 1974.

'Industrial Democracy: Fantasy, Fiction or Fact?' Times management lecture, 1970.

Wall, T. D., and Lischeron, J. A. *Worker Participation: a critique of the literature and some fresh evidence.* McGraw-Hill, 1977.

Warr, P., Fineman, S., Nicholson, N., and Payne, R. *Developing Employee Relations.* Saxon House, 1978.

Watkins, D. *Industrial Common Ownership.* Fabian Society, 1978.

Williamson, O.E. *Markets and Hierarchies: analysis and anti-trust implications.* Free Press, 1975.

Wright, D. E. *Cooperatives and Community: the theory and practice of producer cooperatives.* Bedford Square Press, 1979.

Index